Trading online

Trading online

online

a step-by-step guide to cyberprofits

Alpesh B. Patel

FINANCIAL TIMES
PITMAN PUBLISHING

FINANCIAL TIMES

MANAGEMENT

LONDON • SAN FRANCISCO
KUALA LUMPUR • JOHANNESBURG

*Financial Times Management delivers the knowledge,
skills and understanding that enable students,
managers and organisations to achieve their ambitions,
whatever their needs, whevever they are.*

London Office:
128 Long Acre, London WC2E 9AN
Tel: +44 (0)171 447 2000
Fax: +44 (0)171 240 5771
Website: www.ftmanagement.com

An imprint of Pearson Education Limited

First published in Great Britain 1999

ISBN 0 273 63541 7

British Library Cataloguing in Publication Data
A CIP catalogue record for this book can be obtained from the British Library.

10 9 8 7 6 5 4 3 2

Typeset by Northern Phototypesetting Co, Ltd.
Printed and bound by R R Donnelley & Sons

The Publishers' policy is to use paper manufactured from sustainable forests.

About the author

Alpesh B. Patel is a barrister-at-law who now trades equity derivatives full time. As a barrister, Alpesh was involved in advising banks, building societies and pension funds on financial services. He has extensive experience of both the UK and US derivatives and stock markets and holds equities in the UK, India, France and the USA.

He is an associate of the Society of Technical Analysts, an affiliate of the Market Technicians Association (USA), a colleague of the International Federation of Technical Analysts and a member of the Global Association of Risk Professionals, as well as a member of the Bar Association of Commerce, Finance and Industry.

When not trading, Alpesh likes to lecture on trading strategies, trading psychology and using the internet as part of a trading system. Alpesh also holds several directorships in Indian and English companies, including TraderMind Derivatives Ltd.

Alpesh has a degree in Law from King's College, London, and a degree in Philosophy, Politics and Economics from Oxford University. He is the author of *The Mind of a Trader* (Financial Times Pitman Publishing, 1997) and *Your Questions Answered: Money, Savings and Financial Planning* (Rushmere Wynne, 1997). More details about those books are available at two web sites:

> http://www.numa.com/bookshop/books/4748.htm
> http://www.batsford.com/books/sbn/35706

If you have any comments regarding this or Alpesh's other books or lectures on trading psychology contact him at his e-mail address: alpesh-patel@msn.com

Contents

···

SECTION 5 The truth is out there

SECTION 6 Appendices

Foreword

··

by Patrick Henry Arbor
Chairman, Chicago Board of Trade

A mere ten years ago, few people could have imagined a global network connecting everyone and everything, providing a boundless data stream accessible to all at virtually no cost. Today, as we prepare to cross the threshold of the twenty-first century, the internet looms as the most important, revolutionary development since Benjamin Franklin tied a key to a kite string.

Ours is an age of information. Knowledge informs our lives, creating pathways of successful, ordered living. As the grand neoteric tool of connectivity and information, the internet is redefining the future scope of communications, day-to-day living, and business.

This profound impact makes Alpesh Patel's *Trading Online* such an important book for those of us who make our way in the global trading community. *Trading Online* is not so much a reference book as a road atlas to cyberspace, identifying the most direct routes to high-quality, low-cost information for the online trading of financial instruments. By taking the time to read *Trading Online*, readers will save hours of time lost on the back roads and blue highways of the internet.

Trading Online provides a variety of routes to online investment, leading to numerous applications for the trading of equities, bonds, and assorted financial instruments. A thoughtful and practical writer, Alpesh Patel includes ample information by which computer neophytes can acclimatize themselves to this brave new world of internet trading. However, Alpesh Patel does not linger unnecessarily long on the footpaths leading to cyberspace – it is just long enough to quickly bring Internet newcomers up to a comfortable cruising speed. He then quickly transports readers in Section 2 to the road down which all traders wish to travel – the road to profit.

In the section *The Road to Profit*, Alpesh Patel offers practical advice regarding what goes into a sound trading strategy, analyzing different methodologies and offering tips on constructing action plans. This pragmatic approach will help prepare anyone for cyberspace, from the tyro to the trade master.

It has been said that time is possibly the most precious commodity of all. That being the case, *Trading Online* services readers well by saving readers a lot of unnecessary time wending their way through the labyrinthine passages of the internet. Alpesh Patel offers a wealth of practical information on where to find what in the online labyrinth, and details exactly how to access that information. This makes *Trading Online* a unique resource for intrepid internet travellers.

Critically, the information dispensed in *Trading Online* bears tremendous relevance to the sprawling international financial markets. As chairman of the world's oldest and largest futures exchange, I know exactly where the financial markets have been, and have a vision of how they will develop in the future. Technology is rapidly transforming the financial markets, infusing traditional trading methodologies with electronic lifelines that span the globe. Without question, internet access is becoming an increasingly important component of these financial markets. The savvy trader will seize the opportunity today to learn about this development, for in doing so, he or she will seize the future. *Trading Online* presents a treasure trove of information for those wishing to seize the future today.

Logically presented and well thought out, *Trading Online* supplements its extensive information cache with cross-referencing, itemized tables and comprehensive appendices. It is this attention to detail and Alpesh Patel's exhaustive approach that characterize this volume, making *Trading Online* an indispensable map to the internet's open road and, in a very Mercatorian sense, an atlas for the future.

November 1998

Ba
Sushilaben Rambhai Patel
for your 70th birthday

and

Papa   Mummy
Bipinchandra Rambhai Patel   Ramilaben Bipin Patel

for your 50th birthdays

Thank you for all your sacrifices

United your resolve, united your hearts;
United be your mind, Thus you live long together.

(*Rig Veda*, 10: 191-4)

Acknowledgments

· ·

A note I must make of my gratitude,
the following have graciously helped without bad attitude,
come first and forth dear uncles,
your wisdom and counsel through the years have I heeded,
indeed often it has been much needed.

Next up on the stage of appreciation,
a publisher with insight and vision
after all, did he not this book commission,
and forsee the growth of cybertrading with precision.

Beholden this writer, too,
to the team at Financial Times Pitman Publishing,
names too many to mention and met have I too few,
but essential remains each from start to exhausting finishing.

Finally must I turn to dear reader,
about internet trading seek you truth and discernment,
thank you indeed for your purchase and payment
it is visible you show foresight and clear judgment.

Janak Kaka and Yashvin Kaka – thank you for continued non-stinting support. I must have learned something (although probably not enough) from all those talks on the way to Skipton and Tumblers.

Thankyou Richard Stagg, my publisher, for confirming that the market needed such a title, for your help and advice in what should be included and the emails and photocopies of relevant articles.

Unlimited thanks to Selina who will now become the book's most ardent and shameless publicist.

Thanks also to Sugra, my agent, for the work to date on contracts; particularly screenplay rights.

A book is always a mammoth partnership, yet no author ever complains that it is his name alone that appears on the cover. To reverse in some small way this injustice I must thank the following at Financial Times Management for their essential help in making this book a success: Elizabeth Truran, Penelope Allport, Helen Baxter, Maria Bertacchi, Kate Jenkins, Amelia Lakin, David Hart and Colin Reed. I hope to meet in due course those individuals whose names are not included – I trust they will forgive the omission.

Preface

··

Private information is practically the source of every large modern fortune.

Oscar Wilde

Five years ago internet trading did not exist. Today, it has come of age. Recent media comment reveals the importance of trading online: "Cost of online share deals falls," "Informed traders in new empowered marketplace," "Day traders take Wall Street by storm," "Trading online is the most exciting and profitable job I have ever had," "Future at your fingertips."

What's all the fuss about? Well, imagine trading and investing without having to speak to a broker, no more scouring newspapers, journals, tip sheets, plotting charts or updating portfolios by hand. No more rummaging for opinion and analysis. No more wondering: If only there were someone you could bounce ideas off; Have I missed some late-breaking pertinent information. Instead, imagine everything available on your desk each morning to the next – up to the minute, real-time *all* the time.

Would it be a quicker, cheaper, easier and more profitable way to trade and invest? You'd better believe it. So, in the words of A-T Attitude, the internet trading company, ask yourself: "Are you *still* thinking about using the power of the internet to make a difference to the way you trade?"

This book aims to be your route map for fully utilizing the internet advantage as a lucrative trading resource.

This book aims to be your route map for fully utilizing the internet advantage as a lucrative trading resource. For net virgin to seasoned expert, the internet provides an unbelievable opportunity to profit from trading and investing. Forrester Research estimates that 14 million individuals will have online trading accounts by 2002, wielding a massive $688 billion in assets. That figure alone justifies the online broker E*Trade's claim that "Someday, we'll all invest this way." And they won't be using the internet because it's trendy, but because used properly it is lucrative. But you need more than a computer and a modem to succeed.

Why you need to read this book

To avoid being overwhelmed by information, you need clear, simple "how-to" action plans to quickly find the type of information you need, and then manage it effectively for profit. The competitive advantage that the internet offers will be rapidly eroded without such an efficient professional approach.

This book provides the approach and framework necessary to trade as profitably as possible on the internet, using the unique combination of skeleton plans and action plans as part of a trading strategy. With an action plan you know where to go, what you're looking for, why you need it, and what to do with it when you've got it.

By the end of the book you will have a professional approach which you can refer to each time you want to trade, and know which sites to visit for precisely the type of information you want.

Without such plans, you will at best waste hours tied up in the net jungle, at worst you will lose money. After all, access to a law library does not make a lawyer anymore than access to the latest financial information makes a profitable trader. You need the guidance of someone who has been there, done that and done it profitably. Introducing *Trading Online*.

How this book is organized

Section 1: In the beginning

This is the pre-start, the trading equivalent of foreplay. In this section we get everything ready: hardware requirements, deciding on internet service providers and a browser.

Since many readers will already have internet access and be rather impatient to get on with the trading meat of the book, this section is summarized in Chapter 1 and the rest can be safely skipped and returned to later.

The section is really for the novice or the trader who wants to make sure all his equipment is up to spec.

Section 2: The road to profit

This section details the essence of the book. We examine what action plans are, how they fit in with a trading plan and a skeleton plan, and the steps involved in forming one as well as trading best practice. Advice is given on choosing data providers, performing fundamental and technical analysis, planning trades, executing them, monitoring positions and keeping abreast of market developments.

By the end of this section the reader should have a thorough grasp of what it takes to be committed and professional about trading and how to drive home the internet advantage.

Section 3: The skeleton plans

This section has diagrams of skeleton plans for various products which the reader can then use as a framework for making their action plan, taking out most of the hard work. You go through the skeleton plan and choose the sites you like, based on the advice given, and that becomes your action plan.

Section 4: The sites

In this section are sites recommended in the skeleton plans that are then described, reviewed and rated so the reader can get an idea of what they offer before visiting them and deciding on which ones to focus for his individual needs. What a time saver!

Section 5: The truth is out there

To make sure you are well equipped to venture alone into the internet jungle, this section describes and comments on two important web resources: directories and search engines, so you can go forth and ever increase your knowledge. Even here, the aim is not merely descriptive but to actually impart valuable cost and time-saving experience.

The aim is not merely descriptive but to actually impart valuable cost and time-saving experience.

Section 6: Appendices

The final section contains entries on technical analysis, fundamental analysis, the basics of futures, the basics of options, orders, an alphabetical list of sites, and finally, recommended reading on and around the subject of this book.

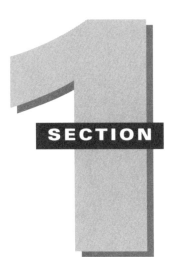

SECTION 1

In the beginning

1

The quick guide: section 1 summarized

❝ *I think emotions are far more important than brains in being a good trader.* **❞**

Bernard Oppetit
Global Head of Equity Derivatives
Banque Paribas

In this chapter

Those who are familiar with the basics of the internet and computer hardware can skip Section 1 and go straight to the heart of the book. Alternatively they can read this chapter – which summarizes the whole of Section 1.

Objectives

The summary of Section 1 provides a quick guide to:

- computer hardware: computer, modem, monitor, printer
- internet service providers
- browsers

Hardware

Computer

A PC is to be recommended rather than a Mac. For reasons best known to Bill Gates and Steve Jobs, most trading software is not Mac compatible. It makes far more sense therefore for you to stick with a PC (which are always Windows compatible) than to buy a Mac and be disappointed.

For trading a classic Pentium processor 100MHz is sufficient.

Soundcard and speakers can be useful for online news broadcasts but are not essential. Many internet sites provide live broadcasts and a soundcard and speakers will add even more value to the internet. Fortunately, these are often thrown in with new computers or are available pretty cheaply.

Modem

Internal or external modem, it makes little difference. It does not matter from a trading point of view whether the modem is some electronic wizardry inside the computer or a separate attachment outside it. The latter option may be better if you are not keen on opening the computer up.

At least a 56k modem is recommended. You do not want to be waiting all day to receive trading news and information. The speed of your modem is important to ensure you can have an outside life too.

Consider ISDN if you can afford it. This is a dedicated line that is faster than a normal modem. It is lightning fast, but can be expensive.

Monitor

A monitor of 15″ minimum is required – beyond 15″ and monitors start getting very pricey; less than 15″ and you start needing a magnifying glass.

Anti-glare and anti-radiation filters are essential. The radiation emitted from the trading screen all day may cause you to grow a second head, but there is no evidence that two brains would improve your trading performance. So buy a filter, and keep your unihead good looks.

Processors

Although there are as many new processors produced each year as there are sex allegations brought against Bill Clinton, it remains the fact that old is best (when it comes to processors at least). Newer, faster processors are great for games but are not necessary for trading.

It is not necessary to buy the latest PC as it will go out of date quickly and you will be paying a premium. Instead buy a cheaper PC and upgrade later.

16Mb RAM is a minimum requirement. RAM is the temporary memory in which your computer runs programs; a little like a play room. The more room the computer has, the quicker it can get things done. However, 16Mb is more than enough. You can, of course, buy more, but you do not strictly need it for your trading.

3GB hard drive or larger is best. The hard drive is where all the programs and other things you save are stored. Storage space is useful as over the years we all tend to collect clutter, such as bric-a-brac, spouses, etc. 3GB would probably last most traders until they decide to upgrade their computers (and their spouses).

Windows 95 operating system is recommended. When it comes to programing trading software, most programers use the latest version of Windows. Although Windows 98 is strictly the latest version, since it is so new I still recommend using Windows 95.

CD drive is useful, x4 or faster. Most programs and much data are provided on compact discs. A four-speed one is more than adequate although many computers now come with nothing slower than 32-speed.

Printers

Laser printers are the most expensive, but are best for drawing charts. These printers have dropped dramatically in price and are best when it comes to printing out all those trading charts and for reading text.

Inkjet is a minimum requirement. If the purse strings are tight an inkjet is likely to be adequate for printing charts and text.

Internet service providers

ISPs provide access to the internet, but they also have their own member-only content, rather like an online magazine. Many organize events such as online special guest stars.

Internet access providers

Unlike internet service providers these do not have their own content but only provide internet access. However, they are cheaper than ISPs and are sufficient for trading purposes.

Unlimited online time plan

ISPs and IAPs usually have different charging plans, many charging by the number of hours spent using their services. Since as traders we may spend a lot of time online the cheapest pricing option is almost always the "unlimited" time plan since there is only a monthly flat fee for access.

Free trial of internet service providers

Try before you buy is the advice here. Almost all ISPs and IAPs permit a one-month free trial and it is best to use this to test their reliability.

Compare access providers

You can do this by using www.consumerratings.com. This web site ranks internet access providers according to numerous variables. It is a good pointer for narrowing down the providers you would like to test before actually subscribing.

Browsers

Browser software turns data into pictures and so lets you view sites in graphics, sound and video. They are a great and essential part of trading, as important to trading as the remote control is to television viewing.

The latest versions of Internet Explorer or Netscape Navigator are recommended. If you are looking for a browser then you want the most sophisticated one and one that is catered for by almost all internet sites: Internet Explorer and Netscape Navigator are highly recommended for this reason. They are available free from cover CDs of most internet magazines.

It is essential to familiarize yourself with bookmarks in Netscape Navigator or Favorites in Internet Explorer for the purposes of managing information. Details are given on how to do this later in the book.

Summary

This chapter covers the basics for those already familiar with computers and the internet. The summaries in the remaining chapters of Section 1 will expand further. If you are not in a rush, why not join the novices and read the remaining chapters of Section 1 in full?

2

Absolute beginners to internet professors

❝ No one has information first. A guy sitting in his living room in Kansas watching TV can see information as fast as a trader on a trading desk now. Ten years ago, because I was at Salomon, because I had this kind of technology, I had an edge over a lot of people. ❞

Bill Lipschutz
former Global Head of Foreign Exchange
Salomon Brothers

In this chapter

This chapter can be skipped and returned to later if you are itching to set up to trade. First, there is a brief description of the internet and how it developed. The description is purposely brief because there can be few traders who do not know what it is and fewer still who are overly concerned about its origins. After that, things get really heavy as I analyze the internet – present and future development.

Objective

■ Non-essential to trading: an analysis of the internet

What is the internet?

In the early 1970s, when fear of global thermonuclear war was the subject of news and not history, ARPAnet (Advanced Research Products Agency, part of the US Defense Department) was created as a means of sending vital military information during a nuclear conflict, presumably so that if everything was vaporized, including humans, at least the computers could have a chat about how the weather had suddenly changed for the worse.

Since, in the event of war, a route between any two computers could be disrupted, a system had to be developed which could reroute data without passing through any single solitary hub. Consequently, research and inventions proceeded for some 20 years into developing what is recognizable today as the internet (see Illustration 2.1).

One definition of the internet could be that it is "an *inter*national *net*work of computers communicating information between each other." But that would be a dull and boring definition that would fail to capture the essence of the "net." The internet is the means to tour the world in seconds, the possibility to find information about virtually anything from anywhere at any time. It is far more important for its consequences than for what it is. We shall examine those in a moment.

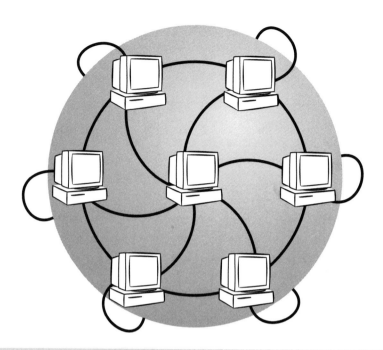

Illustration 2.1

The internet simplified

Why is the internet so popular?

That the internet is hugely popular is beyond doubt:

- IntelliQuest Information Group estimates some 62 million US adults are online.
- eStats reckons US users represent two-thirds of all users, and that internet traffic doubles every two days.

That the internet's growth rate has been exponential and phenomenal is also beyond doubt:

- There were 3 million online users in 1994 – there were 100 million by the end of 1997.
- It took radio 38 years to reach 50 million listeners, television took 13 years to reach 50 million individuals. The internet achieved 50 million users in 4 years.

Moreover, make no mistake about it: the internet is big money:

- Forrester Research estimates 14 million individuals will have online trading accounts by 2002 wielding $688 billion in assets.
- It also estimates internet commerce to exceed $300 billion by 2002.
- Not surprising when you consider that, according to the *Economist*, Dell already sells $1 million of computers daily.

What makes it so popular is the combination of elements present in other successful products.

Coca-Cola Strategy: accessibility and palatability

You only need access to the basic hardware: phone line, computer, modem. None of which is difficult to get hold of. Distribution is an essential component of success: ask Coca-Cola. The other aspect of accessibility is that a product, if used as a luxury consumer good (as opposed to a business input), has to appeal visually – the advent of the browser with its graphics, sounds and videos made the net palatable. A little like drinking a black liquid from an attractive bottle (again, ask Coca-Cola) – Java, applets, sound, videostreaming are all part of the Coca-Cola Strategy of palatability.

Schwab Strategy: relative cheapness

Like a discount broker the internet is cheap: access to the internet is via a local call, and local call charges are negligible in most parts of the world. Access to computers is ubiquitous given their falling costs combined with technology improvements.

The 7–11 Strategy: convenience

Every part of the internet is open 24 hours a day. Additionally, unless you own a 7–11, it is available at a place you visit without going out of you way, i.e. home or work.

Barnum Strategy: give 'em what they want – a service

When we talk about the popularity of the internet, we actually mean the popularity of certain activities and certain sites. No one wants to see John Doe of Pensicola's site, except Mrs. Doe. There has to be a reason to use it and there is: the internet sites contain vast amounts of stored information.

The Newspaper Strategy: currency

So far, what we have said could apply to a library. What makes the internet unique is that it is possible to obtain the most current information available. In fact, the internet is far more current than any newspaper.

In essence, the internet is a new and unique combination of elements that already help many businesses succeed. Those elements are present in this product, but they are also present in abundance in each category: hence the explosive growth rate. Take any one of those elements away and the internet would be a whole lot less successful.

Extrapolation of this analysis could lead us to envisage how the internet may grow in new, lucrative ways. For example, why not the "Budweiser Strategy: sponsorship" to reduce costs, i.e. if local phone calls were sponsored by a company, such as Budweiser sponsoring the SuperBowl, then even lower costs would increase use.

But the issue as to why the internet is popular (and, therefore, what makes for successful internet sites and home pages) goes beyond analyzing elements of successful businesses. The success of the internet is an issue about what drives it.

What drives the net?

Profits drive the net. We are here to make money. It is no wonder the full fruits and promise of the internet were realized first and foremost by Americans and they remain the most popular users of it. Henry James once observed: "To make so much money that you won't, that you don't 'mind', don't mind anything – that is absolutely, I think, the main American formula." (*The American Scene*, 1907). James Bryce wrote in confirmatory tones when he said: "How does Wall Street tell on the character of the people? They are naturally inclined to be speculative. The pursuit of wealth is nowhere so eager as in America, the opportunities for acquiring it nowhere so numerous." (*The American Commonwealth*, 1888).

Sure, there are the idealists who proclaim the internet a great democratizer, a leveler, where the most humble can cast the shadow of a giant by setting up a home page next to that of General Electric or IBM or any other Fortune 500 company. But they are not what drive the internet. Theirs are not sites of popularity. They are indulging in a self-gratifying ego-massage.

And, to be sure, the availability of information drives the net. Those informers of information sources are the most popular and lucrative sites on the internet, but their raison d'être is not altruism. Search engine Yahoo! is a listed company with shareholders making money from selling advertising virtual estate (i.e. internet real estate). The internet provides information; that is provided for the purpose of profit and profit is the purpose of the internet. As Walter Wriston, former chairman of Citibank noted: "Money is just another form of information." (*Risk and Other 4-letter Words*, 1986). Despite the praise heaped upon it, the internet has not prevented man, woman, and corporation remaining economic agents out to make a buck.

Why do we want so much information?

To profit. Information about stocks, information about cars, cinema tickets, is sought because we perceive the benefit to outweigh the costs of obtaining the information – i.e. a personal profit. But that leads us to the most interesting issue of all: what is the importance of the internet – for us as people and for the economies in which we live.

The consequence of all this information

Inadequate information stifles trade

Asymmetric information between buyer and seller results in a no sale or fewer sales than would have been the case with perfect information. The result is an inefficient market, i.e. one in which both parties would have benefited from the trade but it failed to take place because of inadequate information, and they did not get the information because the costs of obtaining it would outweigh the benefits of doing the trade.

I am far less likely to buy a second-hand car from you if I have no way of knowing its quality. That is why you permit me to visually inspect it. That low-cost method of obtaining information about the subject matter of the trade results in my buying it. Inadequate information is the reason why brand new cars depreciate as soon as they are taken from the showroom, because as soon as they have an owner, any future buyer will have inadequate information about the car and be less willing to buy it, so the owner is forced to reduce the price to entice buyers.

The internet is a source of cost effective information about a host of goods and services. Whereas before there may have been inadequate information stifling trade, now the internet provides low-cost information facilitating trade. The seller wants to provide the information because he wants a sale and the purchaser want the information because he wants to buy.

Consider stocks: is it any wonder that trading online is one of the success stories of the internet when you consider that people are more likely to buy stocks when they can research them rather than if they cannot. I will not buy a stock if my information is inadequate. Hey presto! Along comes an internet broker and provides free information about a stock. Why? Because he gets the benefit of a sale. Remember: profit not altruism drives the internet.

The chain of reasoning is simple: the cost of obtaining information from the internet is lower than the benefit of doing the trade and therefore the internet helps those trades which would otherwise not have occurred. The internet makes an inefficient market more efficient. The internet increases trade.

The internet is a remover of inefficiencies. To test if something can work on the net, consider the current way it is done and any inefficiencies associated with it, and then consider if the internet would reduce those inefficiencies without increasing costs so as to wipe out benefits of the trade. If so, all other things being equal, it will work on the internet.

Transaction costs: another inhibitor of trade

Consider another inefficiency of most markets: transaction costs. The labor market has a transaction cost: the cost of commuting. Hence, with the advent of computers we have telecommuting, removing the inefficiency but delivering labor nevertheless.

Brokerage commissions are another transaction cost. The result? Deep discount brokers. But why not a step further? Why not connect my computer directly to the order book so buyer and seller can meet? Already happened. The NYSE and International Petroleum Exchange are onto it. Charles Schwab is onto it. (Let us not forget online banking: the transaction costs of traditional banks maintaining a building, paying staff, etc. And look at the transactional costs of the traditional bookstore!)

Again the simple test applies: transaction costs are reduced, so I trade where before I may not have. Trade increased. The equation is whether my transaction costs are reduced such that I enter a trade which I would not have otherwise. The equation for the person facilitating the reduction in transaction costs is whether the benefits of trades as a result of his activity outweigh the cost of reducing transaction costs.

The questions are:

- What are the information and transaction costs?
- Will the internet reduce them to such an extent that trade is increased?
- Does the increased trade offset the costs to the service provider?

Put another way: can I get marginally more benefit than before per unit cost?

The result?

The result of increased trade through improved information is increases in growth on a macroeconomic scale. Reduced transaction and information costs mean increased productivity. Reduced costs alone should lower inflation.

A report by the US Department of Commerce, entitled *The Digital Economy* (1998), implies that inflation in the USA would have been 1% greater if not for the online economy. Is it coincidence the internet heralded the commencement of the Goldilocks economy? We must beware that the internet does not imply a guarantee of lower inflation: a mismanaged economy can lead to recession. But the internet has resulted in possibly an important structural change in the global economy: releasing the benefits of lower inflation and higher trend growth through making more markets efficient with the resultant increase in global trade and hence wealth. That is the glory of the net.

In terms of market efficiency the internet is similar for world trade to what the derivatives market in Chicago was for farmers. It reduced transactional costs of search and delivery and informational costs by contract standardization, thus increasing trade, not only for the farmers, but also for the USA. The internet is more like a stock or derivatives exchange in that it is a near perfect market.

Happy now?

Will the reduction of transaction and information costs mean more leisure time? No, that is what we naively thought 20 years ago. We believed computers and technology would mean the same work could be done quicker and, therefore, there would be more time for leisure. But as we know, man, woman and corporations are not altruistic. Profits run markets, and if the same amount of work can be done in half the time then twice as much can be done in the same time. More profits.

As T.S. Eliot pointed out:

> *Where is the Life we have lost in living?*
> *Where is the wisdom we have lost in knowledge?*
> *Where is the knowledge we have lost in information?*
>   *The Rock,* 1934

So is it raining money if you provide information?

All the statistics about billions of dollars streaming through the internet and its huge popularity do not mean that you have only to set up a site and money will follow. Many sites on the internet fail to meet the strategies already discussed. How many sites are just plain old difficult to navigate making their product unpalatable? Moreover, if someone else is doing the same thing on the net, but better, you will be beaten to the finish line anyway.

It is no wonder that whole books have been written on designing internet sites. Information is not enough. Presentation is all. If information were the point of arrival, there would be no lawyers. The client could place the depositions on the judge's table and leave. Presentation of information is one direction in which the future of the internet is going. How can we convey information to the end user better? That is why so many web sites allow customizable pages. We are all artists and psychologists now.

No more big boys?

Does all this information mean that the playing field for traders is now level, or at least, leveler? Does all this information mean the individual investor and the professional trader are similar? No more so than placing an individual in a law library makes him a lawyer, or placing him in a medical library makes him a surgeon. If the provision of information was all, then this book would not find a market; you would just go to the internet.

The trading playing field is not level, but the slope is a little gentler. Information is not knowledge and is even further removed from experience and further still removed from wisdom. The internet provides the private investor with information, some sites provide knowledge, and some, through trading games, may provide experience, but the professional trader remains at a significant advantage. Were it not so, Merril Lynch would not spend hundred of thousands of pounds on training programs for its traders; it would just give them access to the internet.

Individual traders are bound in ignorance to think they can compete with the big boys based on information alone. It has been an objective of this book to impart knowledge and wisdom; how the information is to be used, not only where to find it. The internet is not good at genetically engineering talent. Nor is it good at training; the classroom and personal effort remain the most efficient ways of doing that.

And so it is not the case, as is commonly predicted, that the middleman, intermediary, in all things will vanish because of the internet. Sure, their roles will change, but they will remain because:

- Information in the hands of the private investor will not guarantee profit without training and talent. So an adviser, fund manager, may still have a job!

- The division of labor is a market efficiency not an *in*efficiency. It makes more sense for me to pay my adviser $100 to do something which would cost me $200 to do, and so at the same time he is doing it I can go away and earn $300.

Summary

The internet does not mean no more losses for the trader, for information alone is not the answer. It is the purpose of books such as these to provide another field leveler: knowledge.

Getting infrastructure: computer hardware

> **ℭℭ** *I would rather deal with one mistake once rather than the same mistake over and over again.* **𝟿𝟿**
>
> **Jon Najarian**
> *Chairman and CEO*
> *Mercury Trading*

In this chapter

Before we can connect to the internet we need some pretty basic hardware. Most people have this already, but this chapter may nevertheless be useful if you are considering upgrading or desire to know if you have the right equipment.

Objective

■ Understand the types of hardware needed to trade

The computer

Minimum requirements

PC or Mac – Gates or Jobs?

The first thing to decide is which type of personal computer will suit your trading needs best. Although there are other manufacturers, such as Amiga and Acorn, the real decision must lie between the two giants in the personal computing world: the PC or the Apple Mac.

Windows 95 and 98, of course, operate on the PC, and far more software is written for PC users than for Macsters, despite Steve Jobs' return to head the company he formed.

Outside the USA the PC is even more dominant than the Mac. Consequently, I would recommend the PC over the Mac for trading. The simple fact is that there are more users and more software and hardware support for it. Unless you have a particular fondness for the underdog, get a PC.

The processor – the brains in the box

The type of processor or central processing unit (CPU) is one of the most important factors to consider when buying a computer. It will largely determine the speed at which programs will operate and therefore your efficiency. Make the wrong decision here and you could end up with the computer equivalent of Stan Laurel.

There are many processor manufacturers, all with "geeky" technological names, like Protech, Opti, Cyrix. The safest option is to stick with the leader of the pack – Intel's Pentium range.

You have a choice between:

- Pentium with MMX technology
- Pentium Pro
- Pentium II
- classic Pentium.

MMX technology makes next to no difference for trading programs and using the types of internet trading sites listed in this book. So unless you are also going to use your computer for graphic design or playing games then MMX is not needed. If you still really want MMX, then you would be better advised to go for the Pentium II.

The Pentium Pro will generally be faster running with most software. This option gives great performance at sensible prices.

The Pentium II is, in oversimple terms, a combination of Pentium / MMX and Pentium Pro. It's new and therefore a little pricey.

The classic Pentium is the oldest of the series but more than up to the job for our trading and investing purposes. Anyway, it can be relatively easily and cheaply upgraded later when prices for the newer processor fall.

For our purposes, the classic Pentium is more than capable of handling the stresses and strains of trading and investing we will be putting it to. It's the oldest of the range of Pentium processors, but consider it the computing equivalent of having the tried and testedness of Meryl Streep as opposed to the looks and suppleness of Alicia Silverstone.

The speed of a processor is measured by its clock speed. The higher this figure, the faster the processor. Obviously you will want to weigh price against performance. Fortunately, most stockists will probably only sell computers which are more than fast enough to handle internet trading tasks, so you will not have to worry if the computer you are purchasing has a processor that is too slow. For instance, the Pentium II, with 266MHz, is probably now going to be entry level.

For reference, the bare minimum for operating virtually all but the most advanced trading software and surfing the net is probably the classic Pentium 100MHz. If the latest Pentium II 500MHz is a sexy, sleek red Ferrari then the classic Pentium 100 is a rather sensible, yet sufficiently raunchy souped-up Mini.

Out of date on day two
At the end of the day, even the latest, sleekest, hottest, best computer purchased today is going to feel either very expensive or obsolete in 12 months' time.

Processor not for trading
You may want to consider a superior processor if you intend to use your computer for things other than trading, such as playing 3-D games, desktop publishing, designing intercontinental thermonuclear weapons, for instance.

Buy cheap, save and upgrade
Since the price of processors is falling continuously, it can be a good idea not to buy the top of the range one, and therefore the most expensive, but to buy something cheaper and adequate for now and then upgrade in 6–12 months when prices for what was the best thing around have fallen.

Sweet memories

After the processor this is the next most important consideration.

Programs need read only memory (RAM) in which to work when they are running. As programs get bigger and better they need more memory. Another benefit of extra memory is that it improves the performance of the computer, allowing it to work faster. Your computer should have 16MB as an absolute minimum otherwise you may well find it excruciatingly slow and unable to handle some trading software.

The hard disk is where all your software is stored. The larger the memory, the more programs you can happily store on your computer. Think of the hard disk as a wardrobe. With time it starts to get filled with lots of useless, often embarrassing items. Therefore I recommend you purchase as large a hard drive as you can afford, but at the entry level 3GB (gigabytes) should be enough for most applications for at least 12 months. Fortunately, most entry-level PCs now come with 6GB.

> **A big byte**
>
> One byte is one unit of information.
> One megabyte is 1,000,000 bytes of information.

> **A bigger byte**
>
> One gigabyte is 1,000,000,000 bytes of information.

Operating system

This is the software that comes with the hardware. It is the main program through which you work all the other programs. Almost all of the major trading programs highlighted in this book are Windows 95 compatible, and so that is the operating system I would recommend. In any event Bill Gates needs the money. Windows 98 can, of course, run Windows 95-compatible software.

CD drive

With much trading data now available on compact disk, a CD drive is an absolute must. However, don't be fooled by promises of 8 times or 16 times fast drives. A quad speed drive is more than adequate unless you plan to play videos on your drive.

Soundcard and speakers

It would be hard to find a new PC where this did not come as standard. With many internet sites offering audio news a soundcard is an essential component. Unless you are a music junkie or plan to compose a symphony on your PC any soundcard will do.

And the kitchen sink too

Other than these hardware factors, there will be a lot of other matters you will want to consider depending on your own circumstances:

- Is there technical support available? Is it by phone or call out? Is it free?
- How long is the warranty?
- If something goes wrong will the computer be collected or do you have to arrange delivery?

■ What pre-installed software do you get, and is it software you would have bought otherwise?

■ Does someone come to set everything up or do you have to connect it all yourself?

The modem

The modem is the electronic gizmo that is the link between your computer and the internet via your phone line. It is one of the most important "black boxes" for the trader as it is the link to the outside world and the wealth of trading information. As it is the trader's messenger-cum-runner you obviously want it to have the fastest speed possible, otherwise you will find your life full of agonizing minutes of waiting between receiving and sending data, while your messenger is in transit.

Inny or outy?

The first issue is whether you want an internal or external modem. An internal modem is an electronic set of chips that resides inside the body of your computer, so that it is hidden away. An external modem is an electronic set of chips that resides outside the body of your computer, so that it is not hidden away.

Personally I am ambivalent about the choice (see Table 3.1).

Table 3.1 Internal or external modem?

	Advantages	Disadvantages
Inny	• Neat and out of the way • Cheaper	• To get access to it for whatever reason you have to open up the whole computer
Outy	• More easily accessed and therefore more easily replaced for upgrade or repaired • Can be moved from one computer to another	• Takes up an extra port socket in the computer which could have been used for some other add-on • Needs an external power supply – yet another plug socket

The additional benefit of the outy is that you can amuse yourself staring at its flashing diodes while it takes ages to download data.

Faster than a speeding bullet – shot from a runaway train

As the modem is the data messenger of the computer you want to ensure the data are carried as fast as possible. It is better to let the data ride their way from the computer to the internet and back in a Ferrari-like modem than in a horse and

Your lines are slowing

A 56k modem has the speed written on the packaging and it has the real speed. Due to numerous reasons, including phone line quality, ISP technology, the modem will usually run at around 44k.

Betamaxed!
Don't get "betamaxed," i.e. overtaken by technology. Always ask about the upgrade path. Would future upgrade require software download only or a new chip. Is upgrade to the new ITU standard included?

carriage. If you choose a slow modem your internet trading experience will become as stimulating as being ravaged by a wet lettuce.

Modem speeds are expressed in bits per second (bps) this is the Baud rate. As a minimum requirement I would recommend a 56k modem. If you can't afford such an awesome piece of machinery then 36.6k will do, but keep a good book next to the computer to read in between the long waits for data. Speed, cost, availability, and compatibility make the 56k modem the modem of choice – the modem Harrods would sell you.

There are two competing 56k modem formats: K56flex and x2. Choose the modem format supported by your ISP provider. Most of the larger, better-known ISPs can handle both formats, but check to be sure.

Additional features

Ideally you will want to use your modem for sending and receiving more than just data. A data/fax/voice/video modem would, of course, be better and these are becoming standard. At the very least try to get a fax/data modem so that you can receive and send faxes via your computer without having to purchase a fax machine.

Souping up performance: improving modem performance

Integrated services digital network (ISDN)

ISDN can give access at speeds of up to 128k. It can, however, be prohibitively expensive. For a start you need an ISDN terminal adapter instead of your modem. Internal units cost around $100 and external ones $200. But in the UK the cost varies from £175 to £500. You also need an ISDN line for which the phone company will charge you. On top of that there are good old phone rates to pay. In the USA phone rates for ISDN can vary from around $30 per month upwards. To find out local rates look in your local phone book for an information number.

My advice is that, if you can afford it, ISDN can be very time saving, as long as your ISP supports ISDN. It all comes down to how much value you place on your time.

In the pipeline

There is talk of even faster communications hardware than ISDN. As yet most is in development or too expensive for all but large businesses. For example, there are leased lines, there is cable and ADSL (which can carry data at speeds of 15000k.) Satellite and VDSL will be far faster than any trader will need unless he wishes to see live pictures from an exchange floor.

The monitor

If you become a devoted trader then you will probably end up staring boggle eyed for hours at this piece of equipment. It in return will be distinctly unmoved by the overattention heaped upon it.

Minimum requirements

Oh, what a big one you have!

Monitors, like TVs, are measured in terms of the diagonal length of the screen. Entry-level sizes are 15," but 17" or 18" are becoming cheaper every month. The general rule is that the bigger the screen the greater the resolution you can have, and so more information on the screen. The downside is, of course, cost.

Curves or flat features?

When it comes to monitors the most pleasant screen to work with is the flat screen. It provides less distortion at the edges and so less strain on the eye. Even better than a flat screen is the Sony Trinitron screen which provides sharper images, excellent color alignment and no distortion at all at the edges.

Do not stare at the glare

It is better to have a monitor with an anti-glare surface, which thereby reduces reflected light. An anti-static coating is also a healthy precaution. A low-radiation monitor should come as standard, but inquire nevertheless. For a few dollars you can purchase add-on filters which clip on over the monitor – choose ones which reduce glare and radiation.

hot tip

Ergonomics! Ensure you position the monitor at eye level. You should not have to twist your neck or require undue head movements to look at the monitor from the keyboard. Avoid direct sunlight reflecting onto the monitor screen as this can reduce visibility of image.

The printer

There are three main reasons why an online trader will require a printer:

1 For printing hard copies of information discovered on the internet.

2 For printing charts of technical analysis software (see Diagram 3.1) (discussed in detail later).

3 Other household or business printing, e.g. correspondence to dear senile aunt Cecilia.

Regarding the first reason listed the quality of the print is irrelevant, as long as you can read the print of course. For the second reason the quality can be very important because you would be drawing fine lines. For the third reason the type of print will be a matter of personal taste.

Diagram 3.1

Fine lines of charts

We will now examine various printer options and discuss for what trading needs they are best suited. The key features to remember when choosing a printer are:

- the cost of purchase
- the running cost, e.g. to replace cartridges
- the quality of the print
- the print speed.

Dot matrix

Dot matrix ribbons

Dot matrix printers use ribbons in the same way as traditional typewriters (remember those?) The replacement of the ribbon tends to be the largest running cost.

These are as old as the hills. They are the cheapest in terms of initial purchase cost and subsequent running cost. However, their quality is generally the lowest too.

Their name derives from their print method and not the inventor (there was no Dr. Dot Matrix as far as I can tell.) The printer head produces a series of dots, using pins, to produce letters. The more pins, the finer the lines (i.e. higher the resolution). Standard numbers of pins is nine, going to over 24.

If you plan to use your printer only for printing information from the internet and not charts and do not plan on creating correspondence then a dot matrix should suit you fine. They are not known for their speed, but they are faster than the internet so an extra second here or there won't matter.

Inkjet

Inkjet printers spray a jet of ink onto the paper to produce characters – hence the name ink + jet! (When it comes to naming printers the manufacturers are hardly known for their cutting wit and repartee.)

Inkjet resolution tends to be far superior to that of dot matrix printers and comparable to low-end laser printers. Inkjet printers come between most laser printers and dot matrix printers in terms of initial purchase cost, running cost and quality.

This type of printer is going to most suit the individual who will be printing charts and also writing private correspondence where the appearance of the letter should be at least semi-professional.

Color inkjets are also widely available, but other than making your charts look prettier they are not necessary for trading.

Laser printer

This is the printer of choice. This printer is what the Tomahawk cruise missile is to the Scud. They are the most expensive of all the types of printers we have considered, but they also produce the highest quality print – for when only a professional appearance will do.

All laser printers use toner cartridges. These contain fine powder that is then "heat fixed" to the paper in the shape of a character or part of a graphic. The method used for fixing can be either laser or light emitting diode (LED). LED "laser" printers are cheaper than other laser printers, all other things being equal. Their quality can often be as good.

Emulation

This can be considered printer language. Before you even consider buying a printer it should be Hewlett-Packard LaserJet II emulation. That does not mean it is a HP Laserjet or even that it is made by Hewlett-Packard but that it can "talk" the industry standard basic minimum printer language. Without it you may have problems printing from certain software.

Remember memory

Memory is important for laser printers because of the way they work – they download data from a whole page, memorize them, and then print. The minimum RAM should be 1MB and always make sure this can be upgraded. While you're at it, ask about the cost and availability of upgrades.

Speed

For laser printers, the speed is measured in pages per minute (ppm). Since we will not be in a rush for our print jobs this does not concern us too greatly and we may therefore save costs by getting a printer with a low ppm.

The laser printer is best suited to the individual who, as well as drawing price charts, is going to conduct private correspondence, and in situations where professional appearance is important.

Inkjet ink cartridges

Inkjet printers use ink cartridges – replacing these when they are used up is their major running cost. Always ask the cost and availability of replacements.

---

hot tip *Ask, ask, ask* *With any type of printer always ask about the cost, longevity and availability of replacing "consumables." A consumable is something like the ribbon in a dot matrix printer or the laser toner in a laser printer or the ink cartridge in a color inkjet printer.*

DPI – the measure of quality

Dots per inch (DPI) is a measure of print quality. 300 dpi is at the bottom range of laser and LED printers. 600 dpi is at the top end and produces a very professional look. Top-end inkjets produce 300 dpi. The difference between 300 and 600 dpi is noticeable with the naked eye.

Summary

Getting the correct hardware is a precursor to trading. If done correctly the trader can forget about the equipment and concentrate on the important task of trading. In order to purchase the correct hardware the issues to consider are:

- PC or Macintosh
- processor speed and type
- size of hard drive and of RAM
- operating system
- speed of CD drive
- modem (internal or external) and speed
- normal telephone line or ISDN
- monitor size
- printer quality.

With the correct hardware, issues of actually connecting to the internet arise. That brings us to internet service providers, examined in the next chapter.

Gatekeepers to the net: internet service providers

" *I think the best traders are those that don't read the newspapers.* "

David Kyte
Chairman
Kyte Group

In this chapter

With hardware at hand, we now need to access the internet. In this chapter we explore the providers of access and what to look for and look out for, including charges and the best subscription plans for traders.

Objectives

- Understand how to choose an ISP
- Awareness of how to save costs

What are internet service providers?

You have a PC and a modem, and you know about the internet. But how do you get the internet "into" your computer? This is where an internet service provider (ISP) comes in. ISPs provide a way for your PC to connect via your modem to the internet and vice versa. They are companies that you dial up from your PC and they do the rest (see Illustration 4.1).

Most ISPs give you free software which takes you through the registration process and, once loaded, produces a pretty icon on your screen desktop and only needs to be double clicked, usually, for it to come to life and dial out via your modem to the ISP and get you connected to the net (see Diagrams 4.1–3). Browsers (see next chapter) such as Netscape Navigator or Internet Explorer or the ISP's own browser are also usually included free and they convert all the data streaming up and down your phone line into pictures and text that you can understand.

Popular ISPs include America On-line, MSN, Compuserve, Prodigy, although there are many reputable country-specific ISPs as well, such as Virgin.Net in the UK and of course the ever-popular sleeping giant of the internet world, ZAM-NET in Zambia.

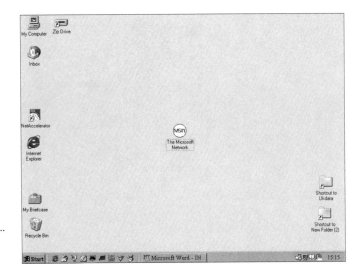

Diagram 4.1

Connecting using the ISP (screen 1)

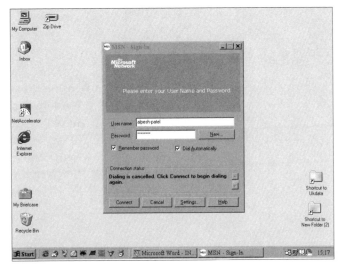

Diagram 4.2

Dialing the ISP (screen 2)

Diagram 4.3

Connected! (screen 3)

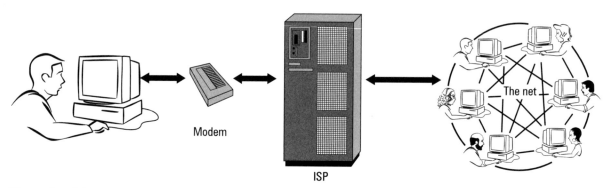

Modem

ISP

The net

Illustration 4.1

The world of ISPs

ISPs and IAPs

Technically, there is a difference between an internet service provider and an internet access provider. ISPs, as well as providing access to the internet in the manner described, also provide special internet-based content for members only, often through their own software provided free on subscription. Such content will be sections on entertainment, news, weather, sport, computing, business, etc. They will often have lots of chat "forums" producing a community feel (see Table 4.1).

Table 4.1 Internet service provider or internet access provider?

Internet service provider	Internet access provider
Special content for members only	ISP type of content often available elsewhere on web
Well organized by the ISP	Often cheaper
Chat forums and "community"	Chat forums available on web
Easy to use ISP proprietary software interface	
Lots of assistance	

IAPs are better for those with web experience who know there way around and so are happy to use a browser to find what they are looking for. ISPs with their own helpful member-only special content areas are better for the novice who wants to be led to the best of the web and experience readily what it has to offer.

Charges

When you connect to the internet you have two main charges:

1 the charge of the phone call for the period you are online

2 the charge the ISP levies for providing you its services.

Phone charges

These are levied by your phone company, for example MCI, AT&T, Ma Bell, Cable or British Telecom, etc. in the UK. If you want to know how much they are then you need to speak to that company and tell them which number you are dialing to connect to your ISP.

ISP charges

Most ISPs have various charging programs. Sample charges of some of the main providers are given later to give you some idea of the typical choices. These prices are, of course, subject to change and please see the web addresses or call the provider for particular terms. The pricing plans listed earlier apply only to members in the USA. All pricing plans are subject to applicable taxes. Appendix 6 lists more exhaustively web addresses of the major providers and sites so you can inquire about current charges and free software.

AT&T WorldNet

www.att.com/worldnet

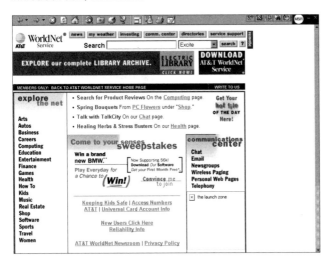

Diagram 4.4

AT&T WorldNet

■ $19.95 per month, with unlimited usage.

■ You can register for the Hourly Price Plan and get 10 hours of internet access for $9.95 per month, at $2.50 for each additional hour.

IBM Internet Connection

`www.ibm.net`

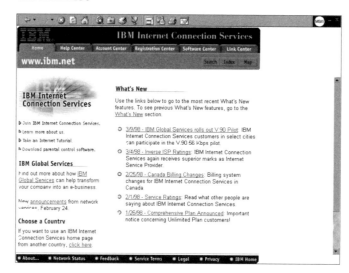

Diagram 4.5

IBM

- Unlimited Plan monthly subscription charge $19.95.
- Basic Plan monthly subscription charge $4.95 plus $1.95 per hour, for hours in excess of 3 per month.

MSN

`www.msn.com`

Diagram 4.6

MSN: un peu international

■ MSN Premier Plan $6.95 per month. You receive 5 hours of MSN and internet access. Each additional hour is $2.50. Or you can choose the annual version of this plan for a yearly rate of $69.50. The annual plan gives you the same monthly access hours and the same additional hourly rate. (That's 12 months for the price of 10.)

■ MSN Premier Flat Rate Plan $19.95 per month. For one all-inclusive price, you get flat-rate access to MSN and the Internet. Everything's available to you whenever you want, for as much time as you want, with no additional hourly charges.

■ MSN Premier Destinations Plan $6.95 per month. If you already have internet access, you can continue to use that service and get full access to MSN's pro-graming. Or you can choose the annual version of this plan for a yearly rate of $69.95. (That's 12 months for the price of 10.)

■ MSN Premier Flat Rate ISDN Plan $49.95 per month. So, if you have an integrated services digital network (ISDN) adapter, you'll receive flat-rate internet access – single or dual channel, with hundreds of access points around the world.

AOL

www.aol.com

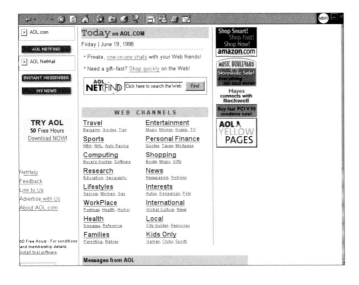

Diagram 4.7

AOL

■ $21.95 per month standard plan providing access to AOL and the internet, without hourly fees.*

■ $19.95 per month ($239.40 1-year prepaid subscription) providing access to AOL and the internet, without hourly fees, for members who pay in advance for 1 year.*

Pricing plans do not include premium services, which carry additional charges.

- $9.95 per month "bring-your-own-access" plan providing unlimited access to thousands of unique AOL features,* including access to the internet, for individuals who already have an internet connection or access through the work or school environment.
- $4.95 per month light usage plan providing 3 hours of AOL, including the internet, with additional time priced at just $2.50 per hour.*
- $9.95 per month limited usage plan providing 5 hours of AOL, including the internet, with additional time priced at just $2.95 per hour.*

Pricing plans do not include premium services, which carry additional charges.

And not to forget our British readers.

MSN (UK)

www.msn.com.

- **Monthly pass:** If you don't want to worry about how much time you spend online, your best option is the monthly pass (the most popular pass among UK members). For just £14.95 this pass gives you unlimited use of MSN and the internet for an entire month.
- **Annual pass:** The annual pass gives you 12 months of unlimited use of MSN and the internet for just £149.95. This works out to less than £12.50/month. Best of all, there's no clock watching or access charges for a whole year.
- **Hourly pass:** If you prefer to pay by the hour, the hourly pass gives you use of MSN and the internet for your first 3 hours each month for £4.95. Additional hours are billed at £1.95 each.
- **UK destination pass:** If you already have internet access, the destination pass is for you. You can continue to use your existing access provider (or use MSN access at £2.50/hr) and still enjoy unlimited use of MSN shows and services for just £4.95 per month.

Since we are going to be using the net for trading and researching our trades we will almost always want unlimited access.

Comparison of unlimited time plans

- MSN: $19.95
- AT&T WorldNet: $19.95
- AOL: $19.95 (if you pay 1 year in advance)
- IBM: $19.95.

Clearly, the price competition between some of the leading providers is fierce (perhaps a little tacit collusive price fixing?) This begs the question: Other than charges, what should we look for in internet service providers?

What to look for in an internet service provider

ConsumerRatings.Com (www.consumerratings.com) provides rankings of internet service providers according to user responses (see Diagram 4.8). It's worth a visit for updating. Of course it's not a scientific poll, but better than nothing.

U.S. Nationwide Internet Access Providers

	Score	#of Resp.	Software	Value	Availability	Stability	Web Page Speed	News/Chat Speed	E-mail	Tech Support	Web Hosting	Customer Service
AT&T WorldNet Service	81	203	4	4.1	4.5	4	3.8	3.9	4.2	4.1	3.7	4
Microsoft Network	73	132	3.8	3.8	4.1	3.9	3.5	3.4	3.6	3.4		3.4
AOL - America OnLine	61	634	3.4	3.2	2.7	2.5	2.8	3.4	3.7	2.9	2.9	3.1
IBM Global Network	55	174	3.1	2.4	3.4	3.1	2.7	2.4	2.9	2.5		2.3
	Score	#of Resp.	Software	Value	Availability	Stability	Web Page Speed	News/Chat Speed	E-mail	Tech Support	Web Hosting	Customer Service
Relative weights (3=very important, 2=important, 1=somewhat important, 0=not important)			2	2	2	2	2	2	2	2	2	2

Diagram 4.8

ConsumerRatings.Com

Free trial

You want an ISP that is willing to give you some free time to check out its services. The usual free offers range from 1 month free or 25–50 hours free online.

*nb *Free time online offered by ISPs never refers to the phone call charges to connect to the ISP which are charged by your phone service provider, e.g. MCI, AT&T or British Telecom.*

hot tip *Obtaining free trial connection*
Most ISPs offer a free trial for a limited time. To take advantage of these you need to obtain their software. This can be done either by calling the ISP numbers in the appendix, or looking in your local phone book under "internet" and calling them to send you their software. Alternatively you can buy virtually any internet or PC magazine which will almost certainly have a cover CD that includes one of these trial offers.

Local access number

You connect to your ISP by having the modem dial the ISP's phone number. Obviously you want that phone number to be a local phone number. While it is perfectly possible to live in Los Angeles and dial an ISP's London number each time you want to connect, it is not to be recommended. All the big and many of the smaller ISPs provide local access phone numbers. Indeed, some even have toll-free access numbers.

Unlimited connect time plans

As noted earlier, for our purposes the unlimited time plans are going to be the most useful. You will want an ISP offering these.

Low cost

Shop around, find the cheapest unlimited online time ISP. This may not be one of the big providers, but a local provider particular to your own area.

Technical support number

This is something I would emphasize far more now than I would have done 18 months ago. ISP software and browsers are becoming more and more complex and so tend to give PCs more headaches. Many colleagues mention problems with connecting to their ISPs because of software-related problems. That is where technical support becomes essential. If you cannot connect, trading becomes very difficult.

E-mail

How many e-mail accounts can you have? If other members of your family want to receive e-mail, it can be useful to have multiple accounts so they can have their own postboxes – and privacy.

Modem support

You must ensure the ISP supports your modem connection type. Does it support ISDN or 56k speeds, if you have those connections.

Web space

Many ISPs offer the subscriber free web space on which to create personal web home pages.

hot tip   *Magazine guides*
Look in internet magazines for listings of ISPs and their pricing plans. These magazines usually carry information specific to your local area as well as national information. Some of the local providers listed there may be far cheaper than the bigger ISPs. But do try them on a free-trial basis. The smaller companies may not be as reliable as one of the bigger providers.

nb   *There are presently two 56k standards: Flex and x2. Ensure your ISP supports the one compatible with your modem, otherwise you will only connect at regular speeds – and probably not realize it.*

Summary

For trading alone an internet access provider providing unlimited online time at competitive rates is the trader's ideal.

If the rest of the family is also going to be using the internet then you will probably have to consider an internet service provider that provides special content.

In choosing how to connect to the net, because of fierce competition it is always in the interests of the trader to shop around and get free trials.

A good source of ratings of ISPs is www.ComsumerRatings.com – visit it during your free-trial access period.

Check for:

- local access number
- unlimited time plans
- low charges
- technical support availability
- e-mail
- modem support
- free web space.

With internet access sorted we need some software now with which to view the internet. This is where the browser comes in.

The acceptable face of the internet: browsers

‟ Okay you blew it. Stand back and re-evaluate. ”

Paul RT Johnson Jr.
Vice President
ING Securities, Futures and Options, on trading losses

In this chapter

We've got our computer and some nice company has provided us with internet access, so we now need some software to view the internet on our screens. Enter the browser. The latest browsers really do help speed things up when we are researching. And as every trader knows there are some crunch times when time is of the essence.

Objectives

■ Get to know a browser's workings intimately

■ Understand how to manage (trading) information in a browser

■ Know how to speed up internet browsing

What are browsers?

A web browser, such as Internet Explorer or Netscape Navigator, is an essential item of software for any trader using the internet. Indeed, it is essential for anyone using the internet. It is essential because it converts all the data documents and data files that swim around in the internet not only into boring old text, but but hugely more interesting pictures. Like most children we all secretly like picture with our text (see Illustration 5.1 and Diagram 5.1).

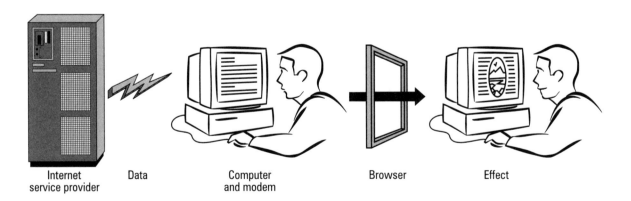

| Internet service provider | Data | Computer and modem | Browser | Effect |

Illustration 5.1

The browser effect

Browsers make your web experience more fulfilling and enriching! As well as pictures, browser add-ons allow you to hear financial news broadcasts, and even watch them as a live video feed. A browser does to the web what Windows did to DOS.

Although the World Wide Web is actually a part of the internet, both terms are often used interchangeably. I shall continue to propagate that enduring mistake, because for our purposes it matters not.

Diagram 5.1

Text and pics using the Internet Explorer 4.0 Web browser

Know your browser: a browser tour of duty

As with people, the best way to get to know a browser is to play around with it.

Hyperlinks

When text in a browser is <u>underlined</u> it usually means that clicking on it with your cursor will "link" you to another page elsewhere. This is a useful technique to ensure web pages are uncluttered, yet permit great depth of information.

You can tell you are on a hyperlink because the cursor will usually change shape.

Home pages

This is the page your browser automatically opens on. It will usually be your ISP's home page and will be full of hyperlinks to take you to wherever you wish to go. You can, of course, ignore the home page and type in your own URL.

URLs ("you are 'ell")

You will already have come across a universal resource locator (URL) without realizing it. For example: http://www.drjsplanet.com/ is a URL. It is the address of a particular web page.

Hypertext markup language (HTML)

Just as you do not need to know how a television converts tv signal into pictures, so you do not need to know what HTML is. However, for the terminally curious, HTML is the code web site writers use to make their web sites so appealing and attractive. It is to web sites what make-up and concealer are to an acned teenager.

hot tip *Never say "earl" when referring to a URL. Most people usually say "web address" when they mean "URL." When telling someone a web address, you can be really cool and ignore the "http://" bit.*

Refresh — Reloads the current page

Stop — Stops downloading data

Home — Takes you to your browser's home page

Search — Click to get a list of search engines

Favorites — Keeps a list of all the sites you record as your favorites. More about this later

History — Lists sites and pages you have visited

Back — Takes you to the preceding page

Forward — Takes you to the subsequent page you visited

Diagram 5.2

Playing with the browser

What to look for in your ideal browsing partner

- Video and radio support
- ability to display forms
- ability to support Activex, VRML and Java; makes your browser display more interesting bits – such as moving icons, 3-D effects etc.
- support frames can be very important when viewing trading sites displaying data
- ability to open multiple windows so you can read one page while another loads
- security features
- free?

■ speed: does the web page load text before pictures – which always take longer – so that you can start reading while waiting for the pics. A poor browser would display nothing until everything is downloaded, meaning you can be waiting longer to get started.

Which are the best ones?

There are many different software companies that will provide you with browsers. However, by far the two most pervasive and popular are Internet Explorer 4 and Netscape Navigator 4. They meet all the criteria listed earlier. While doubtless there are other browser providers, a particularly popular one being Air Mosaic, they either do not meet all of these criteria or are from companies smaller than Microsoft (IE4) or Netscape (NN4) leaving one with the possibility of less compatibility and/or support.

Using Internet Explorer 4 and Netscape Navigator 4 together
Contrary to popular belief, and some pervasive conspiracy theories, you can install Internet Explorer 4 and Netscape Navigator 4 together on the same PC. They are not incompatible, and Internet Explorer does not kick the hell out of Netscape Navigator at 3am when you are not looking.

Diagram 5.3

Internet Explorer 4

To use Internet Explorer 4 (Diagram 5.3) or Netscape Navigator 4 (Diagrams 5.4, 5.5, 5.6) effectively you will need a Pentium processor, Windows 95, 16MB RAM and around 90MB free hard disk space. Although both browsers will run on lower specs, I do not recommend it. It will slow you down. The alternative is to use an earlier version of either browser – available from friends or the Internet Explorer and Netscape Navigator sites.

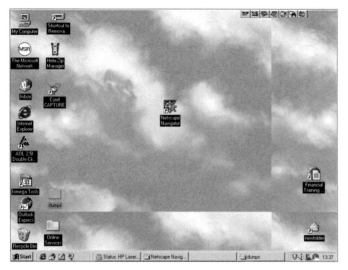

Diagram 5.4

**Netscape Navigator 4
(screen 1)**

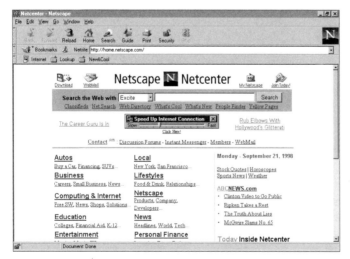

Diagram 5.5

**Netscape Navigator 4
(screen 2)**

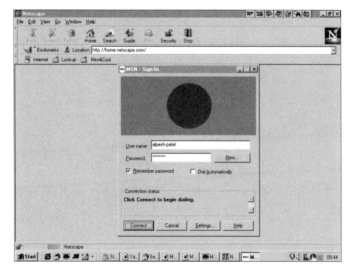

Diagram 5.6

**Netscape Navigator 4
(screen 3)**

Gimme, gimme, gimme: getting hold of web browsers

The shops

Many software stores sell browsers. However, they are usually part of an internet package and so are not free. Why pay for something when you can get something else just as good for free?

IE4 and Navigator 4 are free. Read on to discover where to get them from.

The internet – or Catch 22

You can download browsers from web sites, but you usually need a browser in the first place to locate the site! Obviously, this method is best suited to those who already have a browser and wish to choose an alternative.

Downloading off the web can be slow and tedious. I have usually found that after the download is complete, for some incomprehensible reason/excuse the program cannot start anyway. Download software off the net only as a last resort – and only ever from reputable sources. For present purposes, Microsoft counts as a reputable source.

Downloading off the net is simple. You go to the relevant address (e.g. www.microsoft.com/ie/download or www.home.netscape.com/) and follow the simple instructions.

Magazines

If you have ever bought a computer magazine, whether it specializes in hardware, software or the internet, you will have noticed CDs taped to the cover. Very often these will have copies of the latest browsers for free, and almost always IE4 and Navigator. In the UK *.net* has a copy of both IE4 and Navigator on its CD each month. All you have to do is download them.

To find out whether the CD in question contains the browser you are looking for, skim through the magazine contents pages before buying it.

Netscape Navigator and Internet Explorer 4 guides

The browser is like a car which is going to drive us around our internet destinations. Like anyone who spends a lot of time in the car, we want to make sure it is running efficiently and the interior is just how we want it and suited to financial browsing. In this section we will familiarize ourselves with the two most popular browsers. As well as comfort and ease of use, we want to ensure we can use the browser to quickly get to where we want to go. That is the aim of the rest of this chapter.

Inside Bill Gates's world of net experiences – guide to Microsoft Internet Explorer 4.0

IE4 alters the state of Windows 95, making it a little closer to Windows 98. By the end of this chapter you will have the potential to do all of the following. Don't worry if it all seems a little overwhelming now, there will be step-by-step guides and a summary and checklist later. All the jargon will be explained as well. With Internet Explorer 4 you can:

1 Treat Windows like a browser: you will find **back** and **forward** buttons.

2 Open multiple windows and panes so you can work on one thing while another downloads. Click the **Search** button on the toolbar: the **Explorer bar** appears in the left side of the browser window. Then you can click a link to view that page on the right side of your screen while still viewing the list of search results on the left. You can similarly browse through your **Favorites** and **History** folders, channels, or your documents.

3 Start programs by clicking icons on your **taskbar**.

4 Keep your most used web pages handy; with as few mouse moves as possible connect to the net and your favorite site; create a button on the **Links** toolbar just by dragging a link to it from the **Address bar** or a web page. You can easily customize the Links toolbar to display buttons the way you want them. Or add a web page to your list of favorites for easy access from the **Favorites** menu or **Explorer bar**.

5 If you have installed the Windows **Desktop Update**, you can also view the **Channels** right on your desktop or as your screen saver; update your favorite web sites and view them at your leisure; **subscribe** to your favorite sites so that the content is automatically updated whenever you want – daily, weekly, or monthly. Internet Explorer can download updated web pages or entire sites in the background while you do other work on your computer, or even while you sleep. Then you can look at them later online, off-line, at work, at home, or on the road.

6 **AutoComplete**: when you start typing a frequently used URL in the Address bar, Internet Explorer completes the address for you. And if a web address you type or click in a web page is wrong, Internet Explorer can search for similar web addresses to try to find a match.

7 Keep a web component on your desktop so you can have updated news using **Active Desktop**.

Treat Windows like a browser: you will find back and forward buttons

Wherever you are in Windows the back/forward buttons now work exactly as they do when you are browsing the internet (Diagram 5.7).

Diagram 5.7

A web look to control panel

hot tip **New Internet Explorer 4 components**

You can download new add-ons for your Internet Explorer 4 browser from www.microsoft.com/ie/ie40/Check out

This will help you maneuver around your files a lot quicker. You will also notice an **up** button which moves you to the superior folder if you are in a sub-folder. Once you get used to these buttons, you really will find them indispensable.

1   Click on the **My Computer** icon on your desktop.
2   Click on **Control Panel**.
3   Now click on the **back** button on the browser.
4   Click once again on **Control Panel**.
5   Now click **up**.

Open multiple windows and panes so you can work on one thing while another downloads

If you go into **View** then scroll down to **Explorer bar** you will see a pop-up menu containing **Search**, **History**, **Favorites** and **Channels**. If you click on say, **History**, then another pane should appear. (See Diagram 5.8). Alternatively click on **History** button on the browser.

View > Explorer Bar > History

If you click any **Links** on the left-hand pane, the relevant pages appear displayed in the right-hand pane. This means you can look at a search results list on the left while actually investigating some of the results in the right-hand pane. The handy thing about that is you don't lose your original list if you want to return to it. With a bit of practice using this should become second nature.

> **The Explorer Bar** is a way to browse through a list of links, while displaying the pages those links open on the right-hand side of the browser. These links may be contained in **History** or **Channels** or **Search** or **Favorites**.

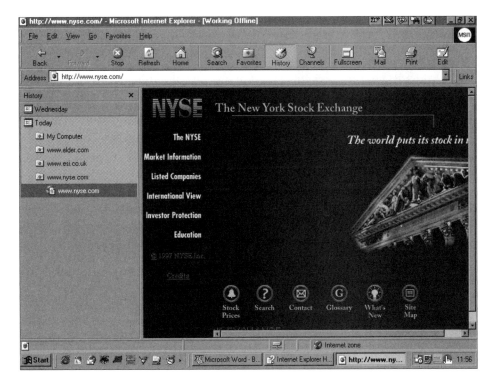

Diagram 5.8

IE4 Explorer bar

1 Visit a few different internet pages and links. It does not matter which.
2 Now make the explorer bar appear with **History**.
3 Go through each of the sites you just visited by clicking on the links in the left-hand History pane and watch them appear in the right-hand pane.
4 Make the **Explorer bar** appear with **Search**.
5 Search for the term **Traded Options**.
6 Click through several of the results listed and watch the results on the right-hand pane.

We will return to searches later, so do not worry too much about them for now.

Use the Taskbar to Quick Launch programs

This can be time-saving device to open your favorite trading software. The taskbar is at the bottom of the Windows screen (see Diagram 5.9).

Desktop Button

Diagram 5.9

Typical taskbar

Outlook Express

Internet Explorer 4

The essential aspects of a taskbar are:

■ Clicking the desktop icon minimizes all windows and shows your desktop. Consider it the computer equivalent of having a lightning fast secretary come in and clear your desk for you.

■ Any file, folder, document or shortcut dragged and dropped into this area of the taskbar (known as the **Quick Launch Area**) will immediately be activated when clicked. A very useful time-saving device.

■ You can rearrange the icons by pointing the cursor at it, holding down the left mouse button and moving it to a new location on the **Quick Launch Section** or onto somewhere on the desktop.

■ To add a new icon to the Quick Launch Area you first create a shortcut to the desktop and then drag the icon to the Quick Launch Area.

■ To make the Quick Launch area wider just drag the vertical line more to the right.
Start > Programs > Windows Explorer > right click on program's icon *> Send to > Desktop as a shortcut*

exercise

1 Click on **Outlook Express** in the **Quick Launch Area**.
2 Click on **Desktop** icon in the **Quick Launch Area**.
3 **Drag** and **Drop** the **Outlook Express** icon next to the **My Computer** icon.
4 Return the **Outlook Express** icon to the **Quick Launch Area**, but this time to the other side of the **Desktop** icon.
5 Shorten the Quick Launch Area. Notice the arrow that appears.
6 Click on arrow and notice the effect.
7 Widen the Quick Launch Area until the arrow disappears.

Drag and drop

To drag something you point your cursor at the icon, hold down the left mouse button and move or "drag" the icon around (while still holding the left mouse button). You drop it as soon as you release the left mouse button.

Making Links and Favorites one click away

This topic is so important for the online trader that we will discuss it separately later, when we discuss managing information.

Use Subscriptions and Channels to stay up to date with your favorite web sites

One of the main problems with using the internet as a source of information is that we don't always know when that information has changed unless we monitor a site regularly. To circumvent this problem, some clever nerds decided that it would be a good idea to have a net site come to you each time it changed, rather than have you go to it. This can all get a bit confusing, so here are some basic facts to help clarify things.

Creating a shortcut

To create a shortcut to a program, first click on **Start**, go to Programs, then Windows Explorer and find the program. Right click on the program's icon and choose the **Send to** option. Choose **Desktop as a shortcut**.

- Subscription simply means having your designated sites automatically update for you; no fees are involved.
- You can subscribe to a site as well as a channel.
- You do not need to subscribe to a channel or a site to view it.
- A channel is like any other web site, but is a little bit more geared up for receiving subscriptions.

Good, with that out of the way we can proceed.

A channel is a web site designed, like all web sites, to deliver content from the internet to your computer.

- Use the **Channel Guide** on your desktop **Quick Launch Area** or in the browser to view a list of channels available through the Microsoft Web site. This list is updated frequently with the latest offerings from new and existing content providers.
- The instructions which follow are fairly self-explanatory. Add channels to your Channel bar. If you want to, you can also subscribe to a channel when you add it to your Channel bar.

■ If you decide to subscribe to a channel you will be given the option of when you would like the updates, how you wish to be informed, e.g. by e-mail, and how you would like to see the consequent display, e.g. as a screen saver, an icon on your desktop. The Subscription Wizard is very straightforward and self-explanatory.

Automatic updates under subscription

These are really designed for people who have a constant link to the internet (for example, at work on a dedicated line) and for people with a fast link e.g. through ISDN. Otherwise subscriptions can be time consuming and seriously annoying! Consequently, they do not form an essential part of our trading action plans.

■ The Channel bar displays all channels installed on your computer, whether you subscribe to them or not. Organize your channels as you would your favorite pages or any other folder – add and delete web sites and specify which web sites are listed.

■ View a channel, whether or not you have subscribed to it, just by clicking it in the Channel bar.

Subscribing to a non-Channel site is very straightforward:

1 Log on to the site in question.
2 Right click on your mouse and click on **Add to favorites** (see Diagram 5.10).
3 When in Add to favorites click on **Subscribe**.

Diagram 5.10

Getting ready to subscribe

exercise

1 Go to www.pointcast.com.
2 Subscribe to the channel and arrange for daily updates.
3 Log off.
4 From the taskbar have the computer update the subscription.
5 Log off.
6 Delete your subscription.

AutoComplete

AutoComplete is a useful device for when you can't remember or be bothered to type in that all-important web address. AutoComplete remembers previous addresses you have typed in and fills them in when you re-type them (Diagram 5.11).

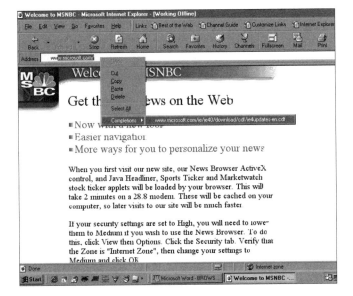

Diagram 5.11

Autocompletion in full flow

1 Start typing in an address you have typed in before into the **Address Box**. Notice how it is AutoCompleted.

2 Continue typing the address. Notice how the AutoCompleted text is overwritten. This is useful when Internet Explorer 4 completes the wrong address.

3 With the characters selected right click on your mouse.

4 Move down to the **completion** sub-folder. Notice the options for completion contained in here.

5 Type in this new address **Pointcast**. And press <enter>. You should be taken to the Pointcast site. Note how Internet Explorer 4 AutoCompletes the **www.** and **.com** bits.

If AutoComplete really annoys you, it can be turned off. Click **View** then **Internet Options** then uncheck the **Use AutoComplete** box.

View > Internet Options > Use AutoComplete

Keep a web component on your desktop so you can have updated news using Active Desktop

If you have fast, constant internet access then this little tool can be a useful and efficient way of monitoring your stocks and general financial news. If you do not have fast, constant internet access then forget it. The **Active Desktop** (Diagram 5.12) will even cause a 56k Modem and Pentium 233MHz processor to scream in strain under the computing pressure you will inflict upon it.

Each time you log on the web component will update. You also can click on parts of the component, say a news headline, to get more in-depth coverage.

Diagram 5.12

Active Desktop with two popular tickers

The steps are relatively straightforward:

1 Turn on **Active Desktop** by right clicking your mouse on the desktop and highlighting the **Active Desktop** folder and then clicking the **View as Web Page** sub-folder.

2 Next log on to www.microsoft.com/ie/ie40/gallery/main.htm.

3 Here you will find a list of Active Desktop components. Simply click and the Wizards will do the rest.

4 Once the component is on the Desktop, to you can move it around and resize using the usual drag and drop.

5 To update your component's content, either click on the update icon on the actual component, or right click your mouse somewhere on the desktop and highlight **Active Desktop**, next click **Update Now**.

Active Desktop > View as Web Page

If you are that way inclined the really clever thing to do is to add web pages as Active Desktop components (perhaps one of the sites from the action plans we cover later?) To do this:

1   Log on to the relevant site.

2   Right click your mouse on the desktop.

3   Go to the **Properties** folder in the pop-up menu.

4   Go to **Web** tab.

5   Click **New** to add a new component.

6   The Wizard will take you painlessly through the remaining steps.

7   To update your component's content right click your mouse somewhere on the desktop and highlight **Active Desktop**, next click **Update Now** (Diagram 5.13).

Right click on desktop > *Properties* > *Web* > *New* > follow Wizard

Diagram 5.13

Making your desktop an Active Desktop

Managing information on Internet Explorer 4

As traders and investors using the full host of internet resources at our disposal, we will need some convenient way of accessing these sites, without for instance, resorting to scraps of paper stuck on our monitors.

In this section we examine some easy ways of doing this using **Favorites** and **Links**.

Favorites

Favorites is a folder containing the addresses to all your favorite web sites which you can access by double clicking on your mouse. This will come in especially handy once we have a systematic action plan for trading and need to methodically visit certain sites each time we are going to enter, monitor or exit a position.

Viewing favorites

To view favorites in Internet Explorer 4 (Diagram 5.14) you can either click on the Favorites icon in which case the **Favorites** appear in the Explorer bar or you can

Information equals profit

Pay close attention to information management – successful trading depends in no small part on proper information management. Using folders effectively can make the difference between a successful and a loss-making trade.

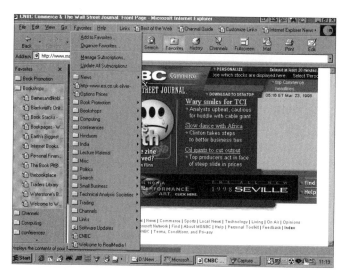

Diagram 5.14

Two ways to view your Favorites

click on the pull-down text menu marked Favorites in the top row of the Internet Explorer 4 browser.

Keeping favorites handy

You can keep shortcuts to your favorite web sites on your desktop, so they are only a click away and your browser is opened up immediately for you. Just open the drop-down Favorites menu and drag the favorites you wish to your desktop.

Another way to get a favorite site to your desktop is to right click on it from the site's shortcut in the Favorites drop-down menu, and from the pop-up menu that appears, select **Send to** and **Desktop as Shortcut**.

Links

hot tip

Links and Favorites

Links can be treated just like Favorites. They are in fact both shortcuts to sites. The only difference is in the way they are displayed.

You can arrange it so that some of the shortcuts to your favorite sites appear on the browser itself. To do this you first need to drag open the **Links** bar. It's the one marked **Links** funnily enough. Next open the drop-down Favorites menu and drag a favorite site to anywhere in the link box. (Tip: You may need to jiggle the mouse about a bit in the format of any existing link site, so that room can be made for your new site.)

Adding a site to Favorites

There are numerous ways to add a site to your Favorites:

1 You can visit the site and then go to the pull-down Favorites menu and click on **Add to Favorites**.

2 Without even visiting a page you can right click your mouse on a link and from the pop-up menu choose **Add to Favorites**. This will add the **Target page** of the link to your favorites.

3 You can click and drag the small page icon in the top left corner of the Internet Explorer 4 window (or the one in the Address box next to the URL address) on to the Favorites drop-down menu.

Using folders

To manage and keep tidy a number of sites that have a common theme you will need to use **Folders**.

To create a new folder, click on the **Favorites** text menu. The drop-down Favorites menu should appear. Click on **Organize Favorites**. To create a new folder click on the **New folder** icon. (It resembles a closed folder with an asterisk at its top right corner.)

An alternative way to create a new folder at the same time as adding a Favorite site is to right click the mouse making the pop-up menu appear. Click on **Add to Favorites**. Next click on **Create In**. Then click on **New Folder** (Diagram 5.15).

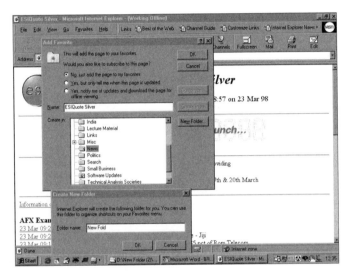

Diagram 5.15
Creating a new folder

Moving things around in Favorites

Once in the drop-down Favorites menu you can move various favorites sites into it (for instance, because you want the one you access to be nearest the top, or because you want to create a new folder) by using the usual drag and drop method. A black horizontal line will appear to mark the new destination.

To move a site or folder into another folder, display the drop-down Favorites menu and click on **Organize Favorites**, then click on **Move**.

Deleting a favorite site

Should one of your favorite sites become an ex-favorite site then to delete it you can either:

1 Go into the drop-down Favorites menu and right click on the site. A pop-up menu will appear which will include the option to **Delete**.

hot tip **Back up favorites**

You will want to make a back-up copy of all your favorites, after all you will have collected quite a few addresses and should they be deleted accidentally, will you recall what they were? Your Favorites folder should be stored at C:\WINDOWS\Favorites. Find this using Windows Explorer (see your Windows 95 handbook if you are unsure.) Next make a back-up copy onto a floppy by right clicking on the Favorites folder and from the pop-up menu that appears select **Send to** and then **31/2 Floppy (A:)**.

2 Go into the drop-down Favorites menu and click on **Organize Favorites**. Highlight the site in question. Click on the delete button.

3 Display Favorites in the Explorer bar (by clicking on the Favorites icon in Internet Explorer 4). Highlight the chosen site by right clicking on it. From the pop-up menu that appears, click on **Delete**.

Renaming your favorites

Since Internet Explorer 4 chooses the site name to assign to a favorite, your favorites list could have some long and unusual names which will mean little to you and which will not help you in recalling exactly why you added that site to your list. To rename a Favorite folder or site, display the drop-down Favorites menu and click on your chosen site and then click on **Rename**.

exercise

1 Log onto CNBC.com.
2 Add this site to your Favorites folder.
3 Log on to FT.com.
4 Using your Favorites folder, log back on to CNBC.
5 Now create a new folder entitled **News**.
6 Add CNBC and FT to that folder.
7 Delete both CNBC and FT from the folder.

The underdog Netscape Navigator 4.03

It is a testament to the strength of Microsoft that after entering the internet market a lifetime too late in internet terms it still managed to overtake one of the earliest starters in that market. How? Because Microsoft had a more diversified computing base which it could use to create "integrated" packages and offer net services as part of them.

And for the conspiracy theorists: could it be that Microsoft, being aware of its phenomenal power, entered the internet market late to permit fledgling weaker companies to gain strength so that it would only have to fight monopoly threats later – after earning a substantial amount of money first? Don't forget Microsoft started working with Apple to strengthen it when it appeared that the Justice Department would attack Microsoft in a world with a weak Apple.

We will now take the Netscape Navigator for a spin and put it through its paces.

Open multiple windows and panes so you can work on one thing while another downloads

A **Frame** is a self-contained area of a window in a browser that can work independently from the other frames (Diagram 5.16). With Netscape Navigator you can:

■ Update the contents of one frame without having to reload the entire window. Simply right click inside the relevant frame and on the pop-up menu click on **Reload frame**.

■ Save the contents of a single frame. Right click your mouse button on the relevant frame and on the pop-up menu click on **Save Frame As**.

■ Print the contents of a frame without printing the whole window. Right click on the relevant frame and on the pop-up menu click on **Print**.

■ Open another window to view another site simultaneously. Right click on any link and on the pop-up menu click on **Open Frame in New Window**, or launch Navigator again and type in the desired site address.

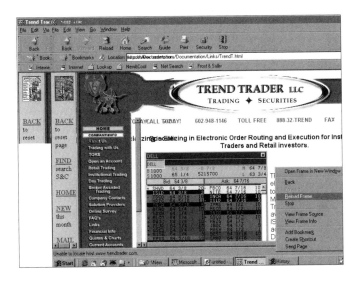

Diagram 5.16

Netscape getting ready to play with frames

1 Go to www.moneynet.com.
2 Select a frame.
3 Print that frame.
4 Save that frame.
5 Open a link in a new window.

Use keyboard shortcuts

With Navigator you can use some nifty keyboard shortcuts to avoid messing around with the mouse too much, trying to find minuscule links:

■ Get rid of the status bar by clicking [Ctrl] + [Alt] + [S].

■ Click [Tab] to move from link to link – elegantly and with much finesse.

■ [Ctrl] + [N] opens up a new window.

■ [Ctrl] + [Alt] + [T] tells you what you are waiting for to download – handy if you're bored (Diagram 5.17).

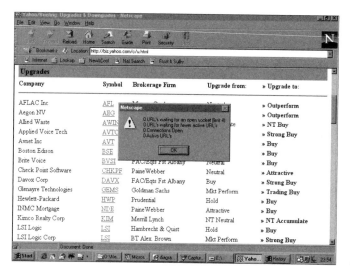

Diagram 5.17

**Netscape and Ctrl +
Alt + T**

Increase viewing space

This is for when you just gotta absolutely positively have those extra few inches
(Diagram 5.18):

▓ To hide toolbars go to **View** drop-down menu and click on **Hide** whichever
toolbar.

▓ To make toolbars smaller go to **Edit** drop-down menu, then **Preferences** and
then go to **Appearance** and next check the button next to **Show toolbars as
pictures only**.

▓ To temporarily hide a toolbar click on the tab to its left.

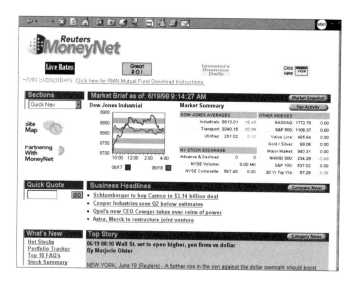

Diagram 5.18

Full screen ahead

Searching made a teeny bit easier

To simplify your searching Netscape Navigator has some useful features:

- Under **Bookmarks** menu you can go to **Search** and click on some of the best search engines on the web. You can also search people's names and e-mail addresses here.

- A question mark inserted in the location box will take you to a randomly chosen search engine.

- Enter two or more words in the location box that are not a URL address and Netscape will automatically place them in a search engine.

exercise

1 Type trading psychology in the location box.
2 Type ? in the location box and in the search engine that appears type **trading stocks.**

Channels and subscriptions – again

As in Internet Explorer, Netscape Navigator has channels to which you can subscribe and have information delivered automatically as by magic to your desktop. To use this facility you need to do the following:

1 Launch Netscape Netcaster which comes with Netscape Navigator by clicking on the **Window** pull-down menu and then clicking on **Netcaster**. It may be that a trial version of the Netcaster has expired on your Navigator, in which case you will be instructed to visit www.home.netscape.com. If you can download anything from here without being bombarded with advertisements and annoying registrations in triplicate and then eventually led up 16 blind alleys, you'll be lucky. I gave up after half an hour. At this stage you may wish to just go ahead with Internet Explorer 4. Anyway, for the sake of completeness, this is what I understand is supposed to happen if you manage to get onto Netscape Netcaster.

2 A **Channel Finder** should appear on the right-hand side of your screen. This pop-out menu will list all the channels (a channel is an internet site with special design features and content – see definition in Internet Explorer section) available for subscription (subscribing to a channel means arranging for automatic download of the sites contents at specified times, see definition in Internet Explorer section.)

Off-line browsing

With Netscape Navigator, as with Internet Explorer, you have the useful facility of automatically saving pages you have visited for browsing later. Useful if you want to store them for later review or if your local phone company charges for phone calls:

■ Click the **Window** pull-down menu and then click on **Netcaster**. Open the **Channel Finder** and click on **New**. Add the URL of the desired page you want to download for off-line browsing. This site will now be located in your channels and Navigator will download it and cache it for later off-line browsing.

■ In future right click on the site from the **Channel Finder** and select **Start Update** from the pop-up menu.

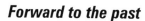

exercise

1   Add www.moneynet.com to your channels.
2   Download the content.
3   Log off and view the pages.

Forward to the past

Netscape has some nifty features that make it quick to go back to sites you've recently visited. This is particularly useful when you have been searching for financial information and have not printed or saved every site you visited and want to return to it.

There are several ways to visit sites previously viewed:

hot tip
Visit now, browse later
Browsing or "surfing" sites quickly before deciding which bits you need and then returning to them is a lot faster than saving or printing each page.

■ Press [Ctrl] + [H] or click on the **Window** then on **History** to get the History list. You can then click on any of the sites you have visited to have them appear again.

■ To quickly search through the history folder click [Ctrl] + [F] (Diagram 5.19).

■ Click on the down arrow at the right-end extreme of the location box. A drop-down box appears with the URLs of your recent excursions.

■ Right click your mouse button on the browser **back arrow** key to get a pop-up menu of recent URLs.

■ Of course you can just click on the **back arrow** key.

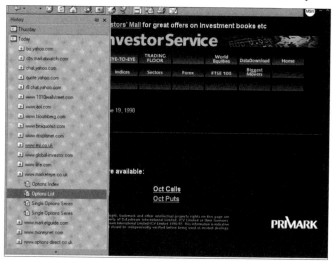

Diagram 5.19

Out of the history folder

Managing information on Netscape Navigator 4.03

Using **Bookmarks** and **Links** we can manage tidily all those sites we find the most useful, so that we can return to them conveniently at a later time. This may appear trivial, but since financial information is the prerequisite to successful trading, we must ensure we place sources of information in places where we can find them readily.

Bookmarks

A **Bookmark** is the equivalent of **Favorites** in Internet Explorer 4. It is a folder containing the addresses to all your favorite web sites which you can access by double clicking. As with **Favorites** you can have sub-folders for placing addresses which are in the same categories, e.g. all news-related web sites in a news sub-folder within **Bookmarks**.

Viewing bookmarks

To view bookmarks in Netscape Navigator (Diagram 5.20) you have two options:

1 Click on the **Bookmarks** icon, which then pulls down a menu.

2 Click on the **Window** pull-down menu and then click on **Bookmark**.

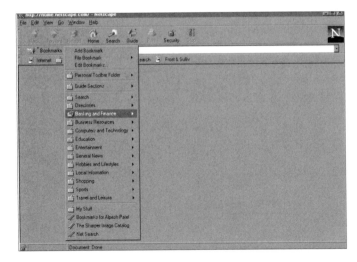

Diagram 5.20
Netscape Bookmarks

Keeping bookmarks handy

You can view your bookmarks inside your browser. Go the **File** drop-down menu. Next click on **Open Page** then **Choose File** in the box that appears. Go to Netscape's program directory then click on **Users**. Next click on **your name**. Click on **Open**. Finally choose **Add Bookmarks** in the bookmarks menu.

The next time you want to view the bookmarks easily you can open the bookmarks folder and access the list from there and have it appear in the browser window.

In Netscape Navigator you have something called a **Personal Toolbar**. This is a small strip of icons below the bar containing the location box. (In some cases the **Personal Toolbar** may be above the location box.) You can make your favorite bookmarks appear as icons on the **Personal Toolbar** by doing the following:

■ To the left of the location box is a green bookmark icon. When your mouse cursor is above it the cursor will change into a hand. Click and drag the link to your **Personal Toolbar**.

■ Another way to get bookmarks into your **Personal Toolbar** and so keep them hand is to click on the **Bookmarks** drop-down menu and then click on **Edit bookmarks**. In the pop-up menu you can then move bookmarks around by dragging and dropping them on to the **Personal Toolbar**.

You can conveniently place links to your desktop by placing the cursor over the green bookmark icon to the left of the location box. Click and drag the link to your desktop. Clicking on the icon which will be automatically created will launch Netscape Navigator and take you to the relevant site.

Adding a site to Bookmarks

To add a favorite site to your bookmarks do one of the following:

■ Having reached your favorite site, right click your mouse. In the pop-up menu click on **Add Bookmark**.

■ Click on the **Window** drop-down menu. Next click on **Bookmark** and finally in the pop-up menu that appears click on **Add Bookmark**.

■ Place your cursor over the green bookmark icon to the left of the location box. Drag and drop the link to the **Bookmark** icon on the toolbar.

Using folders

To manage and keep tidy a number of sites with a common theme, use **Folders**. To create a new folder is rather a long-winded process:

1 Click on the **Bookmarks** icon in the toolbar.

2 Click on **Edit bookmarks**.

3 Click on **File** drop-down menu or right click on the screen and a pop-up menu will appear.

4 Finally and at long last click on **New Folder**.

exercise

1 Go to www.reuters.com.
2 Now to www.cnbc.com.
3 Using the **History** folder return to the Reuters site.
4 Create a new folder entitled **News** in **Bookmarks**.
5 Place the Reuters site in the **News** folder.

Moving things around in Bookmarks

Click on the **Bookmark** icon. Now click on **Edit bookmark**. Once in the Edit bookmark menu you can move various bookmarks sites in there (for instance, because you want the one you access most to be near the top, or because you want to create a new folder) by using the usual drag and drop method. A black horizontal line will appear to mark the new destination.

Deleting a bookmark

Should one of your bookmarks become an ex-favorite site then to delete it you click on the **Bookmark** icon. Next click on **Edit bookmark** and in the screen that appears highlight the site or folder you want to delete. Next right click your mouse and click on **Delete**.

Bookmark > Edit Bookmark > Bookmark your name > File > Save As

The Battle of the Browsers: Netscape Navigator or Internet Explorer?

If you are new to browsers and have yet to get used to the idiosyncracies of a browser, or you are thinking about changing your browser then you may want to read the next bit.

So, having examined both the Netscape Navigator and the Internet Explorer, which is better? In my opinion it is the Internet Explorer, and here's why:

1 Internet Explorer is a lot more intuitive, you can right click on many more items and have pop-up menus displayed for much of what you may want to do.

2 Because of lack of right click functionality in Netscape Navigator the same task in Navigator can take three or four more clicks than in Internet Explorer.

3 With Internet Explorer you have the option of changing the whole feel of Window 95 to something more like a browser with back and forward buttons.

4 **Active Desktop** in Internet Explorer is a very useful feature.

5 Channel subscription in Netscape Navigator appears far too long winded.

6 Moving bookmarks is far more difficult in Navigator than in Explorer.

hot tip *Back up bookmarks*

*You will want to make a back-up copy of all your bookmarks, after all you will have collected quite a few addresses and should they be accidentally deleted, will you recall what they were? Click on the **bookmark** icon, next click on **edit bookmark**. Next click on the highest level bookmark icon; it should be entitled something like **bookmarks for your name**. Next click on **File** and in the drop-down menu on **Save As**. Next make a back-up copy onto a floppy.*

Summary

The browser is the primary contact the trader has with the internet and therefore its importance cannot be underestimated. It even more important because used correctly it can be a filing system for managing information:

- The latest versions of Netscape Navigator and Internet Explorer have all the features that a good browser should have and will keep pace with web site developments.

- The most important thing to become familiar with on your browser is the Favorites or Bookmarks facility, because information management should be second nature to a trader.

Feeling the need for speed: speeding things up

ff *That is also why a lot of people leave early or at certain times. Because if you hang around the quiet market, you get bored and you start buying when you shouldn't.* **"**

Paul RT Johnson Jr.
Vice President
ING Securities, Futures and Options

In this chapter

Everything is running smoothly, you're surfing cyberspace, cruising down the electronic superhighway, hovering along the information virtual motorway – feeling slick, looking good. But wait – isn't the scenery passing just a little bit slowly, is not getting to your destination taking too long to be cool? The problem with the internet is that, for the private investor working from home, things can drag as the World Wide Web becomes the world wide wait – slower and longer than a political convention.

In this chapter we examine some quick tips which may help tune up the computer and squeeze that extra iota of performance out of it and the browser. No promises of turning your Chevvy into a Porsche though.

Objective

- Learn some quick ways of speed surfing

Tips

Open the browser at your destination

In both Internet Explorer and Netscape Navigator you can determine at which page the browser first opens when you launch it. This can save a vital few seconds because it means you can start at your favorite and most usual home page:

- In Internet Explorer click on **View** drop-down menu and then click on **Internet Options** and on the **General Tab** enter the site of your choice next to **Home Page Address**, or click on **blank** for a blank screen – saving lots of downloading time.

- In Netscape Navigator click on **Edit** drop-down menu and go to **Preferences** and then in **Navigator** enter the home page of your choice or a blank screen to save even more time.

Cache clear

The sites you visit are stored in your computer's hard disk. To speed things up when downloading web pages you can:

■ In Internet Explorer 4 (Diagram 6.1) click on **View** drop-down menu and then click on **Internet Options** and on the **General Tab** click on **Delete Files** and on **Clear History**.

■ In Netscape Navigator (Diagram 6.2) click on **Edit** drop-down menu and go to **Preferences** and **Navigator** then click on **Clear History**, on the **Advanced** go to **Cache** and then click on **Clear Memory Cache** and **Clear Disk Cache**.

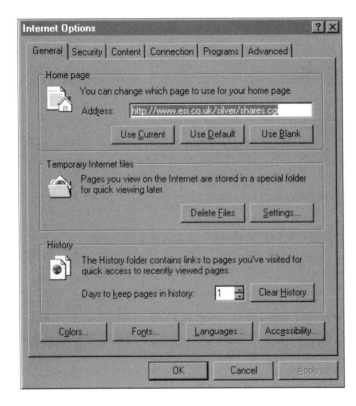

Diagram 6.1

IE4 with Options folder open

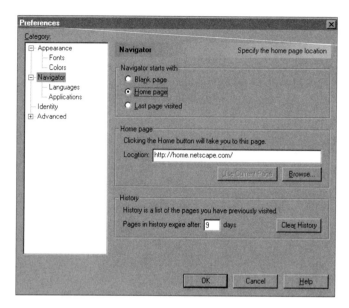

Diagram 6.2

NN4 with folder open

Turn off graphics

Pages load a lot faster if you are not downloading graphics:

■ In Internet Explorer 4 click on **View** drop-down menu and then click on **Internet Options** and on the **Advance Tab** scroll down to **Multimedia** and clear the **Show Pictures** box.

■ In Netscape Navigator click on **Edit** drop-down menu and go to **Preferences** and under **Appearance** then click on **Text Only**.

Consider an internet accelerator

Go to any software vendor and they will have some software called an internet accelerator. Most of these download links which lead off your current page when your modem is not doing anything else and you are reading a particular page. That way, when you click on one of the links, hey presto! the page is already downloaded (see Table 6.1).

I am dubious about their value for money but they occasionally speed things up marginally.

Table 6.1 Selection of internet accelerators

Name of accelerator	Address
Blaze	www.xspeed.com
Net Accelerator	www.imsiuk.co.uk
Peak Jet	www.peak-media.com

Open multiple windows

Remember you can launch multiple copies of your browser simultaneously, so while surfing one page you can wait for another to download.

Time your time on

Internet speed slows down around 7–10am EST (US) and 4–7 pm EST (US) when internet traffic is horrendous. Browse around 3am EST for best results!

Increase cache size

Pages you have visited already are saved on your hard disk and loaded from there before being downloaded by your browser if you visit them again. Since downloading from a cache is quicker than from the internet you should increase the size of your memory cache:

- In Netscape Navigator click on **Edit** drop-down menu and go to **Preferences** and **Advanced** and then **Cache** and **Increase size**.
- In Internet Explorer 4 click on **View** drop-down menu and then click on **Internet Options** and on the **General Tab** click on **Settings** and adjust size of cache.

Defrag

Downloaded web pages get scattered around on your hard drive which means your computer gets slower and s-l-o-w-e-r at finding them from the cache. Defragment your hard drive to reduce this and speed things up.

In Windows 95 click on **Start** then on **Programs** next go to **Accessories** then **System Tools** then **Disk Defragmenter**.

Get faster hardware

You could always get a faster modem, computer processor or RAM, or use ISDN. See the section on hardware in Chapter 1 and Chapter 3 in its entirety.

Summary

There are various things you can tweak on your browser to make things happen a little faster. We explored them in this chapter. Most internet magazines, and the help files in browsers, usually contain a good splattering of tips and tricks too.

The road to profit

Making your action plans

❝ If you go into a trade with a wishy-washy attitude then you are going to be wishy-washy in execution. ❞

Phil Flynn
Vice President
Alaron Trading

In this chapter

Action plans are the unspoken aspect behind successful and professional trading. They may not be called that by everyone, and professional traders may only apply them sub-consciously, but the term is the label for the approach we investigate in this chapter.

Objectives

- Understand the importance of action plans
- Learn how to use skeleton plans to make action plans
- How not being one of the big institutional traders can be an advantage

Why action plans?

Our aim is simple: to trade, to make profit. In order to make full use of the internet and realize our aim we have to have a framework, an approach, that is professional. Our trading research has to be focussed by our framework to ensure we are efficient, accurate, thorough and so above all profitable.

The action plan is our systematic professional approach. It ensures that we have a route map through the internet jungle so that we are not sidetracked or lost in reaching our destination of trading profits. An action plan is a procedure or checklist which can be used each and every time you wish to trade. This ensures you know exactly what you are looking for, where to get it, how to use it and also ensures you have not missed any important steps.

An action plan:

- provides a professional approach
- permits efficiency
- ensures you can quickly get the information you need
- helps manage the vast quantities of information
- makes sure you do not forget anything.

Skeleton plans

Later I provide skeleton plans for trading. The skeleton you use depends on the product you wish to investigate or trade. The flesh on these skeletons is provided by you with my help; you select the net sites you like from my recommendations. After that, the skeleton plan becomes an action plan, which can be used as a systematic process, procedure and checklist which can be used each time you wish to trade (see Illustration 7.1).

Skeleton plan

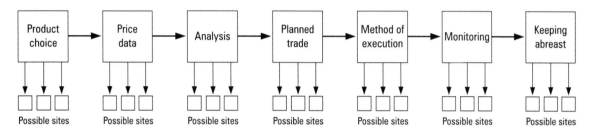

Action plan

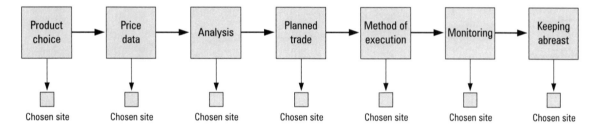

Illustration 7.1

From skeleton plan to action plan

What all action plans need

There are certain key elements which our action plans will cover. These are listed in the box to the right. We shall go through each item in the chapters that follow.

Steps in the action plan

1 product choice
2 price data
3 analysis
4 trade planned
5 method of execution
6 monitoring
7 keeping abreast/educational

Advantages of not being a trading Goliath

At this point, some individuals may question whether action plans and the internet can really compete against the might of the institutional traders. As a piece of motivation, inspiration, and reassurance, I would like you to read the following excerpt from *The Mind of a Trader*. Bill Lipschutz who is being interviewed used to be Global Head of Foreign Exchange at Salomon Brothers and he averaged $250,000 in profit a day, each trading day, for his employers for eight years.

Most traders of course do not work for the leading investment banks. Most traders are private individuals who toil in whatever spare time they have to make a few accurate trades. These "Davids" compared to the investment bank "Goliaths" lack the same infrastructure, the support staff, the research capabilities, the state-of-the-art information and analysis software and hardware and they lack the benefits of being surrounded by highly experienced colleagues. But the Davids do have a few advantages over the Goliaths. To trade successfully and defeat Goliath effectively at his own game, these few advantages must be "driven home" and capitalized upon.

Advantage 1: The ability to sit on your hands

Uncomfortable, yet profitable. That is the consequence of sitting on your hands. As Bill explains, the private trader has definite benefits over his full-time investment bank counter-part in not having someone looking over his shoulder.

"When you work for a big company you don't see many traders saying, 'oh man, I don't really have a good idea about the market, gee I'll read the newspapers today.' Because your boss is walking by, saying, 'How come you're not trading?' The fact of the matter is, if most traders would learn how to sit on their hands 50 percent of the time, they would make a lot more money.

"Let's say you place 1 bet each day over a period of 250 trading days in a year. You know what it's going to come down to? It's going to come down to five bets; three of which are going to be horribly wrong and you are going to lose a fortune, two of which are going to be amazingly right and you are going to make a fortune. And in between, the other 245 times are not going to matter, you'll make a little and lose a little. They will be all those times when you should probably be sitting on your hands, and you'll be scrambling to get out even, or you are not paying attention and you **** up, and you get out even when you should have made a little bit of a profit. It all really comes down to a few decisions.

"You really need to understand the benefit of 'being out of the market' if there is nothing to do, if there is no high probability trade. The whole game of trading is to continuously work for an edge. Continually take the high probability bets. Take those all the time, and by definition you will come out ahead, as long as your risk of ruin is low enough so that you do not get blown out with any one or two or three bad bets, a bad streak. So if you have someone at a big company, looking over your shoulder and saying, 'how come you're reading the paper, shouldn't you have a position?' The real answer is, 'no.' But management is not too much into that."

Advantage 2: Decision-making control

On your own, with your own funds, you are the "trigger man." It all depends on you and you alone. Similarly, if you do not work on the trading floor, but instead have individual investors, you could have some freedom.

"Individual investors are not going to call you every day, because they don't really want to know what your positions are, whether you are long, short or out of the market. Now you, Alpesh, you are the sole decision-maker at every level; what to commit, when to commit, if to commit. I am smiling because just like you I was in university for a long time, I traded on my own; you, me, probably every other trader you are going to interview, we were all up 480 percent, at some point and the funny thing is of course you are looking at a universe of all successful people. If you weren't up 480, or 200 or 80 percent or whatever it was when you were on your own, you would never have made it."

The point Bill is making is that you ought to be having exceptional returns, probably better than your professional colleague at a bank, if you are in total trading control. If you can't do it on your own, it's unlikely to be better when you have someone over your shoulder. This is a point with which Kaveh Alamouti, Head of Derivatives and Arbitrage at Tokai Bank, also agreed when I spoke to him about the sizable returns my trading was producing, compared to some of the "star" traders in investment banks. I reflected that unfortunately the stars had a "little bit" more capital at their disposal than I!

Advantage 3: Information is Profit

The greater availability of information to the private investor than ever before has meant that, rather than being at a disadvantage to his professional colleague, he is on almost level terms with him. So strictly this is not an advantage, but not a disadvantage any longer either.

"In 1997 information is available instantaneously far more than any of us can absorb. No one has information first. A guy sitting in his living room in Kansas watching TV can see information as fast as a trader on a trading desk now. 10 years ago, because I was at Salomon, because I had this kind of technology, I had an edge over a lot of people. I was one of the first handful of traders in New York to have a Telerate and Reuters machine in my home. And now it's commonplace.

"I wanted it at home because I knew other traders would get into work and they would have to call colleagues in London and ask them how things had looked overnight. And it occurred to me that you were going to get a second hand interpretation doing things that way. So when I had the Telerate at home, I could come to work and know what the markets were doing. Today, almost everyone has access to that kind of information and the edge of many traders is gone."

Do not let information availability become a disbenefit. Although you may be able to obtain information as quickly as a professional trader, they have the resources to manage it. The information problem up until the 90s has been one of availability, cost and promptness. In the 90s and beyond the information problem is not really about those things, it is about information management. Do not just sit back in complacency because you have the same information at the same time as Salomon, remember you have to manage all the information available to you, otherwise it will be under-utilized.

Advantage 4: Flexibility and agility

As most people know, big things take longer to change and adapt than small things. Those are the laws of inertia and momentum. A similar law applies in trading, to the advantage of the trading "Davids."

"You can very quickly reorient what your firm is doing. Many small firms will trade many different markets. If for example a certain market is currently yielding certain opportunities or going through structural change, big firms are much slower to realize these opportunities. For big firms there are generally many more decisions which are not related to the issue at hand that have to do with reorienting a department. That is the nature of big organizations."

It is important as a trader to monitor industry-wide changes, in the same way the CEO of Coca-Cola would monitor changes in the nature of the soft-drinks market. You ought then to be better placed to change product, or market if what you are trading should prove to be unprofitable, perhaps because of regulatory or other structural changes. It is an advantage which you may only utilize but once in your trading career, but it is worth bearing in mind.

Advantage 5: The pressure to Perform

The small trader with his destiny in his own hands may often have less pressure exerted on him than others. However, this is not necessarily an absolute benefit.

"As far as professional traders versus the individual traders are concerned, the individual trader, of his own account, does not have the same kind of pressure of someone looking over his shoulder and saying, 'you ought to do this or that.' But then again no one is going to force a discipline on you, no one is going to say, 'you have to cut your losses, this is too big or this is too little.' Now that is probably a bad thing. You will not have, as an individual, a superior who has a dispassionate view on your positions, who can advise. A small trader who has never worked in a big firm and learnt the discipline of the big firm has trouble with discipline. He will say, 'I know this is a great trade, I am going to stay with it.' Whereas in a big firm you often have a dispassionate superior who will say, 'It does not matter, it is too big, you have got too much of a loss, you have to be out of it.'"

Consequently, if you are an individual private trader, you must ensure that you recognize what beneficial outside influences (such as an imposed trading discipline) are placed on you, and then ensure you impose them on yourself.

Summary

A more detailed explanation of each stage is provided in subsequent chapters, however for an overview the following summary should be of value.

After choosing the type of product you wish to invest through, e.g. stocks, the next stage is obtain some historical and daily prices for a range of stocks. With these basics you need to conduct some research and analysis of your chosen product so that, for instance if you chose to invest in stocks, you can settle on a particular company. The two principal methods of analysis are technical analysis and fundamental analysis. This is the most detailed and demanding aspect of trading.

The next step, after analyzing various options and deciding upon an investment, is to plan the trade from entry to exit: entry prices, likely exit price, duration you are willing to hold the investment, best, worst and expected scenarios.

Having planned on paper your intentions and aspirations you now need to place the order with a broker, after which you regularly monitor the position to decide when to exit. Finally, whether holding a position or not, you need to keep abreast of trading and market developments which could affect your investments, so that you can constantly re-evaluate your views.

Step 1
What's your pleasure?
the product choice

❝ If you get up in the morning and don't want to come to work then you are in the wrong job. ❞

Brian Winterflood
Managing Director
Winterflood Securities

In this chapter

The first thing you have to do when deciding to trade is to determine what type of product you think you may want to trade. Is it to be futures, options, stocks, bonds or what? At this stage we are not selecting a particular stock or a particular futures contract, we are only deciding the type of product category in which we are going to be interested.

Objective

■ Understand how to choose a product to trade that is a "personality fit"

Questions, questions, questions: choosing a product

There are some key questions you ought to ask yourself before coming to a decision on which product to trade in.

Do I know enough about this product or do I need to investigate further?

Clearly it helps to know something about futures, stocks or options before thinking you can plunge into the murky and complex world of futures trading. The skeleton plans include recommended sites for beginners and those wanting to investigate a type of product. If in doubt, stick to what you know.

It may sound like a good idea to trade futures, but remember the analysis you have to do, the information you need, the understanding of macroeconomics and/or technical analysis required to trade such instruments, the start-up capital and risks. Consequently, in investigating a particular product you would be advised to examine other aspects of the skeleton plan as well, for example visit a few broker sites and find out minimum capital you require, or visit a few data vendor sites and see if the cost of data is prohibitive. At this stage you only need to be aware of these issues. We will return to them later.

Does this product fit my personality?

This point is a little bit more subtle. It is best explained by an extract from *The Mind of a Trader*:

> Trading with a system or a product that does not suit your personality inevitably results in fighting both the system and yourself. Without an appropriate system you will wear yourself and your finances down. It is a little like playing football with someone else's gear on, or going in to battle wearing someone else's armor. It is self-evident that even if the football gear belongs to Joe Montana and the armor to Julius Caesar, you will not perform as they did.
>
> As Martin Burton states, Chairman of Monument Derivatives and former Director of County NatWest,
>
>> "The key thing is that you have to trade within your personality. It may be that your personality is flawed as indeed I am sure mine is. The flaw in my personality is that there will be times where I may be too aggressive or too quick to react. There is no point me trying to play tennis like Bjorn Borg if I am John McEnroe. Therefore I try to trade according to my personality, a personality that is capable of being aggressive on occasions or quick to react. To me if I occasionally release anger I am doing myself a favor, even if I am not doing anyone around me a favor, because I am releasing all the poisons I have. Then as soon as I have released them I am totally free.
>>
>> "If you are a certain type of a person you have to identify what you are. Come to terms with yourself as a personality, genuinely and without lying, and not something you would like to be. Trade with what you are. That to me is a really big key issue with traders. I am what I am and I have no pretensions as to what I am and I am happy to trade within my own personality. That is a very important point for me."
>
> Your system must play to your personality strengths and mitigate the influences of your personality weaknesses. You first need to ask yourself what are your personality strengths and weaknesses, and what do you like and dislike about trading. For instance are you patient or impatient, do you believe in technical analysis, do you enjoy plotting charts, do you prefer a diverse or concentrated portfolio?
>
> Next decide if your system plays to your attributes. For instance, if you are impatient, then when devising your system, you would obviously not be looking at long-term investments. You would want a system, probably based upon technical analysis, that indicates imminent price movements. A system based on projections of likely long-term demand for a company's products is hardly likely to suit your personality and would probably lead to frustration.

A further example of harmonizing your personality to your trading system is if your personality is very risk averse you may consider options a better instrument than futures. If you are indecisive you may want a system which spells out in detail when exactly you ought to enter and exit. If you are not a very quick thinker, you should probably not to be an intra-day futures trader.

The message is to stick to what you are comfortable with.

Action plan

1 Decide if you have chosen with confidence the product you will trade or whether you want to investigate products further.

2 Consider in the light of what you have just read whether this product suits your personality.

3 Read the section in the book where the skeleton plans for your product are located.

4 Surf all the sites or the ones which most closely match what you are looking for.

5 If you are undecided about a product, use the sites to learn more about it and how it works – depending on experience already gained.

6 After making your decision as to product, keep a note of the sites you found most useful in the bookmark/favorites section of your browser for future reference.

7 Go to Step 2 (Chapter 9).

Summary

There are a lot of financial products one can invest in, from stocks to futures. However, selecting one is not just a question of arbitrary choice. If a product and timeframe are chosen that suits your individual personality the likelihood of substantial profit increases significantly. Some important questions to bear in mind are:

▪ Are you relatively risk averse?

▪ Are you looking for a short-term trading or long-term investing?

▪ Do you prefer examining charts or accounts?

Step 2
Traders' bread and butter: price data

❝ *Don't you tell me you know this stock is going up. You do not.* **❞**

Brian Winterflood

Managing Director
Winterflood Securities

In this chapter

Trading is about price. Price data are essential components to every trading activity. We examine the types of data available and their sources.

Objectives

■ Comprehend the variety of sources and types of data

■ Position selves to choose the best type of data for chosen type of trading

Price data

Price data can be real-time, delayed (e.g. 20 minutes), end of day or historical (e.g. daily data going back 2 years). Which one of these would be most useful to you depends on several factors, as shown in Table 9.1.

Table 9.1 Comparison of types of price data

Type of trader	Most useful form of data	Methods of viewing
Open and close position in 48 hours	Real-time quotes	Internet site or software on PC
Open and close position in 7–14 days	Real-time or delayed quotes	Internet site or software on PC
Technical analyst (see later)	Historical and end of day charts	Internet site or software on PC

Before you can analyze any product you need to have some way of examining its price. For this three components are essential and the skeleton plan provides lists of sites for accessing each:

1 A data provider that can provide the price data daily or intra-daily, and provide historical prices.

2 Some way of viewing the prices, whether at the data provider's internet site or on software downloaded on your computer.

3 Software which can convert the data into graphical format and chart them over time.

Sometimes, internet data providers also provide charts online, reducing the need for separate software on your PC (see Illustration 9.1). However, as these charts are held by the site itself, there is far less you can do with them than with actual software. Nevertheless, they are a cheap alternative to software and worth considering. Consequently, the skeleton plans refer to some of these sites as well.

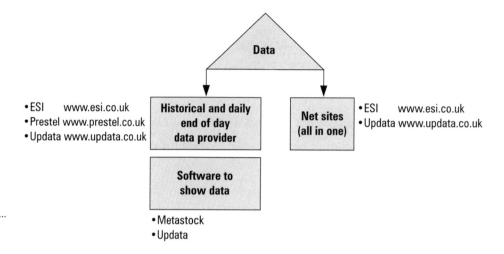

Illustration 9.1

*Internet data
providers*

Data providers

When you are choosing a data provider, whether real-time, delayed, end of day or historical, to provide prices for futures, options or stocks, that provider ought to meet certain criteria. All the recommended sites in the skeleton plans meet the criteria:

- accurate
- cost effective
- in readily accessible data formats for a wide range of software
- several modes of delivery, e.g. internet delivery may be supplemented with satellite, or radio signal or phone line delivery of data.

Software charting and analyzing data

Most trading software companies provide ample illustrations of their software on their sites. Some permit demo downloads and online ordering. These sites are good places to shop around in from the comfort of your PC monitor. The skeleton plans for each product recommend software which meets certain criteria that ought always to be your minimum requirements when trading:

1   cost effective, preferably a one-off fee and not an annual licensing fee

2   value for money – with as many functions per dollar as possible

3   easy to use – user-friendly intuitive displays (Diagram 9.1).

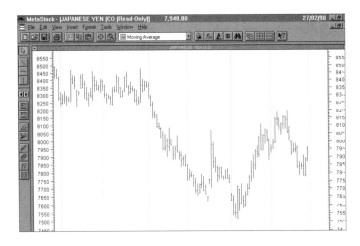

Diagram 9.1

....

Typical charting and analysis software

Online data

As mentioned already there are numerous sites that provide what are often termed **Fast Quotes** or **Quick Quotes**. These sites let you type in a ticker symbol, say for a stock, mutual fund or option and then they display the real-time or delayed price. Some provide historical charts as well. In recommending these sites I have ensured, unless there was a good reason to the contrary, that

1 The service was free.

2 The quotes were delivered quickly.

3 There was the option for a real-time quote as well as delayed.

4 The delayed quotes were not overly delayed.

5 The chart service was as detailed as possible.

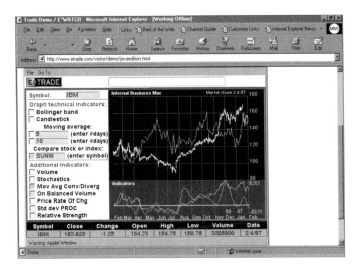

Diagram 9.2

....

Typical online charting and analysis

Action plan

1   Decide for what products you need data – is it stocks, options, mutual funds, bonds, futures, or what?

2   See the skeleton plan in Section 4 for that product and visit sites that provide such data.

3   Visit sites that most match your requirements.

4   Decide whether you want your own software to display data or whether you want internet sites to do that.

5   If you want your own software, visit sites offering that service and read their online brochures; download or order any demos.

6   Choose software which you feel most comfortable with and which provides the best value for money for what you want to do, bearing in mind the recommendations in this book.

7   Choose a data provider that provides compatible data for your software (if you are going to be using your own software) based on the price of such data and the recommendations given in this book.

8   Go to Step 3 (Chapter 10).

Summary

- There are real-time, delayed, end of day and historical data.
- Data are needed for quotes and for charts.
- The main choices involving data relate to how they will be viewed and their source.
- In terms of viewing, software offers more flexibility than the internet.
- The internet is ideal for cheap real-time or delayed quotes, with some sites offering charts as well.

With data sorted we next move onto doing something with it: analysis, getting ever closer to making the fateful trading decision.

10

Step 3
Doing the hard
work: analysis

*❝ Don't be scared to feel you don't know
anything, because you don't know
anything until you learn. ❞*

Brian Winterflood
Managing Director
Winterflood Securities

In this chapter

In this chapter we examine the major forms of analysis: what they are, what most traders look for and how they fit into the skeleton and action plans. We then look at building a trading strategy. This will help to clarify what it is you should be examining when prospecting for trading opportunities.

Once you have chosen a particular type of product in which you wish to invest and have access to some basic price data regarding it, you need to be able to decide what specifically to buy. No matter what you trade your aim is, of course, to buy low and sell high. However, you need something more than telepathy or a flash of inspiration to determine when and what to buy and sell.

This is where analysis comes in. You need to analyze various products to determine what looks like a buy that you will be able to sell at a higher price. For instance, if your product choice is stocks, you need some way of deciding when to buy SmithKline Beecham so that you can sell it within your desired timeframe at a profit. There are essentially two forms of analysis, fundamental analysis and technical analysis and this chapter examines both.

Objectives

- Overview of fundamental and technical analysis
- How to use fundamental and technical analysis
- Appreciation of what fundamental and technical analysts commonly look for
- Appreciation of what option traders look for
- Learn to build a trading plan and strategy

Fundamental analysis

What is it?

When you undertake fundamental analysis you are examining micro- and macroeconomic factors that affect the product's price (Diagram 10.1). For example, if you are interested in frozen concentrated orange juice futures (and who isn't?) you will be interested in, among other things, the weather forecasts for the Florida region. If you are interested in Intel stocks or options then you will be interested in, among other things, the p/e ratio of Intel, its last set of accounts, overseas demand for personal computers.

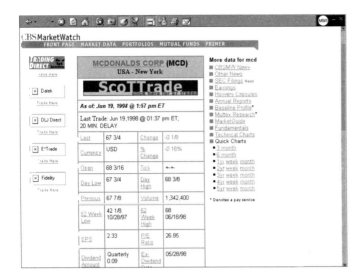

Diagram 10.1

Fundamental data relating to a stock

How do I do it?

There is a variety of types of sites that provide the different forms of fundamental analysis that would be needed for any given product. Therefore, sites have been chosen which provide as much useful information as possible that a fundamental analyst would be interested in, for as little cost as possible (often free). Once you visit the sites suggested by the skeleton plan it soon becomes obvious what you should look for (promise!) Additionally, to make your task even easier under each skeleton plan, there are sub-categories to guide you through what you need to do and examine.

The next section, "Some popular methods of how people choose what to buy," examines what fundamental analysts usually look at and why. This will give you some idea of what it is you should be doing.

hot tip

Fundamental analysis of stocks

Since fundamental analysis of stocks is going to be a very important topic for many readers I have included an appendix providing some advice on factors of importance.

How does this fit in with the skeleton plans?

All will be clear as you progress through the skeleton plans, but to give you an example, under fundamental analysis in the skeleton plans for stocks there will be a sub-category relating to screening, etc. So you will know these are the things to examine and also which sites to go to to get the information. When a skeleton plan directs you to a site the section in the book covering the sites will tell you what fundamental analysis data that site contains, thus further reiterating what exactly you should be looking for.

The recommended reading list at the back of the book will be useful for those wanting to unearth more about fundamental analysis and know what the great fund managers look for (Diagram 10.2).

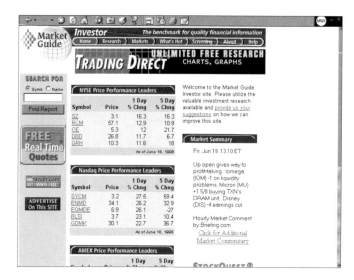

Diagram 10.2

Supplying the demand

Technical analysis

What is it?

Although arguably related to fundamental analysis, technical analysis – or charting as it is often pejoratively and simplistically known – concerns mathematical operations on price data to determine opportune buying and selling points.

With the advent of powerful software you do not even need to know that two plus two equals five before you can use technical analysis (Diagram 10.3). Whether you were interested in FCOJ futures or Intel you would probably examine the same sort of "technicals." For instance, having a price chart for the previous 6 months for a particular stock, you may plot each new day the average price over the last 12 days of that stock (i.e. a moving average) and purchase the stock whenever the price rises above the moving average.

All good technical analysis software vendors have sites that extol the virtues of their software better than any spotty teenager in a software warehouse ever could. This make the internet sites the best way to explore, query, examine and even try out new software before actually paying a penny. The internet comes into its own in the purchase of such software because never before has the consumer had so much information about a product before committing a penny.

As well as the sites of the most popular and best technical analysis vendors, other sites are listed in the skeleton plans which give the novice more information about this form of analysis.

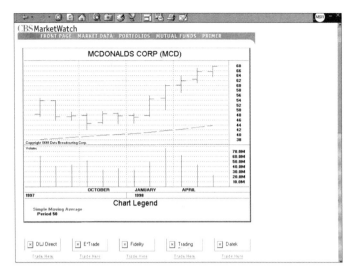

Diagram 10.3
....
Typical technical analysis chart

How do I do it?

Since technical analysis is, well, technical, I have provided more details about it in Appendix 1. This appendix examines what technical analysts usually look at and why. This will give you some idea of what it is you should be doing. And this will tie in with the skeleton plans which will lead you to sites that provide this type of information.

And don't forget to read the recommended reading list (Appendix 7) for more details on technical analysis and visit the educational sites in the skeleton plans.

Some popular methods of how people choose what to buy

Most people, whatever they trade, have several tried and tested methods they use to conjure the inspiration in deciding what to purchase.

What the fundamental analysts examine

There are the fundamental analysts who will have numerous methods, which will include any combination of the following:

■ **Filtering or screening:** fundamental analysts may ask a particular internet site to sift through all the stocks, say, on its database and display the names of those that have certain characteristics. For example, they may ask for the names of all stocks that have a certain price to earning ratio. (Don't worry, these terms, together with what is commonly looked for and why are explained later.)

A typical stock screen

When screening or filtering for stocks (Diagram 10.4) you may decide that you want a company with strong earnings likely to keep a cash reserve (through paying low dividends) which it may use to return value to shareholders by share buy-backs or acquisitions or mergers, in which case you may look for a stock with the following characteristics:

1 a three-year historical earnings growth rate of 20% or more
2 a return on equity (ROE) of 25% or more
3 stocks providing annualized total returns over the past 5 years of 20% or more
4 companies with payout ratios (dividends as a percent of earnings) of 15% or less and dividend yields (dividends as a percent of stock price) of 1% or less.

What would you get? Well, one of the companies listed was Intel. You could then undertake further research.

Diagram 10.4

Stock prospecting using a screen

■ **Newsletters/gurus:** the internet has numerous specialist traders and market commentators (Diagram 10.5) – some of whom are not too bad. Some fundamental analysts scour these utterings and others just stick to their favorites. The types of traders who read these vary from the sheepish – who just want to be told what to buy – to the very independent, who are reading the letters to confirm their own views or get a feel for certain products.

Diagram 10.5

Guru, my guru: a newsletter

Diagram 10.6

Yattering away: a newsgroupie

■ **Newsgroups:** many fundamental analysts will be part of an online community interested in a similar field to their own. They will subscribe to an e-mailing list or bulletin board or news group (all of which are explained later) and discuss whatever concerns them (Diagram 10.6). Such informal arenas are a way to exchange ideas and often form part of a fundamental analyst's toolkit.

■ **Analysts' reports:** many large brokerage houses, such as Lehman Brothers, analyze stocks and commodities to death. Therefore, their recommendations often move markets and can be a good indicator of where things are going (Diagram 10.7). Many fundamental analysts will want to know about upgrades or downgrades by analysts as this is often an important short- and medium-term influence on a stock's price.

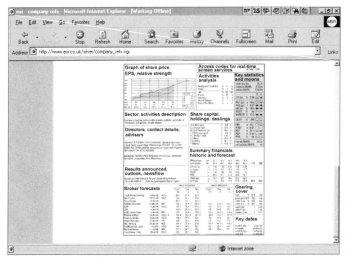

Diagram 10.7

Piggybacking on the big boys: analysts' report

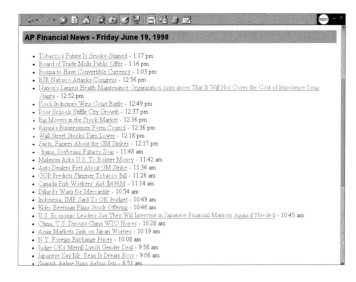

Diagram 10.8

What's new?: a snippet of news

■ **News stories:** part of almost all fundamental analysts' artillery is an examination of stocks, mutual funds, sectors, commodities in the news. Most news sites permit a historical sift through news stories based on keywords. A good site will be renowned for its news coverage and therefore be able to provide breaking news, regular updates during the day (Diagram 10.8).

■ **Data:** plain old data, whether they be company information for the stock trader or weather for the corn futures trader, are essential components of all fundamental analysis (see Appendix 2). For stocks most data are often provided entitled company snapshot or company profile (Diagram 10.9).

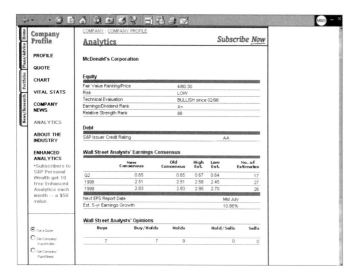

Diagram 10.9

The side shot:
a company profile

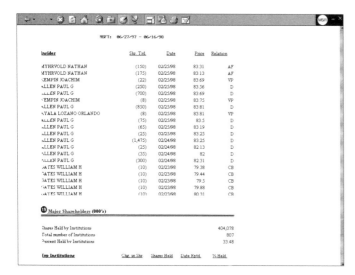

Diagram 10.10

Inside information

■ **Insiders:** many fundamental analysts want to know what "insiders" (i.e. officers, directors, and major shareholders) are doing (Diagram 10.10). This applies to stocks and stock options. If a company's CEO is selling the stock that could well be an important sign of impending price movement down.

■ This is a very simplified "taster" to give you an impression of some of the details of fundamental analysis. (For more details see the recommended reading in the skeleton plans and check out Appendix 2. Tables 10.1, 10.2, 10.3 and 10.4 also contain further details of elements just discussed.)

Table 10.1 Stock and stock option traders

Item**	What signifies positive for the security*
Price and volume	
52-week high	A new high
Growth	
Revenue percent change	An increase (acceleration)
Sales growth rate	An increase (acceleration)
Earnings per share growth rate	An increase (acceleration)
Dividend information	
Dividend yield	An increase (acceleration)
Dividend rate	An increase (acceleration)
Institutional ownership information	
Institutional percent owned	An increase (acceleration)
Institutional net shares purchased	An increase (acceleration)
Financial strength	
Long-term debt to total equity	A decrease (deceleration)
Profitability	
Gross margin	An increase (acceleration)
Operating margin	An increase (acceleration)
Net profit margin	An increase (acceleration)
Valuation ratios	
Earnings per share	An increase (acceleration)
Price to earning ratio	A decrease (deceleration)
Cashflow per share	An increase (acceleration)
Insider trading	
Insider shares purchased	An increase (acceleration)
Insider ownership %	An increase (acceleration)
Management effectiveness	
Return on assets	An increase (acceleration)
Return on investments	An increase (acceleration)
Return on equity	An increase (acceleration)
News	
Company in the news	Unexpected positive story
Sector in news	Unexpected item not in price of individual stocks
Broker report	Upgrade; positive news
Income statements	
Total operating expenses	A decrease (deceleration)
Free cashflow	An increase (acceleration)
Efficiency ratios	
Sales per employee	An increase (acceleration)
Income per employee	An increase (acceleration)

* Conventionally, all other things being equal, compared to similar companies in same sector and compared to self 1/3/5 years earlier and not already incorporated in market expectations.

** See also glossary.

Table 10.2 Mutual fund traders

Item
Management performance over short, medium and long term
Changes in management (could signify changes in performance)
Fees (high fees reduce performance)
Risk profile (is it a high-risk fund?)
Performance relative to market and other funds

Table 10.3 Futures and options on futures traders

Fundamental factor	Fundamental factor
Agricultural	*Oil*
Weather	Weather
Planting intentions	Quota agreements
Price of substitutes	Production levels
Current stocks	Political unrest
Yields	
Probability of crop disease	
Meats	*Copper*
Expected litter sizes	Mining activity
Farrowing intentions	Housing starts
Prices of competing goods	Stocks at the London Metal Exchange
Consumption trends	Probability of unrest in production areas
Present stocks	
Platinum	*Gold*
Automobile production	Political unrest
Mining levels	Jewelry consumption
Jewelry consumption	Inflationary pressures
	Prices of alternative stores of value
Financial futures	
Economy (see later)	

Table 10.4 All traders – the macroeconomy

Macroeconomic statistic	Probable effect
Interest rates	If increase (acceleration) better returns in deposits than stocks, commodities or bonds – so their prices fall; exchange rate appreciates (see below)
Exchange rate	If high, exports expensive so demand decreases (decelerates). Foreign imports more competitive
Balance of payments	If deficit widens, interest rates may be reduced so exports increase (accelerates)
GDP	If high, possible inflationary pressures so possible rise in interest rate (see above)
Foreign markets	If foreign economies sluggish, foreign demand low
Capacity utilization	If high, possible inflationary pressures so possible rise in interest rate (see above)
Jobless claims	If low, possible inflationary pressures so possible rise in interest rate (see above)
Existing home sales	If high, possible inflationary pressures so possible rise in interest rate (see above)
Mortgage lending	If high, possible inflationary pressures so possible rise in interest rate (see above)
Consumer confidence	If high, possible inflationary pressures so possible rise in interest rate (see above)
Construction spending	If high, possible inflationary pressures so possible rise in interest rate (see above)
Factory orders	If high, possible inflationary pressures so possible rise in interest rate (see above)
Non-farm payroll	If high, possible inflationary pressures so possible rise in interest rate (see above)
Retail sales	If high, possible inflationary pressures so possible rise in interest rate (see above)

This is a very simplified illustration; macroeconomic policies vary from country to country and a lot depends on expectations (i.e. were the data in line with what was expected?) This is a basis, however, to help the beginner understand the news stories better and get a firmer feel for fundamental analysis and the fact that everything is connected to everything else – the only issue being how strongly is it connected. See the recommended reading and internet sites for further investigation.

Note, also, what may be considered potentially inflationary factors, such as relatively lower jobless claims, will have the opposite effect in an economy coming out of a recession compared to one which is near the peak of the economic cycle. Therefore, the background economic picture has also to be borne in mind.

Remember the skeleton plans are organized so you can methodically go through this type of analysis, and the sites descriptions have listed what is available on them.

What the technical analysts examine

Look at Appendix 1. And remember, if technical analysis is your particular trading fetish then also see:

■ recommended reading appendix

■ educational sites relating to technical analysis in the skeleton plans.

What options traders examine

Whether they use fundamental analysis or technical analysis or a combination of both, many options traders also use special options analysis software which helps them in making their trading decisions. This software is only useful to options traders as it relates specifically to the technicalities of options. The details of the sites explain what the software does. This will, of course, make more sense to you if you have an understanding of options (see Appendix 4).

You ought to be clear that such software is usually only an optional (!?) extra for more experienced option traders. Many option traders manage adequately without such software.

The vendors of these software packages often have web sites which detail the software and sometimes even allow online demo downloads. These sites are like a shop window and therefore a useful means of comparing products from the comfort of your own home.

Criteria for including sites in the skeleton plans

In examining fundamental and technical analysis internet sites for our action plans, I have sought to include sites which meet the following stringent quality standards! These criteria are also a useful set of guidelines for you to keep in mind when examining other sites not listed that you may find yourself.

Criteria for fundamental analysis sites are:

1 Cost effectiveness: as inexpensive as possible for the quantity and quality of information provided.

2 Extensiveness: one-stop shops are preferable to getting bits and bobs from an array of sources.

3 Quality: good, sound analytical interpretations assist in saving time.

Criteria for technical analysis sites are:

1 Cost effectiveness.

2 Extensiveness: charts on as many products as possible.

3 Customization: does the site allow you to display your own calculations.

What works? Building a trading strategy

So, having examined both fundamental and technical analysis in broad outline together with some common things followers of those techniques use, you may well be tempted to ask what works? Does looking for analysts' upgrades of stock performances work? Does an examination of stock momentum work?

The unfortunate answer is that nothing works and everything works. Nothing works, because if it did it would be consistently profitable and the puzzle of the markets would be solved. Everything works in that all the individual techniques are successful part of the time – that is why they are followed.

A guide to a DIY trading strategy

So where do we go from here? The best advice to give you is, first, read a lot more about fundamental and technical analysis from the recommended reading and the educational sites in the skeleton plans.

Second, develop a trading strategy. A trading strategy is a set of rules which must be met before you enter a trade. In the next chapter we discuss trading tactics which are the actual specific plans for what to do once you enter a trade.

hot tip *Simply be aware and beware*

This is a very simple guide to building a trading strategy to give you some idea of how it ought to be done. As you actually do it you will begin to realize the complexities and your plan will doubtless become more sophisticated. Every individual's trading strategy will vary and likely be unique, based on their own perspectives.

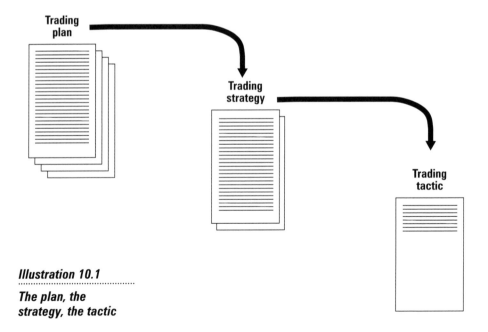

Illustration 10.1
....

The plan, the strategy, the tactic

Steps to building a trading strategy

Select some indicators

Having examined what fundamental and technical analysts commonly look for, and done some reading about those subjects, choose some indicators you think may be potentially indicative of a rising market.

Hypothesize!

Choose some rules you consider worth testing, bearing in mind the period of time you want to be in and out of the market for each trade. Choose a target price for exit, a stop loss figure and other circumstances for exit.

example

A fundamental analyst of company stocks may choose to buy a stock only if the following rules are met:

- P/E ratio less than 7
- analyst recommendations all being buy or higher
- profit margin of 12% or higher
- dividend yield of 12% or higher
- target price: rise of 15%
- stop loss: drop of 10%
- exit if one of these fundamental factors changes adversely.

A technical analyst may choose stock purchase rules based on:

- MACD crossover
- Stochastic crossover
- rising parabolic SAR
- A bounce off a trendline
- target price: rise of 15%
- stop loss: drop of 10%
- exit if one of the above technical factors changes adversely (Diagram 10.11).

Overfitting

There is a tendency when testing trading rules to "overfit" the rules (i.e. amend them) to the data at hand so the results are good for those data only. To avoid this, do some 'out-of-sample testing,' i.e. test the same rules on a completely different set of data. But beware, it may be that your trading rules do genuinely only work with that one company, both historically and in the future, and you may be throwing away a good system by out-of-sample testing. To avoid this, do some paper trades on the same stock as well.

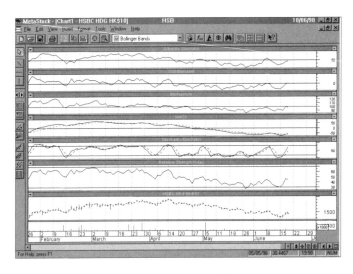

Diagram 10.11

A technical approach

Test

Now test the rules. Select some stocks and obtain their historical price charts (see skeleton plans for sites), next see what would have happened had you used your trading strategy. What would a notional $10,000 have been at the end of 1 year, after dealing costs? Is the return better than bank rates of return? Did you beat the Dow or a typical mutual fund?

How to back test well

1 I tend to test one indicator at a time and add more and more and see how that affects results.
2 Look at a chart and identify areas in which your indicators should produce signals and then find indicators that tend to.
3 Are the results very volatile, e.g. large losses and profits (even though overall profitable)? Can you handle such losses along the way?
4 Do not just test bull markets, test bear and sideways or find a different set of indicators for each type of market (Diagram 10.12).

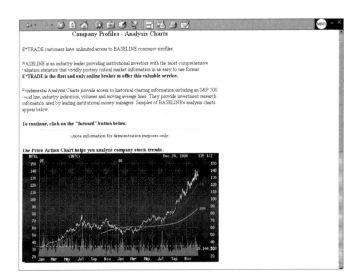

Diagram 10.12

Looking to buy

The preponderance of evidence rule

When testing and developing look for a balance of probability. Examine many different indicators, e.g. news stories on your product, analysts' views, market momentum. When there is a preponderance of evidence suggesting price movement make a paper trade. Keep doing this until you are comfortable that what you are doing works. If it does not find out what aspects do not work, e.g. the technical indicators are always wrong, and either amend or ditch that particular indicator.

Always paper trade with different methods of selecting trades. For instance, you may try to combine stock filters with technical indicators and plot the results together with other systems, and go for what appears to make sense and is profitable.

When you find a trading strategy you are fairly happy with you are then ready to trade.

Action plan

1 Decide if you need or want to find out more about fundamental and technical analysis.

2 Read in this chapter what fundamental analysts look for, and see Appendix 1 as to what technical analysts commonly look for.

3 Examine the sites recommended in the skeleton plan for your chosen product and analysis method.

4 Surf sites which provide analysis for your product choice.

5 Choose site(s) which you like the best for fundamental and/or technical analysis.

6 Develop a trading strategy using the guideline provided in this chapter, then test it to satisfaction (if need be return to Step 4 in this program of action.)

7 Go to Step 4 (Chapter 11).

Summary

The professional trader examines a combination of technical and fundamental analysis as part of a trading plan. It is possible to make a list of factors commonly examined by fundamental and technical analysts and then test these historically against price data as part of a trading plan. The key thing to remember is to enter a position when the evidence is overwhelming in favor of a price move – otherwise stay out.

11

Step 4
The trade
planned

❝ You can't just go out there and wildly speculate. ❞

Bill Lipschutz
former Global Head of Foreign Exchange
Salomon Brothers

In this chapter

This is probably the most important part of any trade. It is also the most neglected. We examine in brief what planning a trade ought to involve. From the previous chapter you have your trading strategy. Now you are going to use it in an actual trade and produce an actual trading tactic. To avoid the many pitfalls of trading we examine keeping a journal, diversification and the types of traders that fail.

Objectives

- Learn to produce and use trading tactics as part of a trading plan
- How to keep a journal as part of profitable trading
- Understand proper diversification
- Examine the types of traders that fail

Action plan for creating a trading tactic

1. Using your trading rules contained in your trading strategy go through the relevant stocks, etc.
2. Select the best possibilities for price moves. Remember the preponderance of evidence rule.
3. For each possibility list the pros and cons (see Table 11.1). Select the best of the best to trade
4. Set an upside target. What do you expect the price to reach and in what timeframe. You may want to attach a rough probability of this occurring.
5. Set a stop loss – a point at which you will exit the trade: either a specific price level or a percentage.
6. Set a point at which you will sell irrespective of 4 and 5 in this list, i.e. you may get negative news on the company and decide to sell even though the stop loss has not been reached.
7. Go to Step 5 (Chapter 12) after reading the remainder of the chapter.

hot tip **Risk – reward** *As a rule of thumb your upside target should be a greater percentage than your stop loss.*

Table 11.1 Part of a simple trading tactic

Pros	Cons
MACD crossover occurred	Sector undergone long bull run
Stochastic crossover	
SAR upward	
Trendline bounce	
All analysts buy or strong buy	
Sector strong	

Journal keeping

hot tip **The mind of a trader**

Stick to your plan. Do not start hoping for price moves, or denying losses. Try to keep objective. Do not get attached to a position: each day is a clean slate. To learn more about trading plans and trading like a professional, you might consider reading The Mind of a Trader (FT Pitman Publishing, 1997).

I am regularly asked by traders what they can do to improve their trading. One of the easiest and simplest steps that can be undertaken is to keep a journal. Imagine all that information and experience you collect as you trade. Without a journal you are throwing so much of it away. Without a journal you are in serious danger of repeating your mistakes. In this regard, keeping a journal is a money and risk management technique. By identifying possible trading problems, you can start to resolve them. So, make journal keeping a goal.

What to record

1 You will want to have a copy of your goals, and note your progress in achieving them.

2 The anatomy of every trade. Write down, from the moment you started analyzing a stock to the moment after you sold it, how you felt at each key moment about every activity you undertook. You may want to compare that with what you know about how you should have reacted, in light of what you have read in this book. For example, how did you feel as you approached your stop loss?

3 Write down what feels good and what feels uncomfortable about what you are doing.

Remember to keep your notes clear and well presented. You will have to return to them at a later date.

Trading types

There are many types of trader. An awareness of the varieties when looking at your trading plan allows you to avoid the pitfalls.

The disciplined trader

This is the ideal type of trader. You take losses and profits with ease. You focus on your system and follow it with discipline. Trading is usually a relaxed activity. You appreciate that a loss does not make for a loser.

The doubter

You find it difficult to execute at signals. You doubt your own abilities. You need to develop self-confidence. Perhaps you should paper trade.

Blamer

All losses are someone else's fault. You blame bad fills, your broker for picking the phone up too slowly, your system for not being perfect. You need to regain your objectivity and self-responsibility.

Victim

Here you blame yourself. You feel the market is out to get you. You start becoming superstitious in your trading.

Optimist

You start thinking, "It's only money, I'll make it back later." You think all losses will bounce back to a profit, or that you will start trading properly tomorrow.

Gambler

You are in it for the thrill. Money is a side issue. Risk and reward analysis hardly figure in your trades, you want to be a player, want the buzz and excitement.

Timid

You enter a trade, but panic at the sight of a profit and take it far too soon. Fear rules your trading.

Diversification

Remember the 4 rules of diversification:

1   **Too much** can be as bad as too little (on the basis that you will be spread too widely to properly monitor your positions).

2   **Correlation**. There is no point buying 10 different stocks, say, if all are in the same sector because they will be highly correlated.

3   **Size of positions**. It is not diversification to have $100 in 9 positions and $10,000 in the tenth.

4   **Risk**. There needs to be similarity of risk between your positions for diversification to be effective. Futures and stocks hardly count as diversifying each other.

Summary

- A good trading tactic results in the selection of the best prospects presented by the trading strategy.
- Upside and downside targets should be set as well as exiting after passage of time.
- Journal keeping and an awareness of the types of failing traders are two additional ways to reduce potential losses.
- Abide by the four rules of diversification.

12

Step 5
Bring forth
the executioner:
method of
execution

❝ *Place the trade and walk away.* ❞

Phil Flynn
Vice President
Alaron Trading

In this chapter

Having analyzed and planned the trade, done all the ground work and preparation, you are ready for the kill. You obviously need some method of putting theory into practice and actually placing the trade. This is where the broker comes in. You have essentially two choices: an online broker or an off-line broker.

Objectives

- Understand the choices available in selecting brokers
- Appreciate the pitfalls associated with each choice
- Know what to look for in a broker

On or off? The chief benefits of online brokerage

Online brokers allow you to place your trade orders via the internet. However, while they are a product of the internet and so even the oldest online broker can claim to be only a few years old, the firms that provide the online services tend to be very well established off-line brokerage firms.

The key benefits of using online brokerage services to execute your orders can be listed as:

- **Cost**. Internet services tend to cost less than comparable off-line services with the lower costs being passed on in part to the consumer, in the form of lower commissions and margin rates and competitive rates of interest on credit balances.

- **Convenience**. You can enter an order at any time night or day and so suit your own timetable. Useful if, like me, you do your analysis late at night.

- **Quick confirmation**. Your trade is usually confirmed electronically, saving you the time to hang around on the phone, or call back busy brokers.

- **Total account keeping and monitoring**. Because everything is done electronically, most online brokers have a facility to permit users to access their accounts and positions on the net. This again is another minor convenience.

If you already have an established relationship with an off-line broker you may not wish to place your orders online. However, online brokers are worth investigating, if only to compare costs. As a small trader, your costs are relatively large compared to the size of your investments and anything which alters that balance in your favor has to be worth examining.

Even if you decide to stay with an off-line broker, there are many off-line brokers with web sites that are worth visiting to find out more about the services they provide and the "free stuff," such as analysis, there.

With these factors in mind, I have listed, as part of the skeleton plans, online and off-line brokers that meet certain baseline criteria. You are encouraged to visit their sites, see what they offer and compare them. To save you time all broker sites listed in this book have descriptions of key services they provide and particularly what is available for free. You will also find a table summarizing these factors for easy comparison. All you have to do is read the relevant section, do some surfing and make your choices.

Pssst ... security: how safe is the process?

The site

All the major online brokers assure their clients that they have unbreachable security in terms of someone placing rogue trades or transferring money out of your account. Security is usually assured through several procedures:

- The broker will have audit trails of all trades and cancellations which are available for you to inspect.

- In addition to this all firms listed in this book have some form of insurance protection (usually Securities Investor Protection Corporation, SIPC), ensuring client funds are either segregated or protected should the firm have financial difficulties. However, as E*Trade points out in its small print "Protection does not cover the market risks associated with investing." Pity!

- Use of firewalls. These are like, well, walls of fire, that prevent access from the outside through links, etc.

- Use of account numbers, user names and passwords.

hot tip *Things to do when placing an online order*
1 *Double-check and read the order carefully.*
2 *If in doubt, check by phone.*
3 *Be careful when clicking on the Submit order button. Do not send a duplicate order.*

The browser

If you are using Internet Explorer 4 or Netscape Navigator 4 then you are using a secure browser. Data passing through your browser to and from your broker will be encrypted. You can tell you are in a secure site because:

1 The URL changes from http: to https.

2 A pop-up window informs you that you are about to enter a secure site.

3 In Internet Explorer 4, a lock icon appears in the bottom left-hand corner.

4 In Netscape Navigator 4, an unbroken key icon appears in the bottom left-hand corner of the browser.

You

The most important thing you can do to help yourself is guard your personal identification number (PIN), account number and username. The PIN is the most important of these.

What to look for

There are over forty online brokers at the time of writing. It is hard to choose between them. To some extent any list, unless it lists all of them (which would be pretty unhelpful) is going to be arbitrary. In deciding the online brokerage firm to include in this book I have considered the following criteria, which are based on what any good trader or investor should have in mind when investigating brokers:

■ Competitive commissions:
  1 check for what size trade the advertised "low" commission applies
  2 any maintenance or handling charges (i.e. hidden costs?)
  3 commissions sometimes vary on the price of the stock, e.g. extra charges for a stock trading less than 50c.

■ Account details:
  1 minimum initial deposit
  2 minimum account balance
  3 interest rates for idle funds
  4 good brokers ought to automatically sweep excess funds to a high interest account
  5 margin and checking accounts:
    – A margin account will allow you to borrow – what are the rates?
    – It would be convenient to be able to write checks.
    – Is there a cost for wiring funds from the account?
  6 availability of account data online
  7 how often is the account up-dated? Intra-daily may be important for the day trader.

■ Established on the net; not new – with potential teething problems.

■ Price quotes.

■ Methods of confirming orders (an online screen and an e-mail at least).

■ Emergency back-up.

■ Types of orders accepted (see appendix on orders).

■ Portfolio monitoring:
  1 How often is your portfolio updated?
  2 Is a tax summary available?
  3 Is an automatic performance measure calculated?
  4 Is a transaction summary available?

- News.
- Research available:
  - What is available, is it free, is it online, or posted?
- Customer support:
  - Phone, fax, e-mail is ideal.

Action plan

1 Read the summaries in this book about the services offered by brokerage firms dealing in your choice of product.

2 For your particular product choice, surf the sites recommended by the skeleton plans.

3 On the basis of these, what you have read in this section and your own preferences, choose whether you would prefer online or off-line brokerage.

4 Settle upon a site, maybe two if you are unsure and want to go through a period of comparing both sites before settling upon one.

5 Add sites to your browser bookmark/favorites which have particularly useful free information for the products you are interested in.

6 Go to Step 6 (Chapter 13).

Summary

With security no longer a major issue, a major benefit of online brokers is the lower cost and greater convenience. However, with such fierce competition it is most important to shop around for one that meets your particular needs.

Step 6
Eyes and ears
open: monitoring

" *It takes a lot of patience and energy and motivation.* **"**

Bernard Oppetit

Global Head of Equity Derivatives
Banque Paribas, discussing trade

In this chapter

Having executed your position after analyzing numerous possibilities, monitoring your open positions and positions you may open is a key part of any trader's time. In this chapter we examine what you monitor, when and why and how it fits into the overall trading approach.

Objectives

- Understand the importance of portfolio monitoring
- Examine how the internet can assist in the task
- Further add to a professional approach

Monitoring what?

Traders monitor two main things:

1 What they own in anticipation of the time when they will want to sell according to their trading plan.

2 Possible other products they may buy but as yet all the factors they look for are not quite aligned, e.g. the price may not be too high or too low as yet.

The key things a trader will monitor are threefold:

1 The price of the product.

2 In the case of an open position, all the fundamental and technical factors which led to the decision to buy and contained in the trading tactic.

3 In the case of a potential position, all the fundamental and technical factors the trader usually examines as part of his trading strategy before entering a position.

In other words, monitoring involves a constant reanalysis and revaluation of a position to see what has changed (Diagram 13.1).

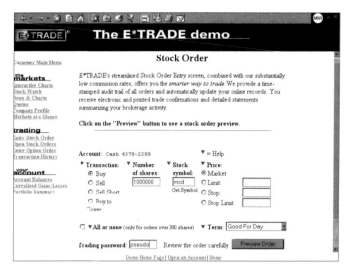

Diagram 13.1

To have or not to have a Big Mac

Having examined fundamentals state what they are. And then if looking to exit in 1 month, say, monitor every 2 days.

Monitoring when?

How often you monitor depends mainly upon two things:

1 Your trading strategy timeframe: are you looking to enter and exit in a short, medium or long period of time? Table 13.1 should help.

2 How close is the position to your stop or target? The closer it is the more regularly you need to monitor.

Table 13.1 Suggested monitoring timeframe

Period expecting to enter and exit	Monitor
24–96 hours	Constant – hourly
1–2 weeks	2 times during day monitor price; end of day monitor everything else
1 month	End of day monitor price; every 2 days monitor everything else
3–9 months	3–4 days monitor price; every week monitor everything else
9 months +	Monitor situation every 3/4+ weeks

How the internet assists

Numerous sites mentioned in the skeleton plans have portfolio monitors or trackers. These usually relate only to stocks. Diagram 13.2 shows a typical portfolio. These are helpful in that you can see all the details for your stock in one place. Most update the price and volume of your stock.

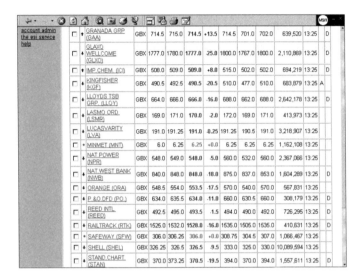

Diagram 13.2

Online portfolio monitor

What to look for when seeking an online portfolio tracker

- Does it recalculate the value of your total holdings?
- How many stocks can you list in one portfolio?
- How many portfolios can you have at one site?
- How often is the portfolio updated?
- Does the portfolio tracker alert you about news, earnings or other related items which may affect your stock?
- Does it monitor and alert you to a change in the technicals of your stock?

Summary

We have now examined what a professional approach to trading requires in terms of monitoring open and potential positions.

- With both the trading strategy and trading tactic in hand, monitor both the open and potential positions.
- Frequency of monitoring depends upon how close the target or stop is and generally on how quickly we expect to enter and exit.
- The skeleton plan lists sites with portfolio monitors which can help reduce the workload.

14

Step 7
Keeping abreast/
education

" The exciting part of being a trader is being involved. "

Jon Najarian
Chairman and CEO
Mercury Trading

In this chapter

Okay, so you have made and executed your order, but before you are ready to go onto making more decisions there is something else that you need to do. No matter what product interests you, whether it is NASDAQ stocks or pork belly futures, you may want to keep abreast of certain market-related information.

In this chapter we examine sources of further information which many traders use to supplement their analysis and which add to an overall professional and thorough approach. Your skeleton plan will lead you to the appropriate sites, but in this chapter we examine the types of information available and its uses.

Objectives

- Understand why and how to use market commentary and online magazines
- Learn how to choose newsgroups and newsletters
- How to incorporate these into an action plan

Market news and commentary

Almost all traders, whatever form of analysis they use and whatever product they trade in, whether bonds or shares, will want to examine daily market news and commentary, as these provide a context for all trading. It is the background against which all trading occurs. Even if you attach little weight to the market commentary it is an important aspect of trading.

The market commentary may relate not only to what is happening to the world economy, but also to the particular product in question. So, for instance, a futures trader in currencies may want to know what is happening to the US macroeconomy and also want commentary on currencies and currency futures generally. The skeleton plans are organized to lead you through each step of what you may want or ought to examine.

If you trade UK stocks you may think it safe to ignore market commentary related to US non-farm payrolls, but you will then have missed why, on so many occasions, stocks with little US exposure, such as domestic electricals, are affected each month when the US non-farm payroll data are revealed. What happens is that the market often uses those data to gauge the likely changes in US interest rates, which in turn affects whether more funds are likely to flow into London or

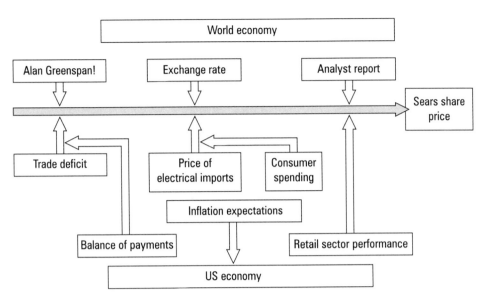

Illustration 14.1

*Everything is
connected to
everything else*

New York and that in turn can affect the share price of companies that have little
to do directly with the USA. The key rule is that everything is connected to everything else (see Illustration 14.1).

This does not mean you have to be an economics whiz to trade, but it does
mean that the better informed you are about what the market is examining the
more likely you are to make better trading decisions. In any event, few people
would argue that more information can do harm. Here endeth the case for following market news and market commentary.

Criteria for including market news and commentary sites in the skeleton plans are:

1 The news providers have to be well known, widely respected and with ample
   resources.

2 Quality commentary on the markets.

3 Categorized news, such as industry, business, commodity, etc. for ease of
   searching.

4 Regular updates during the day.

hot tip *Learning the markets*

*One of the best ways to
learn about the markets
and get a feel for them is
to follow daily
commentary on what
happened in the markets
and explanations for these
events. This should give
you an idea of "what is on
the market's mind." What
data do the market
commentators say dealers
are focusing on? This is
not to say you should try
to second guess them, but
rather get to appreciate
what moves markets. PS.
Nobody ever figures it out
– not even the best.*

Market newsletters

Many traders subscribe to one or more for the particular product they are interested in. The skeleton plans will lead you to the appropriate site.

What are they?

Essentially a market newsletter will contain recommendations as to what to buy
and sell. The individuals who write them are often termed gurus. I suppose
priest, rabbi, imam would be plausible alternatives as well.

Why use them?

A typical newsletter will contain analysis of why a particular stock or other product is recommended. Most traders, if they use newsletters, do so to get a second opinion on their own analysis or to gain ideas. Sometimes a newsletter is a confidence builder for those a little tentative or unsure of their own analysis.

Before you choose to subscribe to any particular newsletter there are some important things to bear in mind.

hot tip *Using newsletters*

Do not merely follow a newsletter, you may as well give your money to the newsletter author – and if you are willing to do that then why not give it to a professional fund manager. Remember, Soros and Buffet do not write newsletters. In other words, the truly successful trade, they do not recommend trades. So I would recommend that you do your own analysis before or after looking at the newsletter you have subscribed to and form an independent view as to the trade.

Product?

Make sure the newsletter trades in the same products as you! Seems obvious – it is! But it also means that if you trade stock options, it will almost certainly be better to have a newsletter making stock option recommendations than one making purely stock recommendations.

Consider the strategy

Are the strategies the newsletter recommends ones with which you are comfortable? For instance, the newsletter may specialize in shorting stocks or spread trading.

Your analysis and guru's analysis

You need to be aware of the type of analysis you believe in and ensure the newsletter follows a similar form. For instance, if you tend to follow earnings surprises and do not care much for technical indicators then it would be perverse for you to subscribe to a newsletter that selected recommendations based on technicals.

Timeframe

You ideally want a newsletter that selects recommendations on a timeframe you yourself like to trade to. An extreme example of a mismatch would be if you prefer to enter and exit trades on a weekly basis and the newsletter is monthly. Its value to you would be limited.

Method of delivery

Are you happy with the mode by which the newsletter is delivered: e-mail, fax, or snail mail?

Comprehensible?

The issue here is do you like the layout and can you understand why the guru is recommending a stock? One thing that will ensure a wasted subscription is if you cannot understand the guru's choice. If you do not fully comprehend how he selects his recommendations you cannot critically analyze them and so are following blindly.

Table 14.1 Checklist of factors for consideration

	My choice	Newsletter 1	Newsletter 2	Newsletter 3
Product				
Strategy				
Analysis				
Timeframe				
Method of delivery				
Comprehensible (score)				
Trial period				
Cost				

You pays your money and you takes your choice

As Table 14.1 makes clear there are an enormous number of factors that determine the type of newsletter best suited to your particular needs. Moreover, for every possible demand there seems to be several suppliers. That being so it would be ridiculous and unhelpful to list, subscribe and review each and every available newsletter. Instead the sites listed are "umbrella" sites which do precisely that. Furthermore, because they are net sites, they are going to be more up to date.

hot tip

Get a freebie
After visiting the sites recommended by your skeleton plan you are strongly recommended to get a free copy or a trial subscription of your shortlisted choices of newsletters which meet these criteria. That is the only way to know for sure if they are any good. Also, ask around in the chat sites in your skeleton plans as to what other traders use. And, if the newsletter does not offer a free trial copy or subscription, be very wary – they may have something to hide.

To give you some idea of the plethora of choices, the list that follows contains just some of the newsletters I came across in the first 30 minutes of researching the issue.

The Addison Report
The Aden Forecast
Adrian Day's Investment Analyst
All Star Funds
Analyst Watch
Asset Allocator
BI Research
Beating the Dow
Bert Dohmen's Wellington Letter
The Big Picture
The Blue Chip Investor
Bob Brinker's Marketimer
The Bowser Report
The Buyback Letter
The Cabot Market Letter
California Technology Stock Letter
The Chartist
The Chartist Mutual Fund Timer
The Clean Yield
Closed-End Country Fund Report
Closed-End Fund Digest
The Contrarian's View
Crawford Perspectives
Dennis Slothower's On The Money
The Dines Letter
Donoghue's Wealthletter
Dow Theory Forecasts
Dow Theory Letters
Elliott Wave Theorist
Emerging & Special Situations
Equities Special Situations
Equity Fund Outlook
F.X.C. Investors Corp.
Fabian Premium Investment Resource
Fidelity Forecaster
Fidelity Independent Advisor
Fidelity Insight
Fidelity Monitor
Financial World
Ford Investment Review
Foreign Markets Advisory
Fund Exchange
Fund Kinetics
Fund Profit Alert
Fundline
Funds Net Insight
Futures Hotline/Mutual Fund
  Timer
Garzarelli Outlook
Gerald Perritt's Mutual Fund Letter
Global Investing
Good Fortune
The Granville Market Letter
Graphic Fund Forecaster
Ground Floor

Growth Fund Guide
Growth Stock Outlook
Growth Stock Winners
Growth Stocks Report
Hot Funds Analyst
Hussman Econometrics
Income Fund Outlook
Independent Adviser for Vanguard
  Investors
Individual Investor Special Situations
  Report
The Insiders
The International Harry Schultz
  Letter
InvesTech Market Analyst
InvesTech Mutual Fund Advisor
Invest With The Masters
Investment Quality Trends
The Investment Reporter
Investor's Guide to Closed-End
  Funds
Investor's World
Investors Intelligence
The Jupiter Group, Inc.
Kinsman's Stock Pattern Recognition
  Service
LaLoggia's Special Situation Report
Louis Rukeyser's Mutual Funds
Louis Rukeyser's Wall Street
The Low Priced Stock Survey
MPT Review
Margo's Small Stocks
Mark Skousen's Forecasts &
  Strategies
Market Logic
The Marketarian Letter
Medical Technology Stock Letter
Moneyletter
Morningstar Mutual Funds
Motley Fool
The Mutual Fund Advisor
Mutual Fund Forecaster
Mutual Fund Investing
The Mutual Fund Strategist
Mutual Fund Technical Trader
NAIC Investor Advisory Service
National Trendlines
Natural Contrarian
New Issues
The Ney Stock and Fund Report
No-Load Fund Analyst
*NoLoad Fund*X
The No-Load Fund Investor
No-Load Mutual Fund Selections &
  Timing Newsletter

No-Load Portfolios
ODDS OEX Fax Hotline
OTC Insight
The Oberweis Report
The Option Advisor
Option Selections & Timing
The Outlook
Overpriced Stock Service
The Oxford Club
P. Q. Wall Forecast, Inc.
The PAD System Report
PEcom Stock Valuation
Personal Finance
The Peter Dag Portfolio Strategy &
  Management
The Professional Tape Reader
Professional Timing Service
Prudence and Performance
The Prudent Speculator
The Pure Fundamentalist
The Red Chip Review
Richard E. Band's Profitable
  Investing
Richard Geist's Strategic Investing
The Ruff Times
Scientific Investment
Sector Funds Newsletter
Short On Value
Sound Advice
Sound Mind Investing
Stockmarket Cycles
Strategic Investment
Switch Fund Timing
Systems and Forecasts
Timer Digest
Todd Market Timer
The Turnaround Letter
US Investment Report
United & Babson Investment Report
Utility Forecaster
The Value Line Convertibles Survey
The Value Line Investment Survey
The Value Line Investment Survey –
  Expanded Edition
The Value Line Mutual Fund
  Survey
The Value Line OTC Special
  Situations Service
Vantage Point: An Independent
  Report for Vanguard Investors
VectorVest Stock Advisory
Vickers Weekly Insider Report
The Wall Street Digest
World Investor
Zweig Performance Ratings Report

The sites

Because of the plethora of choices the sites referred to by the skeleton plans are umbrella sites, namely, sites that list newsletters based upon name, strategy, product and provide a historical performance review.

Action plan

Only after filling in the checklist in Table 14.1, go through the umbrella sites and narrow down your choice of potential newsletters to those you may wish to subscribe to. Then undertake a trial subscription before making your choice.

Chatting to a virtual community: newsgroups

What are they?

A newsgroup is simply a collection of messages posted by individuals to a news server. Posting is the act of putting your message onto the server. News servers are just big computers that host (i.e. store) lots of newsgroup messages for people to view.

You read and post messages using a news reader. A news reader is software much like a browser and the best news is that most browsers include news readers that launch automatically when you want to go to a newsgroup. With Internet Explorer 4 for example the news reader is bundled with the e-mail reader called Outlook Express. In Netscape Navigator it is called Netscape News.

There are some web sites that provide their own news readers and so permit web-based "newsgrouping" (see later) which can be easier for the novice.

There are newsgroups on virtually every topic under the sun from investments to sadomasochism (the dividing line between investment and sadomasochism can be a fine one at times). Some newsgroups are monitored or moderated which means someone sifts through them to ensure the content meets certain quality standards and is not generally scurrilous, libelous and outrageously offensive.

Adding a news server

To add a news server you will first need:

1 the name of the server

2 your account name and password.

In Internet Explorer 4:

■ In Outlook Express click on **Tools** and then **Accounts** and next on **News** and finally follow the on-screen instructions.

hot tip *Web-based newsgroups*
One of the easiest way to use newsgroups without all the trouble of linking to servers and fiddling with browsers is to go to ***www.infoseek.com****. From there you can search for newsgroups and download the **My Deja News** news reader and subscribe to lots of newsgroups.*

In Netscape Navigator:

▪ On the browser click on **Options** and then select **Mail and News Preferences** then on **Servers** (you may need to click on News first if this tab is available.) Next enter the server name in the **News (NNTP) Server** box and follow the instructions.

Subscription

The act of "joining" a newsgroup is called subscription. You do not need to have subscribed to a newsgroup to be able to read and post messages. Subscription just means your news reader creates a special folder for that newsgroup and you can more conveniently send and receive messages by clicking on the icon. No fees are due and there are no membership lists. Before you can subscribe to a newsgroup:

1 Your ISP must have a link with the newsgroup's news server.

2 You have to have set up an account with the news server using your news reader.

Your newsreader will usually download a list of newsgroups available on your news server when you connect. When you see one you may click on it to view a selection of messages and decide whether or not to subscribe (Diagram 14.1).

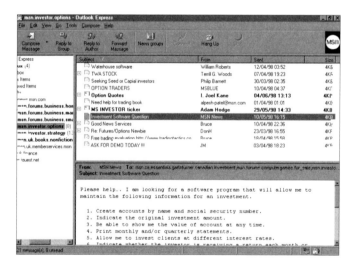

Diagram 14.1

Newsgroupies, newsgrouping

Viewing a newsgroup

In your browser simply type in the URL box **news:name of newsgroup**, e.g. news:misc.invest.

Quality of trading newsgroups

The major problem with newsgroups, which even a short visit will demonstrate, is that:

1 They often get used by a small clique of users who are in fact just talking to each other, with outside messages not replied to readily.

2 The focus of the clique can be quite narrow.

3 The messages can get abusive and personal.

4 Unregulated groups often get posting from unwelcome "get rich quick" schemes.

5 Investors often try to talk up positions they may be holding, so the information is often biased and not credible.

Consequently, for anyone coming to a newsgroup, it can be a little like going to a drinks party and trying to join in a conversation being held by a circle of individuals who have been chatting away for a few hours. My advice would be to use newsgroups only for asking questions, and be wary of the replies even then. They are not, in my opinion, a good source of investment advice on the whole, but better as a source of exchanging knowledge-based background information, such as, say, on the usefulness of Stochastic indicators in technical analysis.

Alternative advice

If you have an investment query then rather than seeking the amateur advice of a newsgroupie, you could always go to a web site dealing with the area of your query (e.g. bonds, etc.) and seek out e-mail addresses of people on them. Often, the advisers who produce the site provide their e-mail addresses and they can be a useful source of free advice on an issue.

Newsgroupie or web chatterer?

Many websites specializing in trading have equivalents to newsgroups but are web based (Diagram 14.2). These often provide higher quality content and are a good alternative to free-for-all newsgroups. The skeleton plans will guide you to the appropriate sites.

Diagram 14.2

Web chatterers

E-zines: electronic magazines

E-zine can be used as a loose term for internet magazines. These may be either internet only or online versions of off-line magazines. Some of the best-known and best-quality e-zines are listed in a later chapter.

Why bother?

The main reasons behind visiting e-zines and then selecting one or two as ones you will visit regularly are the same as following market news and commentary: they provide analysis of the market background against which all trading takes place. Moreover they are an excellent source of education.

The listed sites

The sites included are ones which:

- are highly respected
- provide excellent quality.

Summary

What has been learnt about analysis can be added to fruitfully by examination of market commentary, newsgroups, e-zines and newsletters. These are all useful sources of supplemental analysis. However, with newsgroups and newsletters you must take great care in selection and with newsgroups great care in interpretation.

How it all works in practice

“ *The trouble with a loss is that it's not only a loss of money, but also a loss of ego.* ”

Pat Arbor
Chairman
Chicago Board of Trade

In this chapter

Having discussed skeleton plans and action plans and their importance to trading, as well as what type of information and analysis traders seek, we now examine a couple of examples to make absolutely, positively, totally sure everything is as clear as some very clear crystal.

I would recommend you just skim through the chapter at this stage to get a better idea of what has been discussed so far and how skeleton plans become action plans. Then return to this chapter later and read it more thoroughly when you have gone through Sections 3 and 4.

Objective

- To clarify through the use of example the workings of skeleton and action plans

Example 1: Steve the stock picker

Steve trades stocks. Wisely, he has chosen to improve his trading by using a systematic and professional approach. Sensibly, he read Section 2 of this book and now has a thorough appreciation of the importance of trading plans.

- He turns now to Chapter 16 and starts off by examining the skeleton plan for stocks, equities and indices.
- Under this skeleton plan he realizes the first thing he needs to do is get hold of live data to monitor stocks – because he is going to be trading relatively short term and wants to monitor prices throughout the day.
- Steve does not want historical data yet because he wants to learn more about technical analysis first.
- So Steve looks down the skeleton plan under price data (live, delayed, historical quotes). Since there are quite a few companies listed he decides he will briefly read their descriptions in the book and decide to visit the web pages first of the ones he likes the look of most.
- After some reading, Steve visits some sites, choosing to start with DBC. Steve decides after visiting several more sites and in light of what he read about the sites and service providers in this book to settle for live data from DBC.
- Next Steve moves down the skeleton plan to analysis. He is into fundamental analysis and finds the idea of filters intriguing. So, once again, Steve flicks through the book and reads about the sites referred to in the skeleton plan

under analysis and what they offer. After some thought he decides to visit several of the sites he likes the sound of.

■ Steve decides that he only wants to use one site for its filters and other fundamental analysis because he would be duplicating his work if he visited several different ones. However, he does keep the list of other sites for occasional reference. He particularly liked Microsoft Investor and adds it to his Favorites folder on Internet Explorer 4.

■ As for technical analysis, Steve decides he knows too little for now and wants to educate himself. So he first reads Chapter 18 as suggested by the skeleton plan. He also goes to the recommended reading section of this book.

■ Since Steve knows little about technical analysis, he decides that while he learns more he will not use technical analysis software but online charts instead to save costs in case he decides not to pursue his interest in technical analysis.

■ Steve visits the various sites recommended by the skeleton plan after reading about what they offer in the book. Finally Steve settles on Reuters MoneyNet.

■ Now Steve moves onto method of execution under his skeleton plan. Reading through Chapter 19 and visiting the various sites Steve decides that he wants the cheapest possible online broker and settles on one he likes the look of.

■ Steve moves onto the monitoring part of the skeleton plan. Having read in Section 2 how important this is he works down the list of sites and shortlists some he would like to visit based on their descriptions in the book. Finally Steve settles on Reuters MoneyNet because he is already using that site for his technical analysis and this will mean he does not have to visit too many sites each time he trades.

■ Steve then moves onto the keeping abreast and educational section of the skeleton plan. Starting with news and market commentary Steve visits a few of the sites after reading their descriptions and settles on Microsoft Investor and Reuters MoneyNet as his sources of information. Steve did not want more than two sites as visiting them would be too time consuming, he felt, and duplicative. He was aware that the two he settled on were already being used by him as part of his action plan.

■ Moving to gurus and newsletters Steve reads Chapter 26 as recommended by the skeleton plan and decides to skip those altogether.

■ Steve then moves to discussion forums and likes the idea of bouncing ideas off other stock pickers. He reads Chapter 27 carefully and the advice it gives. He then visits the sites recommended and settles on Market Edge after some detailed investigation of standards of chat.

■ As for e-zines Steve subscribes to the *Economist* and decides for now not to add to his reading load.

■ Steve finally visits the educational part of the skeleton plan and recalls he wanted to know more about technical analysis. He goes to Section 5 and decides to visit a few directories and see some of the sites they mention.

■ Since Steve trades mainly stocks listed on NASDAQ he decided to visit the exchange having got the address from Chapter 22, as indicated by the skeleton plan.

■ Steve now has a systematic procedure and list of sites to visit for his trading decisions and execution. All he has to do now is the hard work of analysis.

Example 2: Olivia the option trader

Olivia bumped into her close but platonic friend, Steve, at a really cool bar one Friday night. As with all conversations in really cool bars on Friday nights, they soon got onto the topic of trading.

Olivia heeded Steve's advice and wisely decided to improve her trading by using a systematic and professional approach. So she bought a copy of the book (because it would have been embarrassingly cheap and crass to borrow Steve's copy) and started by reading Section 2 to gain a thorough appreciation of the importance of trading plans.

■ Olivia turns first to Chapter 16 and starts off by examining the skeleton plan for futures and options.

■ Since Olivia trades stock options, she wants live prices for both the stocks and the options. Olivia also undertakes a lot of technical analysis and so decides she needs historical data as well for stocks.

■ Consequently, Olivia turns first to the skeleton plan for stocks, equities and indices and looks under price data, as well as examining price data under the skeleton plan for futures and options.

■ All in all Olivia decides that for live stock and option prices she will use Reuters MoneyNet and for historical prices she will use Dial/Data because she likes their reviews in the book and their sites the best.

■ Olivia is not a big believer in fundamental analysis, preferring technical analysis, so she next skips directly to technical under analysis in her skeleton plan.

■ Since Olivia is big on technical analysis she has decided she will use special technical analysis software and not online charts. So goes to Chapters 18 and 25 under software in her skeleton plan. Reading those chapters, visiting the sites and downloading some demos, Olivia decides to settle for Metastock, which she knows is compatible with Dial/Data data.

■ Olivia does not like the idea of online execution and decides to stick with her present off-line broker for now.

■ Moving onto monitoring in her skeleton plan, Olivia knows she needs to monitor both the options prices and stock prices. For stock price monitoring she goes back to the monitoring part of the stocks, equities and indices skeleton plan, and chooses Reuters MoneyNet as she is already using that for live prices anyway. For option prices she likewise decides on Reuters MoneyNet.

■ Moving onto keeping abreast and educational aspect of her skeleton plan, Olivia decides that as her main interest is in technical analysis she is going to ignore news and market commentary.

■ However, Olivia does like the idea of a newsletter and visits Chapter 26 as indicated by her skeleton plan under gurus and newsletters.

■ Olivia likes to keep her thoughts to herself and skips discussion forums for now. Similarly, her focus on technical analysis leads her to ignore e-zines.

■ Being a far greater expert on technical analysis than Steve, Olivia does not fancy any research under educational in her skeleton plan, but does want to check out the Chicago Board Options Exchange sites whose listing she gets from Chapter 22, as indicated under exchanges in her skeleton plan.

Summary

This short chapter with its two examples is intended to give you a brief overview of how you may go through the skeleton plans to build up a list of sites for regular visits as part of your trading analysis. Of course, in reality it would probably take several days to go through a skeleton plan and decide on the best sites for your trading. However, the comments about each site are intended to quicken the process. And, of course, remember that I have only included worthy sites worth visiting in the book and not every "Tom, Dick and Harry" site.

SECTION

The skeleton plans

16

Out of the cupboard at last: the skeleton plans

Probably the biggest downfall traders have is that once they have found success, they change their trading rules from what gave them success in the first place.

Phil Flynn
Vice President
Alaron Trading

In this chapter

Having talked about them at length we have finally reached the skelton plans. The way they work is pretty self-evident. Remember, they are modeled on the steps outlined in Section 2. Only sites which are recommended a visit for a particular service are listed and not every site simply because it provides a service irrespective of quality.

To have got this far

hot tip *Visit sites in the skeleton plan which have the highest ranking first and work your way down.*

You will have read Section 2 about making your action plans and gained an appreciation of the steps involved in a thorough trading plan. The skeleton plans are here to guide you to the sites which you will want to examine before finally settling down to your favorite sites.

Stocks, equities and indices

Price data (live, delayed, historical quotes)

- BMI (www.bmiquotes.com) *page 154*
- Prestel (www.prestel.co.uk) *page 157*
- DBC (www.dbc.com) *page 158*
- Dial/Data (www.tdc.com/dialdata) *page 160*
- BridgeFeed (www.bridge.com) *page 162*
- Quote.Com (www.quote.com) *page 164*
- Reuters MoneyNet (www.moneynet.com) *page 165*
- MarketEdge (www.marketedge.com) *page 168*
- Wall Street Journal (www.wsj.com) *page 170*
- MarketGuide (www.marketguide.com) *page 171*
- Financial Times (www.ft.com) *page 177*
- ESI (www.esi.co.uk) *page 178*
- Infotrade (www.infotrade.co.uk) *page 180*
- Market-Eye (www.market-eye.co.uk) *page 182*
- Microsoft Investor (investor.msn.com) *page 185*

Analysis

Fundamental

- Filters
  - Reuters MoneyNet (www.moneynet.com) *page 165*
  - MarketEdge (www.marketedge.com) *page 168*
  - MarketGuide (www.marketguide.com) *page 171*

- Microsoft Investor (`investor.msn.com`) *page 185*
- Zacks (`www.zacks.com`) *page 186*
- Stockpoint (`www.stockpoint.com`) *page 187*
- Wall Street Journal (`www.wsj.com`) *page 170*
- CNNfn (`www.cnnfn.com`) *page 174*
- Standard & Poor (`www.stockinfo.standardpoor.com`) *page 176*
- Financial Times (`www.ft.com`) *page 177*
- ESI (`www.esi.co.uk`) *page 178*
- Infotrade (`www.infotrade.co.uk`) *page 180*
- Hemmington Scott (`www.hemscott.co.uk`) *page 181*
- Market-Eye (`www.market-eye.co.uk`) *page 182*
- Briefing (`www.briefing.com`) *page 183*

Technical

- Online charts
  - *Chapter 18*
  - BMI (`www.bmi.com`) *page 154*
  - Reuters MoneyNet (`www.moneynet.com`) *page 165*
  - ESI (`www.esi.co.uk`) *page 178*
  - Infotrade (`www.infotrade.co.uk`) *page 180*
  - Microsoft Investor (`investor.msn.com`) *page 185*
  - Stockpoint (`www.stockpoint.com`) *page 187*
- Educational
  - *Chapter 18*
- Software
  - *Chapter 18*

Method of execution

- Chapter 19

Monitoring

- BMI (`www.bmiquotes.com`) *page 154*
- DBC (`www.dbc.com`) *page 158*
- Quote.Com (`www.quote.com`) *page 164*
- Reuters MoneyNet (`www.moneynet.com`) *page 165*
- MarketEdge (`www.marketedge.com`) *page 168*
- Standard & Poor (`www.stockinfo.standardpoor.com`) *page 176*
- ESI (`www.infotrade.co.uk`) *page 178*
- Briefing (`www.briefing.com`) *page 183*
- Zacks (`www.zacks.com`) *page 186*

Keeping abreast and educational

- News and market commentary
  - Reuters MoneyNet (`www.moneynet.com`) *page 165*

Bonds

Price data (live, delayed, historical quotes)

Analysis

■ *Fundamental*

- *Chapter 23*
- Bloomberg (www.bloomberg.com) *page 173*

■ *Technical*

■ Online charts
- *Chapter 18*
- *Chapter 23*
- BMI (www.bmi.com) *page 154*
■ Educational
- *Chapter 18*
■ Software
- *Chapter 18*

■ *Method of execution*

- *Chapter 19*

■ *Monitoring*

- *Chapter 23*
- DBC (www.dbc.com) *page 158*

■ *Keeping abreast and educational*

■ News and market commentary
- *Chapter 23*
- Exchanges
  - *Chapter 22*
- Wall Street Journal (www.wsj.com) *page 170*
- Bloomberg (www.bloomberg.com) *page 173*
- CNNfn (www.cnnfn.com) *page 174*
- Standard & Poor (www.stockinfo.standardpoor.com) *page 176*
- Financial Times (www.ft.com) *page 177*
- ESI (www.esi.co.uk) *page 178*
- Infotrade (www.infotrade.co.uk) *page 180*
- Market-Eye (www.market-eye.co.uk) *page 182*
- Briefing (www.briefing.com) *page 183*
- Microsoft Investor (investor.msn.com) *page 185*
■ Gurus and newsletters
- *Chapter 26*
■ Discussion forums
- *Chapter 23*
- *Chapter 27*
- MarketEdge (www.marketedge.com) *page 168*
- ESI (www.esi.co.uk) *page 178*

- E-zines
  - *Chapter 28*
- Educational
  - Research
    - *Section 5*
  - Exchanges
    - *Chapter 22*

Mutual funds, investment trusts and unit trusts

Price data (live, delayed, historical quotes)

- *Chapter 20*
- BMI (www.bmiquotes.com) *page 154*
- Prestel (www.prestel.co.uk) *page 157*
- DBC (www.dbc.com) *page 158*
- Dial/Data (www.tdc.com/dialdata) *page 160*
- BridgeFeed (www.bridge.com) *page 162*
- Quote.Com (www.quote.com) *page 164*
- Reuters MoneyNet (www.moneynet.com) *page 165*
- MarketEdge (www.marketedge.com) *page 168*
- Wall Street Journal (www.wsj.com) *page 170*
- ESI (www.esi.co.uk) *page 178*
- Infotrade (www.infotrade.co.uk) *page 180*
- Market-Eye (www.market-eye.co.uk) *page 182*

Analysis

Fundamental

- Filters
  - *Chapter 20*
  - Reuters MoneyNet (www.moneynet.com) *page 165*
  - MarketEdge (www.marketedge.com) *page 168*
  - Microsoft Investor (investor.msn.com) *page 185*
  - Stockpoint (www.stockpoint.com) *page 187*
  - *Chapter 20*
  - Reuters MoneyNet (www.moneynet.com) *page 165*
  - MarketEdge (www.marketedge.com) *page 168*
  - Wall Street Journal (www.wsj.com) *page 170*
  - Bloomberg (www.bloomberg.com) *page 173*
  - CNNfn (www.cnnfn.com) *page 174*
  - Standard & Poor (www.stockinfo.standardpoor.com) *page 176*

- ESI (www.esi.co.uk) *page 178*
- Infotrade (www.infotrade.co.uk) *page 180*
- Hemmington Scott (www.hemscott.co.uk) *page 181*
- Market-Eye (www.market-eye.co.uk) *page 182*
- Microsoft Investor (investor.msn.com) *page 185*
- Stockpoint (www.stockpoint.com) *page 187*

■ *Technical*

  ■ Online charts
- *Chapter 20*
- BMI (www.bmi.com) *page 154*
- Reuters MoneyNet (www.moneynet.com) *page 165*
- MarketEdge (www.marketedge.com) *page 168*
- ESI (www.esi.co.uk) *page 178*
- Infotrade (www.infotrade.co.uk) *page 180*
- Market-Eye (www.market-eye.co.uk) *page 182*
- Microsoft Investor (investor.msn.com) *page 185*

  ■ Educational
- *Chapter 18*
- *Chapter 20*

  ■ Software
- *Chapter 18*
- *Chapter 20*

■ *Method of execution*
- *Chapter 19*

■ *Monitoring*
- *Chapter 20*
- DBC (www.dbc.com) *page 158*
- Quote.Com (www.quote.com) *page 164*
- Reuters MoneyNet (www.moneynet.com) *page 165*
- MarketEdge (www.marketedge.com) *page 168*
- Standard & Poor (www.stockinfo.standardpoor.com) *page 176*
- ESI (www.esi.co.uk) *page 178*
- Infotrade (www.infotrade.co.uk) *page 180*

■ *Keeping abreast and educational*

  ■ News and market commentary
- *Chapter 20*
- Reuters MoneyNet (www.moneynet.com) *page 165*
- Wall Street Journal (www.wsj.com) *page 170*
- Bloomberg (www.bloomberg.com) *page 173*
- CNNfn (www.cnnfn.com) *page 174*
- Standard & Poor (www.stockinfo.standardpoor.com) *page 176*

- Financial Times (`www.ft.com`)   *page 177*
- ESI (`www.esi.co.uk`)   *page 178*
- Infotrade (`www.infotrade.co.uk`)   *page 180*
- Market-Eye (`www.market-eye.co.uk`)   *page 182*
- Briefing (`www.briefing.com`)   *page 183*
- Microsoft Investor (`investor.msn.com`)   *page 185*

■ Gurus and newsletters
- *Chapter 20*
- *Chapter 26*

■ Discussion forums
- *Chapter 20*
- *Chapter 27*
- MarketEdge (`www.marketedge.com`)   *page 168*
- ESI (`www.esi.co.uk`)   *page 178*
- Market-Eye (`www.market-eye.co.uk`)   *page 182*
- Microsoft Investor (`investor.msn.com`)   *page 185*

■ E-zines
- *Chapter 28*

■ Educational
- Research
  - *Section 5*
  - *Chapter 20*
- Exchanges
  - *Chapter 22*

Foreign exchange

Price data (live, delayed, historical quotes)

- *Chapter 24*
- BMI (`www.bmiquotes.com`)   *page 154*
- DBC (`www.dbc.com`)   *page 157*
- BridgeFeed (`www.bridge.com`)   *page 162*
- Quote.Com (`www.quote.com`)   *page 164*
- Wall Street Journal (`www.wsj.com`)   *page 170*
- Market-Eye (`www.market-eye.co.uk`)   *page 182*

Analysis

■ *Fundamental*

- *Chapter 24*
- Wall Street Journal (`www.wsj.com`)   *page 170*
- *See news and market commentary (following)*

■ *Technical*
- Online charts
  - *Chapter 18*
  - *Chapter 24*
  - BMI (`www.bmiquotes.com`) *page 154*
- Educational
  - *Chapter 18*
- Software
  - *Chapter 18*

■ *Method of execution*
  - *Chapter 19*
  - *Chapter 24*

■ *Monitoring*
  - *Chapter 24*
  - *See quote sites (earlier)*

■ *Keeping abreast and educational*
- News and market commentary
  - *Chapter 24*
  - Reuters MoneyNet (`www.moneynet.com`) *page 165*
  - Wall Street Journal (`www.wsj.com`) *page 170*
  - Bloomberg (`www.bloomberg.com`) *page 173*
  - CNNfn (`www.cnnfn.com`) *page 174*
  - Standard & Poor (`www.stockinfo.standardpoor.com`) *page 176*
  - Financial Times (`www.ft.com`) *page 177*
  - ESI (`www.esi.co.uk`) *page 178*
  - Infotrade (`www.infotrade.co.uk`) *page 180*
  - Market-Eye (`www.market-eye.co.uk`) *page 182*
  - Briefing (`www.briefing.com`) *page 183*
  - Microsoft Investor (`investor.msn.com`) *page 185*
- Gurus and newsletters
  - *Chapter 26*
- Discussion forums
  - *Chapter 27*
  - MarketEdge (`www.marketedge.com`) *page 168*
- E-zines
  - *Chapter 28*
- Educational
  - Research
    - *Section 5*
  - Exchanges
    - *Chapter 22*

Futures and options

Price data (live, delayed, historical quotes)

- For price data of underlying product (e.g. stock, foreign exchange, bonds) *see appropriate skeleton plan earlier*
- *Chapter 21*
- BMI (`www.bmiquotes.com`) *page 154*
- Prestel (`www.prestel.co.uk`) *page 157*
- DBC (`www.dbc.com`) *page 158*
- Dial/Data (`www.tdc.com/dialdata`) *page 160*
- BridgeFeed (`www.bridge.com`) *page 162*
- Quote.Com (`www.quote.com`) *page 164*
- Reuters MoneyNet (`www.moneynet.com`) *page 165*
- Wall Street Journal (`www.wsj.com`) *page 170*
- ESI (`www.esi.co.uk`) *page 178*
- Market-Eye (`www.market-eye.co.uk`) *page 182*

Analysis

Fundamental

- For fundamental analysis of underlying product (e.g. stock, foreign exchange, bonds) *see appropriate skeleton plan earlier*
- *Chapter 21*

Technical

- Online charts
  - For technical analysis of underlying product (e.g. stock, foreign exchange, bonds) *see appropriate skeleton plan earlier*
  - *Chapter 18*
  - *Chapter 21*
  - BMI (`www.bmiquotes.com`) *page 154*
- Educational
  - *Chapter 18*
- Software
  - *Chapter 18*
  - *Chapter 25*

Method of execution

- *Chapter 19*

Monitoring

- *Chapter 21*
- *See quote sites (earlier)*

Keeping abreast and educational

- News and market commentary

- Wall Street Journal (www.wsj.com)   *page 170*
- Bloomberg (www.bloomberg.com)   *page 173*
- CNNfn (www.cnnfn.com)   *page 174*
- Standard & Poor (www.stockinfo.standardpoor.com)   *page 176*
- Financial Times (www.ft.com)   *page 177*
- ESI (www.esi.co.uk)   *page 178*
- Infotrade (www.infotrade.co.uk)   *page 180*
- Market-Eye (www.market-eye.co.uk)   *page 182*
- Briefing (www.briefing.com)   *page 183*
- Microsoft Investor (investor.msn.com)   *page 185*
- Gurus and newsletters
  - *Chapter 26*
- Discussion forums
  - *Chapter 21*
  - *Chapter 27*
  - MarketEdge (www.marketedge.com)   *page 168*
  - ESI (www.esi.co.uk)   *page 178*
- E-zines
  - *Chapter 28*
- Educational
  - Research
    - *Section 5*
    - *Chapter 21*
  - Exchanges
    - *Chapter 22*

Summary

The skeleton plans aim to provide a systematic and thorough approach to trading. However, they only really make sense if you have first digested Section 2.

SECTION

4

The sites

Key to flags in this section

A   *Australia*

C   *Canada*

F   *France*

G   *Germany*

HK   *Hong Kong*

Int   *International*

I   *Italy*

J   *Japan*

S   *Singapore*

SA   *South Africa*

UK   *United Kingdom*

US   *USA*

17

Sites with a little bit of everything

Greater the trader, greater the profit, it's as simple as that.

David Kyte
Chairman
Kyte Group

In this chapter

The sites in this chapter are referred to by various skeleton plans and often by the same skeleton plan more than once, because these sites provide different recommended services. By keeping all the sites in one location you can determine that, say if one site is referred to for three different services and another for only one, you will choose the former site because it is more a "one-stop shop."

To have got this far

- You will have read the section on making skeleton plans.
- You will have read in particular about quote vendors, analysis, portfolio monitoring, keeping abreast.
- From reading that, you will be aware what you are looking for.
- Go to skeleton plans appropriate to your chosen product and work your way through selecting sites for each category, e.g. a quote vendor.

Key to star ratings in this chapter:

*** Best site for what it offers, usually lots of freebies and easy on the eye.

** Useful, informative and well displayed.

* Doesn't get an Oscar, but good enough to get a nomination. Sites which would get less than one star * are not included.

BMI (Bonneville Market Information)***

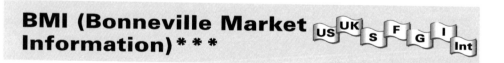

www.bmiquotes.com
3 Triad Center
Suite 100
Salt Lake City
UT 84180
Tel: 800 255 7374
Fax: 801 532 3202

Recommended for

Quotes: real-time, historical, delayed; options, futures, stocks, mutual funds, forex, bonds, international/foreign issues, portfolio monitoring, technical analysis chart.

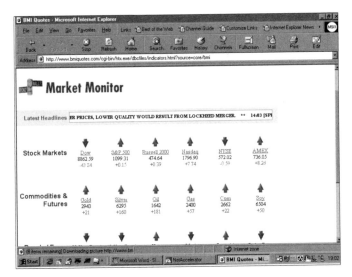

Diagram 17.1

BMI

Exchange and data coverage

■ Stocks, bonds, options, futures, foreign exchanges, indices statistics, mutual funds and more.

■ Futures exchanges: All leading world exchanges.

■ Equity exchanges: All major and many minor international exchanges.

Market data transmitted

■ *General:* open, high, low, close, last trade, total volume, statistics, official volume.

■ *Futures:* nominal open, open ranges, close ranges, open interest, tick volume, cabinet prices, spreads, settlement.

■ *Equities:* P/E ratios, dividends, earnings, yields, X dividend date, 52-week high/low, stock name, full bid/ask time (on NYSE and AMEX), best bid/ask time (on regional exchanges), bid/ask size, incremental volume.

Compatible with which software?

MarketCenter Platinum, SuperCharts RT, Aspen Graphics, Ensign Windows, Ticker Watcher, TradeStation, TradeWind, Vista RT, DollarLink, First Alert. Contact BMI regarding others.

Broadcast methods

■ *Cable:* BMI broadcasts over Superstation TBS and American Movie Classics (AMC) cable networks. BMI states it is the fastest and most accurate cable quote provider in the industry! The financial information comes through cable TV, so installation is relatively simple and easy.

▪ *Satellite (KU Band):* KU Band satellite covers continental USA plus Northern Mexico and Southern Canada. Although it is small and unobtrusive, KU is nevertheless powerful. With a versatile mount, the dish can be placed on a roof, a patio, or a wall.

Other features   free

▪ *Fast quotes:* price quotes based on ticker symbols entered by the user.

▪ *International online quotes:* ADRs, major forex, international stock indexes, international markets, foreign stock quotes.

▪ *CMS bond quotes:* US Treasuries, corporate bonds, mortgage bonds, CMO bonds.

▪ *Mutual fund quotes.*

▪ *News:* news alerts, headlines and full news stories. Apparently during a typical business day, over 12,000 stories are broadcast. Respected equity and futures services such as Dow Jones, Futures World News, S&P MarketScope, Zacks and many others are available.

▪ *Portfolio monitoring:* the web site permits users to create and edit up to 4 portfolios with up to 10 stocks each.

▪ *Historical charting:* web site permits downloading of charts based on type of chart (e.g. bar) and timeframe. Charts for all international/foreign equities as well as the usual, e.g. mutual funds and index charts.

▪ *Fundamental data, news, research:* based upon ticker symbol.

▪ *Trial software download from web site.*

Comment   *BMI is best known for its delivery of quotes and data. It has an 18-year pedigree and is one of the market leaders. Its business is the business of quote and historical information delivery, and therefore perhaps we should not expect too much else besides. However, I was impressed by the news service and all the freebies.*

First, the news service was up to date and of direct importance to the trader. It is clearly written by people who know and care about trading and not just journalists trying their hand at finance.

Second, the freebies were impressive. Even if you don't subscribe to BMI the web site was very easy to navigate and not cluttered. From the same single page you could monitor your portfolio, download a historical chart, obtain fundamental data and get fast quotes. Very well designed.

I was very impressed at the fact that I could download the 1-year candlestick chart of several Vietnamese stocks – for free!

The only complaint I had was the lack of more technical information on the web site – that would have rounded off a very good and straight-to-the-point site.

Prestel Online**

www.prestel.co.uk
Knightsbridge House
197 Knightsbridge
London SW7 1RB
Tel: 0171 591 9000
Fax: 0171 591 9001

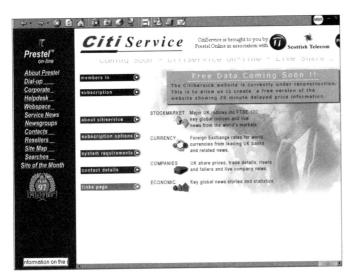

Diagram 17.2

Prestel

Recommended for

Quotes: real-time, historical, delayed; options, futures, stocks, investment and unit trusts.

Exchange and data coverage

- **Stocks, options, futures, foreign exchanges, indices.**
- **Futures exchanges:** LIFFE.
- **Equity exchanges:** London Stock Exchange.

Market data transmitted

- **General:** open, high, low, close, last trade, total volume, statistics, official volume.

Compatible with which software?

- All major formats.

Broadcast methods

- Internet (dial-up).

Comment *Prestel shook up the market for UK-listed company and derivatives quotes a couple of years ago when it started delivering data at phenomenally low prices. I use it myself. No problems to report.*

DBC (Data Broadcasting Corporation)**

US UK C S F G I Int

www.dbc.com
Data Broadcasting Corporation
1900 S. Norfolk Street
Suite 150
San Mateo
CA 94403
Tel: 800 527 7521; 415 571 1800
Fax: 415 571 8507

Lincoln House
Kennington Park
Oval
London SW9 6EJ
Tel: 0171 793 3100
Fax: 0171 793 3101

Diagram 17.3

DBC

Recommended for

Quotes: real-time, historical, delayed; options, futures, stocks, forex, bonds, mutual funds, international/foreign issues, portfolio monitoring.

Exchanges and data coverage

- *Stocks, bonds, options, futures, foreign exchanges, indices statistics, mutual funds and more.*
- *Futures and options exchanges:* all leading worldwide exchanges.
- *Stock exchanges:* New York Stock Exchange, American Stock Exchange, NASDAQ, Options Price Reporting Authority, London Stock Exchange.

Market data transmitted

- *General:* open, high, low, close, last trade, total volume, statistics, volume.
- *Futures:* open, close, open interest, cabinet prices, last spreads, settlement.
- *Equities:* P/E ratios, dividends, earnings, yields, X dividend date, 52-week high/low, stock name, bid/ask, bid/ask size.

Compatible with which software?

A very wide selection of popular software.

Broadcast methods

- *Satellite:* Most conventional satellite receivers should work satisfactorily, with a footprint serving North America, Europe, Middle East and North Africa. A satellite dish is needed!
- *Cable:* Via CNBC, WGN or AMC.
- *FM:* Available in most metropolitan areas in the USA and Canada.
- *Internet.*

Other features – premium/optional

- *News and commentary services* including Dow Jones Online News, ONE Headline Service, Elliot Wave Neowave Report, Hote Stocks Report, Instant Advisor, Vickers Stock Research Corporate, Insider Trading Report, Zacks Earnings Surprises Report, Jake Bernstain Futures Report, MarketLine.
- *Historical charts and analytics.*
- Pager, cell phone, e-mail and desktop alerts on price and volume.

Other features   (free)

- *Fast quotes:* price quotes based on ticker symbols entered by the user.
- *International online quotes:* ADRs, major forex, international stock indexes, international markets, foreign stock quotes.
- *Bond quotes:* US Treasuries, corporate bonds, mortgage bonds, CMO bonds.
- *Mutual fund quotes.*
- *News:* news alerts, headlines and full news stories using CBS MarketWatch.
- *Portfolio monitoring.*
- *Trial software download from web site:* Error! Bookmark not defined.

Comment *DBC provides a very thorough and comprehensive quote delivery service; comprehensive in both methods of delivery and geographical outreach. You can obtain its quotes, using one method or another, throughout Europe, the Middle East and even North Africa, as well as, of course, North America and Canada.*

The FM and cable methods are likely to be most popular since they require the least hardware. Unfortunately, delayed prices are not available online and so the online option is restricted to those with free internet access.

The company is very much geared toward the international as well as the US client and consequently a non-American will feel relatively at ease using this service since the company is likely to know the ins and outs of the user's country.

The premium packages provide an impressive array of news reports and tips, but it's impossible to judge how good these are. They were all individually priced and some appeared rather expensive. The free news service was more than adequate, and had excellent interviews and content.

Dial/Data** US UK C S F G I Int

www.tdc.com/dialdata
Track Data Corp.
56 Pine St
New York
NY 10005
Tel: 800 275 5544/ 212 422 1600
Fax: 212 612 2242

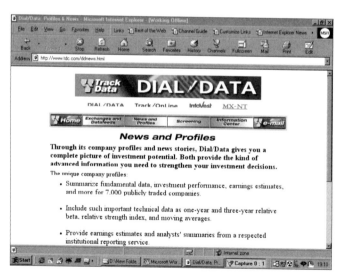

Diagram 17.4
Dial/Data

Recommended for

Quotes: historical, delayed; futures, stocks, options, mutual funds, bonds, ADRs, international/foreign.

Exchanges and data coverage

- **Exchanges:** all major world exchanges.

Market data transmitted

- **Stocks:** open, high, low, close, volume.
- **Mutual funds:** net asset value.
- **Money market:** yield, average days to maturity.
- **Government agencies:** bid, ask, yield.
- **Treasuries:** bid, ask, yield equity options, open, high, low, close, bid/ask volume, open interest.
- **Index options:** open, high, low, close, bid/ask volume, open interest.
- **Market indices:** open, high, low, close, volume.
- **Market statistics:** varied.
- **Futures:** open, high, low, close, volume, open interest.
- **Futures options:** open, high, low, close.
- **S&P industry groups:** weekly, index value, rank.

Compatible with which software?

All major popular software.

Broadcast methods

- **Internet:** If you have the latest downloading (stock price retrieval) from either Omega, Equis, or AIQ you can access Dial/Data through the internet. If you use software from other analysis programs you will have to check with them on availability of Dial/Data internet access.

Other features – premium/optional

- **Company profiles:** The unique company profiles:
  - summarize fundamental data, investment performance, earnings estimates, and more for 7,000 publicly traded companies
  - include technical data as 1-year and 3-year relative beta, relative strength index, and moving averages
  - provide earnings estimates and analysts' summaries from a respected institutional reporting service.
- **The news feature:**
  - displays up-to-the-second headlines and complete text on more than 5,000 daily news stories from Dow Jones Online News and Comtex
  - retrieves news from any company/ticker symbol
  - presents insights into the forces moving stocks that are important to investors.

Other features   (free)

■ *Trial software download from web site.*

Comment   *Although the site is disappointing, lacking the freebies of other sites, functional and informative Dial/Data is one of the most reliable and ubiquitous data providers around. You can be assured the data provided will be screened for errors, and timely. The international coverage is excellent.*

BridgeFeed**   US UK F G I S J Int

www.bridge.com
Bridge
3 World Financial Center
New York
NY 10281
Tel: 212 372 7100 / 800 600 rely

78 Fleet Street
London EC4Y 1HY
England
Tel: 0171 842 4000
Fax: 0171 782 0964

Unicom Electronic Publishing
4F, No.12, Sec.2
King-San Road
Taipei
Tel: 2 321 9209
Fax: 2 341 6188

Earlthorn Investment
Rm.802, Dominion Centre
43–59 Queen's Road East
Wanchai
Tel: 2529 1211
Fax: 2866 2796

50 Raffles Place
19–02 Shell Tower
Singapore 0104
Tel: 222 9992
Fax: 222 4930

Recommended for

Quotes: real-time, historical, delayed; options, futures, stocks, mutual funds, forex, bonds, international / foreign issues.

Exchange and data coverage

■ *Stocks, bonds, options, futures, foreign exchanges, indices statistics, mutual funds and more.*

■ *Futures exchanges:* all leading world futures exchanges.

■ *Equity exchanges:* All major and many minor international exchanges.

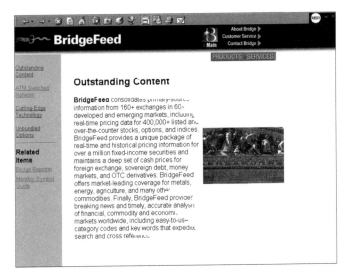

Diagram 17.5
....
BridgeFeed

Market data transmitted

■ *General:* open, high, low, close, last trade, total volume, statistics, official volume.

■ *Futures:* nominal open, open ranges, close ranges, open interest, cabinet prices, spreads, settlement.

■ *Equities:* P/E ratios, dividends, earnings, yields, X dividend date, 52-week high/low, stock name, full bid/ask, bid/ask size, incremental volume.

And for markets that use local market pricing conventions, such as Australia, Germany, Hong Kong, Italy, and Japan, special valuation prices are available.

Compatible with which software?

Virtually all major file formats; check with Bridge, including MegaTech, Metastock, SuperCharts, Reuters Triarch, TIBCO TIB, CSK Software InVision, Telerate TTRS, Bridge MV Link, Midas-Kapiti FIST, and Syntegra OTS.

Broadcast methods

■ *Internet.*

■ *Direct dial-up.*

Other features – premium/optional

■ *News:* BridgeFeed provides breaking news and timely, accurate analysis of financial, commodity and economic markets worldwide, including easy-to-use category codes and keywords that expedite search and cross reference.

■ *Reports and commentary.*

Comment *Again, a web site light on information. However, it is recommended for the quality of its quotes and its service, not its web site. Light on information, and so the best thing to do is contact it with details of what you need and ask for a quote.*

This company is definitely one of the big boys and has just acquired Dow Jones Telerate. It has an international reach and feel. So whether you are based in the USA, Africa or Afghanistan, it can reach you.

Quote.Com *** [US]

www.quote.com
3375 Scott Blvd., Suite 300
Santa Clara
CA 95054
Tel: 800 498 8068/408 327 0700
Fax: 408 327 0707

Diagram 17.6

Quote.Com

Recommended for

Quotes: real-time; futures, delayed data, historical data, stock, mutual fund, options, forex, portfolio monitoring.

Exchange and data coverage

▓ *Stocks, bonds, options, futures, foreign exchanges, indices statistics, mutual funds and more.*

▓ *Exchanges.*

Market data transmitted

▓ *General:* open, high, low, last, net, volume, ask, best ask, size, best bid.

Compatible with which software?

Provided as ASCII, so almost all software should be able to handle.
   Displayed on web site.

Broadcast methods

 Internet.

Other features – premium/optional

 News: Reuters, Marketscope, Businesswire, PR Newswire, S&P News, News-bytes, Edgar Online, Nightly Business Report.

 Historical charting: web site permits downloading of charts based on type of chart (e.g. bar) and timeframe. Charts for all international/foreign equities as well as the usual, e.g. mutual funds and index charts.

 Live charts.

 Live portfolio.

Other features   free

 Fast quotes: price quotes based on ticker symbols entered by the user.

 Mutual fund quotes.

 Portfolio monitoring.

Another sturdy quote site from a specialist in the business. Quote.Com often receives commendations in the press for its services. It concentrates on behind-the-scenes screening to ensure data are "clean;" a thankless task which many quote vendors ignore to save costs.
   It is a mystery why the site does not give more details about Quote.Com. Doesn't it want more business?

Comment

Reuters MoneyNet*** US

www.moneynet.com

Recommended for

Fundamental analysis (stocks and mutual funds), technical analysis (stocks and mutual funds), online quotes (stocks, options, mutual funds, spot currency), news, market commentary, portfolio monitoring, filters.

Online quotes   free

 Fast quotes (delayed 20 minutes)

 real-time quote (subscription fee)

 real-time option quotes (subscription fee)

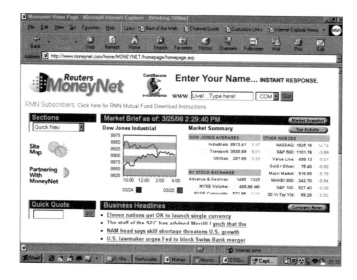

Diagram 17.7

Reuters MoneyNet

- option quotes
- option chains
- currency quotes
- market snapshot.

Fundamental analysis *free*

- Company data:
  1. key financial ratios
  2. accounts
  3. annual reports.
- Company-specific news (up to 30 days):
  1. Reuters Financial
  2. Business Wire
  3. analysts' views; consensus opinion, estimates.
- Filters (see later).

Technical analysis *free*

- Price history – bar charts.
- Intra-day price charts – line charts.
- Technical indicators – bar, candlestick, line charts; moving averages, Bollinger Bands, envelopes, momentum, on-balance volume, price oscillator, price rate of change, relative strength indicators, Stochastic, volume.

News *free*

- Economic calendar
- economic data

- market commentary
- breaking news
- category news – equity, financial markets, industry, international, US government
- companies in the news today.

Filters *free*

- Fundamental:
  1 companies in the news today
  2 stock brokers' research alerts.
- Technical:
  1 most active (volume, %gain/loss, net gain/loss)
  2 bullish/bearish engulfing patterns
  3 stock>/<20% on double volume
  4 moving average crossovers
  5 break-outs
  6 volatility
  7 biggest gainers over the week
  8 oversold/overbought.

Other *free*

- Portfolio monitoring.

Diagram 17.8 shows key financial ratios on Reuters MoneyNet – clean and crisp.

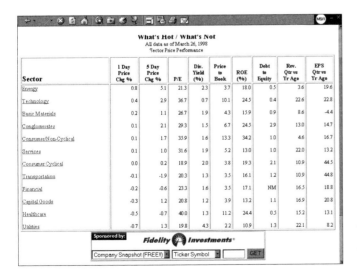

What's Hot / What's Not
All data as of March 26, 1998
Sector Price Performance

Sector	1 Day Price Chg %	5 Day Price Chg %	P/E	Div. Yield (%)	Price to Book	ROE (%)	Debt to Equity	Rev. Qtr vs Yr Ago	EPS Qtr vs Yr Ago
Energy	0.8	5.1	21.3	2.3	3.7	18.0	0.5	3.6	19.6
Technology	0.4	2.9	36.7	0.7	10.1	24.5	0.4	22.6	22.8
Basic Materials	0.2	1.1	26.7	1.9	4.3	15.9	0.9	8.6	-4.4
Conglomerates	0.1	2.1	29.3	1.5	6.7	24.5	2.9	13.0	14.7
Consumer/Non-Cyclical	0.1	1.7	35.9	1.6	13.3	34.2	1.0	4.6	16.7
Services	0.1	1.0	31.6	1.9	5.2	13.0	1.0	22.0	13.2
Consumer Cyclical	0.0	0.2	18.9	2.0	3.8	19.3	2.1	10.9	44.5
Transportation	-0.1	-1.9	20.3	1.3	3.5	16.1	1.2	10.9	44.8
Financial	-0.2	-0.6	23.3	1.6	3.5	17.1	NM	16.5	18.8
Capital Goods	-0.3	1.2	20.8	1.2	3.9	13.2	1.1	16.9	20.8
Healthcare	-0.5	-0.7	40.0	1.3	11.2	24.4	0.5	15.2	13.1
Utilities	-0.7	1.3	19.8	4.3	2.2	10.9	1.3	22.1	8.2

Sponsored by: **Fidelity Investments**
Company Snapshot (FREE!!) | Ticker Symbol | | GET

Diagram 17.8

Key financial ratios on MoneyNet

Comment   *Reuters has developed a very easy-to-navigate site that is a model for what a financial internet site should look like. Without the need to scroll too much you can view a vast amount of information, which simultaneously does not clutter the screen.*

I cannot get over how much information is available free. The technical analysis features are some of the best on the net. The amount of user-defined searches is extraordinary. You can hardly question the quality of news from Reuters.

As is always the case when treated so generously, you cannot help but ask for more. More detailed analysts' views would have been useful, more fundamental filters would also have been welcome.

MarketEdge *** US

`www.marketedge.com`

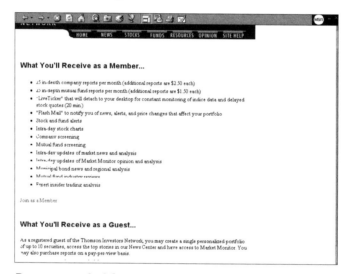

Diagram 17.9

MarketEdge

Recommended for

Mutual funds (reports and commentary), fundamental analysis (stocks and mutual funds), online quotes, filters, portfolio monitoring, discussion groups.

Online quotes

■ Fast quotes; mutual fund quotes

■ market snapshot.

Fundamental analysis

■ Filters (see later).

■ Company data:

   1 key financial ratios

   2 S&P star ratings

   3 accounts

   4 major institutional shareholders

   5 summary investment house reports

   6 insider buying/selling activity.

■ Company-specific news:

   1 analysts' views; consensus opinion.

■ Mutual fund reports:

   1 US equity, international/emerging market, sector funds, municipal/government funds/ corporate funds.

■ Mutual fund analysis and reports (*free*)

   1 week in review

   2 month in review

   3 industry digest

   4 trends.

Technical analysis

■ Charts – net asset value.

Stock alerts

■ Earnings announcements

■ earnings surprises

■ dividend reports

■ price changes > 3%.

Filters

■ Stocks:

   1 financial performance

   2 revenue/market capitalization size

   3 growth (revenue/EPS/DPS)

   4 P/E

   5 insider trading

   6 earnings forecast.

■ Mutual funds (stock, international, taxable bonds, sector, tax free bond):

   1 category

   2 size

   3 age

   4 manager tenure

   5 expenses

   6 relative performance

   7 risk (absolute/relative)

   8 month's top performer.

Other features free

- Bob Gobele's Stock of the Day.
- Columns.
- News – earnings surprises, business, technology.
- Portfolio monitoring.

Discussion group

- Stocks
- mutual funds.

Comment *The two best things about this site are the resources available for mutual funds fanatics, in terms of research and filters, and the variables available for filtering stocks. However, I am inclined to combine the variables available for stock filtering with some of those available in other sites for a truly comprehensive result. While you will pay for the company reports, they are rather good in detail and relatively inexpensive.*

Wall Street Journal Interactive**

www.wsj.com

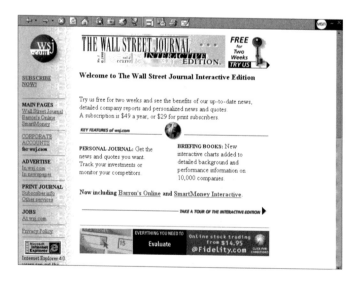

Diagram 17.10
Wall Street Journal

Recommended for

Fundamental analysis and online quotes (stocks, mutual funds, futures (commodities, financial) currencies, bonds, mutual funds, options), news, market commentary.

Online quotes

- Fast quotes (real-time)
- option quotes
- bonds
- mutual funds
- futures
- currencies
- market snapshot.

Fundamental analysis

- Company data:
  1 key financial ratios
  2 accounts
- Company-specific news (14-day searchable archive).

News

- Breaking news
- market commentary.

Filters

- Most active stocks
- leaders
- losers
- earnings surprises.

Other features

- Economic indicators archive
- Federal Reserve monitor.

The Wall Street Journal *is most famous, of course, for its news content, and especially for its editorials and* Heard on the Street *section. As a subscriber to the web site you, of course, receive all this, plus access to a site particularly strong on futures, bonds, currencies and foreign equities.*

It is a real pity there is virtually only the tour that is free on this site. Nevertheless, subscription starts at $29 pa at the time of writing.

Comment

Market Guide *** [US]

www.marketguide.com

Recommended for

Stock quotes, fundamental analysis (stocks), filters.

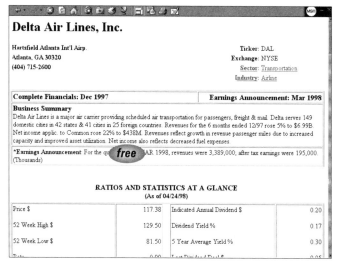

Delta Air Lines, Inc.

Hartsfield Atlanta Int'l Airp.
Atlanta, GA 30320
(404) 715-2600

Ticker: DAL
Exchange: NYSE
Sector: Transportation
Industry: Airline

Complete Financials: Dec 1997	Earnings Announcement: Mar 1998

Business Summary
Delta Air Lines is a major air carrier providing scheduled air transportation for passengers, freight & mail. Delta serves 149 domestic cities in 42 states & 41 cities in 25 foreign countries. Revenues for the 6 months ended 12/97 rose 5% to $6.99B. Net income applic. to Common rose 22% to $438M. Revenues reflect growth in revenue passenger miles due to increased capacity and improved asset utilization. Net income also reflects decreased fuel expenses.

*Earnings Announcement: For the qu... MAR 1998, revenues were 3,389,000; after tax earnings were 195,000. (Thousands)

RATIOS AND STATISTICS AT A GLANCE
(As of 04/24/98)

Price $	117.38	Indicated Annual Dividend $	0.20
52 Week High $	129.50	Dividend Yield %	0.17
52 Week Low $	81.50	5 Year Average Yield %	0.30
	0.00	Last Dividend Decl $	0.05

Diagram 17.11
Market Guide

Online quotes

- Real-time.

Fundamental analysis

- Company data:
    1 key financial ratios
    2 accounts.
- Company-specific news:
    1 analysts' views
    2 earnings estimates.
- Filters (see later).

Filters

Fundamental:

- Hot sectors
- hot industries
- hot stocks (sub-divided into industry, sector and market as a whole)
- variables: EPS; EPS growth; exchange; market capitalization; P/E ratio; price; price high/low; profit margin; ROA; ROE; revenue growth; sales; debt to equity; yield and more.

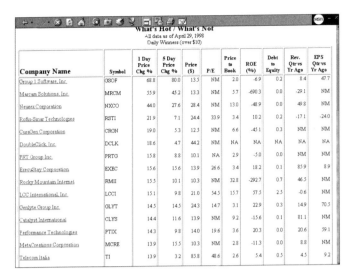

Diagram 17.12

Market Guide's What's Hot

The table in the diagram shows:

What's Hot / What's Not
All data as of April 29, 1998
Daily Winners (over $10)

Company Name	Symbol	1 Day Price Chg %	5 Day Price Chg %	Price ($)	P/E	Price to Book	ROE (%)	Debt to Equity	Rev. Qtr vs Yr Ago	EPS Qtr vs Yr Ago
Group 1 Software, Inc.	GSOF	68.8	80.0	13.5	NM	2.0	-6.9	0.2	8.4	47.7
Marcam Solutions, Inc.	MRCM	55.9	45.2	13.3	NM	5.7	-690.3	0.0	-29.1	NM
Neurex Corporation	NXCO	44.0	27.6	28.4	NM	13.0	-48.9	0.0	49.8	NM
Rofin-Sinar Technologies	RSTI	21.9	7.1	24.4	33.9	3.4	10.2	0.2	-17.1	-24.0
CuraGen Corporation	CRGN	19.0	5.3	12.5	NM	6.6	-45.1	0.3	NM	NM
DoubleClick, Inc.	DCLK	18.6	4.7	44.2	NM	NA	NA	NA	NA	NA
PRT Group Inc.	PRTG	15.8	8.8	10.1	NA	2.9	-5.0	0.0	NM	NM
ExecuStay Corporation	EXEC	15.6	15.6	13.9	26.6	3.4	18.2	0.1	85.9	8.9
Rocky Mountain Internet	RMII	15.5	10.1	10.3	NM	32.8	-292.7	0.7	46.5	NM
LCC International, Inc.	LCCI	15.1	9.8	21.0	54.5	15.7	57.5	2.5	-0.6	NM
Genlyte Group Inc.	GLYT	14.5	14.5	24.3	14.7	3.1	22.9	0.3	14.9	70.5
Catalyst International	CLYS	14.4	11.6	13.9	NM	9.2	-15.6	0.1	81.1	NM
Performance Technologies	PTIX	14.3	9.8	14.0	19.6	3.6	20.3	0.0	20.6	59.1
MetaCreations Corporation	MCRE	13.9	15.5	10.3	NM	2.8	-11.3	0.0	8.8	NM
Telecom Italia	TI	13.9	3.2	85.8	48.6	2.6	5.4	0.5	4.5	9.2

Comment

I found the filters particularly good on this site – and free. You can see the hot sectors and then within those go to the hot industries and from those to the hot stocks. This seems a useful "filtration method" and provides a better context for understanding price moves than the usual hot stocks list.

Also unusual for a site was the free real-time online quotes; albeit limited to only a few exchanges – but beggars can't be choosers.

Bloomberg * US J UK Int

www.bloomberg.com

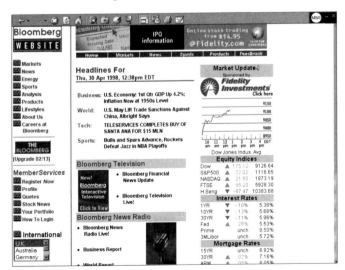

Diagram 17.13

Bloomberg

Recommended for

News, market commentary, fundamental analysis (mutual funds, bonds).

Online quotes

- Indices
- currency
- mutual funds
- bonds.

Fundamental analysis

- Company data (subscription service)
- company-specific news (subscription news).

News

- Category news – equity, business, top stories, mutual funds, tech, companies in the news (some subscription)
- breaking news
- market commentary.

Comment *Bloomberg's site is crisp, colorful and easy on the eye. However, it is clearly an offshoot of their proprietary services and contains that which they deign worthy of the free private investor site scavenger. As such, I would only really consider using it for news; a good collection of category news, and the materials it has on mutual funds and bonds. Much of the rest is subscription only and can largely be gained from free sources elsewhere in a similar format.*

CNN Financial Network *** US Int

www.cnnfn.com

Recommended for

Fundamental analysis (mutual funds, stocks), news, market commentary.

Online quotes *free*

- Fast quotes; mutual funds
- fast quotes; stocks
- market snapshot.

Fundamental analysis *free*

- Company data:
    1 key financial ratios
    2 accounts

Diagram 17.14

CNN research

3   snapshot
4   SEC filings
5   profile
6   upgrade/downgrade (from briefing.com).

■ Company-specific news:
1   from a wide range of sources
2   analysts' views; estimates.

■ Mutual funds:
1   top 25
2   news
3   Morning Star Profiles (star ratings, returns, risk, fees, sector breakdown)
4   value line profile (performance, ranking, risk).

Technical analysis free

■ Charts – stocks and mutual funds.

News free

■ Breaking news
■ category news – economy
■ market commentary.

What I really like about this site is the fundamental analysis information that is available for free for both mutual funds and stocks. What particularly caught my eye was the Morning Star Profiles available for free and the upgrade/downgrade by analysts' listings. To be fair, CNNfn does link seamlessly with www.quicken.com to provide a lot of this free information. The CNN news I found to be better than Bloombergs but not always totally market oriented, unlike say, Reuters MoneyNet.

All in all a great site for stocks and mutual fund fundamental analysts and for economic and general business news.

Comment

Standard & Poor** US

www.stockinfo.standardpoor.com

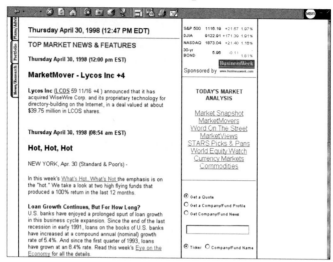

Diagram 17.15

Standard & Poor

Recommended for

Fundamental analysis (mutual funds, stocks), news (commodities, currencies, bonds), market commentary, portfolio monitor.

Online quotes   *free*

▪ Fast quotes; mutual funds

▪ fast quotes; stocks.

Fundamental analysis

▪ Company data:

   1 key financial ratios

   2 accounts

   3 snapshot

   4 profile.

▪ Company-specific news:

   1 from a wide range of sources

   2 analysts' views; estimates.

▪ Mutual funds:

   1 sector overview

   2 trends

   3 news.

Technical analysis

▪ Charts – stocks and mutual funds.

News free

▪ Breaking news

▪ category news – economy, commodities, currencies, bonds, stocks

▪ market commentary.

Other features

▪ Portfolio monitor.

Standard & Poor has a massive database on mutual funds and stocks. And all the access is by payment only, if you find the free sites you have investigated do not provide enough information for you then this site is worth an investigation – there is a free 30-day trial.

Also useful were the period market commentaries on the commodities (mainly directed toward the derivatives traders) – something that is relatively difficult to find on a mainstream site for free.

Comment

Financial Times *** UK Int

www.ft.com

Diagram 17.16

FT.com

Recommended for

Quotes, fundamental analysis (stocks), news, market commentary.

Online quotes *free*

- Delayed
- end of day
- all major stocks throughout the globe
- all major indices, currencies commodities, bonds.

Fundamental analysis *free*

- Company data:
    1. key financial ratios
    2. accounts.
- Company-specific news:
    1. searchable archive.

News

- Category news – companies, world, industry, technology
- market commentary.

Comment   *Financial Times's site, now incorporating FT TV, is one of the most global sites around. Its news commentary is second to none. It is an excellent resource for obtaining quickly a view of what is happening in the markets and economy, together with measured and critical analysis. Although some parts of the site need a bit of work to improve navigation, it is quickly improving.*

Electronic Share Information *** UK

www.esi.co.uk

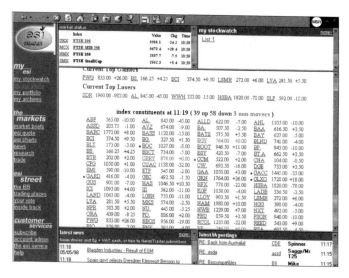

Diagram 17.17

ESI

Recommended for

Fundamental analysis (stocks, investment trusts), technical analysis (stocks, investment trusts), portfolio monitoring, quick quotes, news, market commentary, discussion group, quotes (real-time, historical, delayed, options, stocks, investment trusts).

Online quotes free

- Quick quotes (stocks) (delayed)
- real-time quotes (subscriptions).

Fundamental analysis

- Company data:
  1 broker earnings estimates
  2 analysts' reports (extel).
- Company-specific news:
- AFX News.

Technical analysis

- Charts.

News free

- Category news – market, economic, government, company, industry.

Filters free

- Top gainers/losers
- volume.

Exchange and data coverage

- Stocks, options.
- LIFFE, London Stock Exchange.

Market data transmitted

- *General:* open, high, low, close, last trade, total volume, statistics, official volume.

Compatible with which software?

Most major software packages.

Broadcast methods

- Internet.

Other features *free*

■ Portfolio manager.

■ Quotes.

Comment *In the UK you have very little choice when it comes to internet sites for the trader. Thankfully, there is ESI. Although not comparable to the top US sites, it knocks spots off other similar UK sites. The displays are clear and it often appears as the top UK financial site, beating the likes of the Financial Times.*

Infotrade * UK

www.infotrade.co.uk

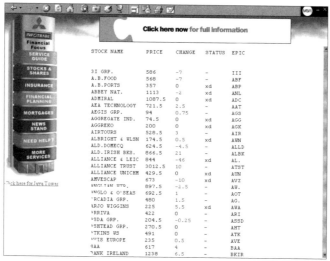

Diagram 17.18

Infotrade

Recommended for

Fundamental analysis (stocks, investment trusts), technical analysis (stocks, investment trusts), portfolio monitoring, quick quotes, news, market commentary, portfolio manager.

Online quotes *free*

■ Quick quotes (stocks) (delayed).

Fundamental analysis

■ Company data.

■ Company-specific news.

Technical analysis

■ Charts.

News

■ News – market commentary.

Other features

■ Portfolio manager.

Infotrade is not quite as good as ESI, but it is worth a visit for comparison purposes, in case you prefer the look or feel of it.   **Comment**

Hemmington Scott * UK

www.hemscott.co.uk

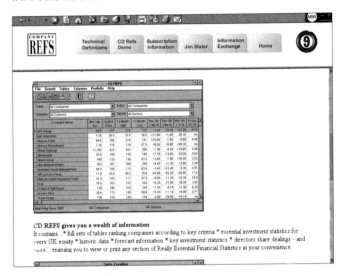

CD REFS gives you a wealth of information
It contains... * full sets of tables ranking companies according to key criteria * essential investment statistics for -very UK equity * historic data * forecast information * key investment statistics * directors share dealings - and more ...enabling you to view or print any section of Really Essential Financial Statistics at your convenience.

Diagram 17.19
....
Hemmscott

Recommended for

Fundamental analysis (stocks, investment trusts).

Fundamental analysis   *free*

■ Company data:

1 key financial ratios

2 accounts

3 annual reports.

■ Company-specific news:

1 analysts' views.

■ Investment trusts:

1 performance

2 profile

3 major shareholders.

Technical analysis

- Charts (stocks and investment trusts).

Comment *This site is strong on UK investment trusts and principally recommended for the vast quantity of fundamental data regarding them.*

Market-Eye ** UK

`www.market-eye.co.uk`

Diagram 17.20

Market-Eye

Recommended for

Fundamental analysis (stocks, investment trusts), market commentary, discussion group, quotes (real-time, historical, delayed, options, stocks, futures, currencies, bonds).

Online quotes *free*

- Quick quotes (stocks, futures, options, currencies) (delayed)
- real-time quotes (subscriptions).

Fundamental analysis

- Company-specific news.

News *free*

- Market news.

Exchange and data coverage

- Stocks, options, currencies, futures.
- LIFFE, London Stock Exchange.

Market data transmitted

- **General:** open, high, low, close, last trade, total volume, statistics, official volume.

Compatible with which software?

Most major software packages.

Broadcast methods

- Internet (direct dial-up).

Other features

- Quotes.

Although not as strong for the stock investor when it comes to data as ESI, very good for the trader in LIFFE products. Seems to be more geared for the semi-professional trader, whereas ESI is more geared for the amateur trader.

Comment

Briefing ** US

www.briefing.com

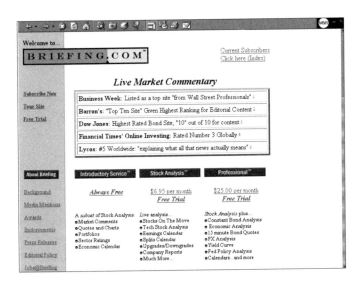

Diagram 17.21

Briefing

Recommended for

Market commentary, fundamental analysis (stocks), portfolio monitoring.

Online quotes *free*

- Quick quotes (delayed)
- real-time quotes (subscription).

Fundamental analysis

- Stocks on the move
- earnings calendar
- upgrade/downgrades
- company reports.

Technical analysis *free*

- Charts.

News

- Running market commentary
- running bond, economic, forex analysis.

Other features *free*

- Portfolio monitor.

 Comment

What makes this site special is the running commentary through the day. It is clear from the commentary that it is written by a trader immersed in the markets and not a journalist. However, to get the live commentary there is a $6.95 per month fee, whereas opening, midday and closing reports are free. Here is a sample:

*12:00 ET Dow +10, Nasdaq -3, S&P +2.87: Not much conviction in today's market thus far as the indices trade in mixed fashion ... Tech sector, specifically the search engines, leading the modest declines ... Thanks to the strong showing from **American Express (AXP +4 5/8),** Dow has managed to hang around the unchanged level for most of the session ... Financial services concern cited by a fund manager in a Business Week article as being able to fetch $130-$140 a share in a takeover situation ... **These days, two magic words get cash flowing in a hurry – takeover being one, and Internet the other** ... As for the tech stocks, they have been listless for the most part, held back by the search engines, and a weak earnings report from Bay Networks ... The thought of another flurry of earnings announcements due next week a likely contributor to today's largely neutral tone as well ... **Lending support to the broader market are the drug, brokerage, and oil drilling stocks** ... 30-yr bond -3/32 at 5.87%, having surrendered modest gains posted shortly after it was learned the **February trade gap widened to $12.1 bln** ... Concern that Asia is not doing the job it was expected to do in slowing the U.S. economy, and the potential for a Fed tightening as a result, keeping a lid on things ... DJTA -17.63.*

Microsoft Investor * * * US

investor.msn.com

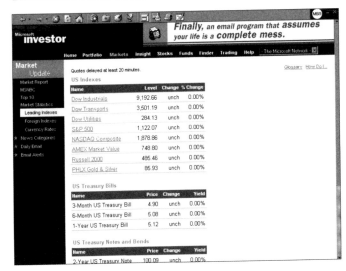

Diagram 17.22

MSN Investor

Recommended for

Fundamental analysis (stocks and mutual funds), technical analysis (stocks and mutual funds), online quotes, market commentary, discussion group (stocks and mutual funds), filters.

Online quotes free

- Fast quotes; mutual fund quotes
- market snapshot.

Fundamental analysis (some free)

- Filters (see later).
- Company data:
  1 key financial ratios
  2 accounts
  3 major institutional shareholders
  4 insider buying/selling activity.
- Company-specific news:
  1 analysts' views; consensus opinion
  2 Reuters news wire
  3 research alerts based on financial ratios.
- Mutual fund:
  1 portfolio composition (Morningstar)
  2 portfolio performance (value line)
  3 screening (see later).

Technical analysis *free*

■ Charts – moving averages, relative performances and few other technicals.

Stock alerts *free*

■ Based on in-house research.

Filters

■ Stocks – 500 criteria!

■ Mutual funds – 300 criteria!

News *free*

■ Companies in the news

■ active stocks

■ biggest losers / winners

■ earnings calendar

■ market commentary.

Comment *There are several very good things about this site – and the best thing you can do is visit it because a home page can paint a thousand words. One of the best things about this site is its screening and filtering tools for stocks and mutual funds. Although subscription only, with filter variables running into the hundreds, it has to be the mother of all filters.*

The market commentary, offered three times daily, is also very extensive and has useful hyperlinks to fundamental data of all companies mentioned. Added to that is an extensive array of columnists on the look out for stocks to give you even more ideas or to confirm your own. A research alert provides useful fundamental information, informing you what is particularly interesting about the site; for instance, if the P/E is twice projected annual growth and that this is generally viewed as bearish. All in all a very good site with numerous original touches.

Zacks ** US C

www.zacks.com

Recommended for

Fundamental analysis (stocks); portfolio monitoring, filters.

Fundamental analysis (partly free)

■ Company data:

    1 research watch: brokerage research reports   *free*

    2 key financial ratios.

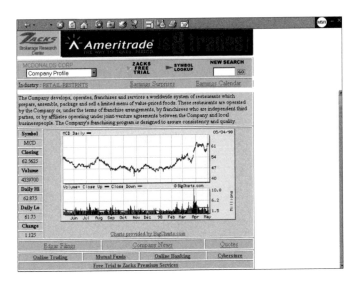

Diagram 17.23

Zacks

■ Company-specific news:

   1 analyst watch: analysts' earnings estimates; brokerage recommendations.

Filters

■ Fundamental:

   1 5000 investment criteria.

This is a sound and sturdy site. It is one of the best, well known, highly reliable and professional.

 Comment

Stockpoint *** [US]

`www.stockpoint.com`

Recommended for

Fundamental analysis (stocks, mutual funds), technical analysis (stocks), filters (stocks, mutual funds).

Online quotes   *free*

■ Fast quotes (delayed) (stocks and mutual funds)

● market snapshot.

Fundamental analysis *free*

■ Company data:

   1 profile

   2 key financials.

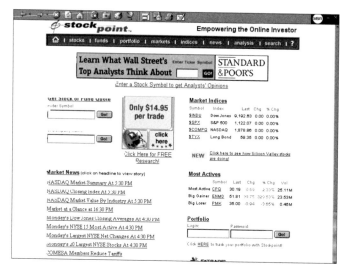

Diagram 17.24

Stockpoint

■ Company-specific news:

1   analysts' ratings (comparison to stocks in same industry)
2   research reports (subscription)
3   news.

■ Filters (see later).

Technical analysis   *free*

■ Price history – bar charts, candlestick charts

■ intra-day price charts

■ technical indicators – volume, on-balance volume, relative strength, Bollinger Bands, price rate of change, MACD, Stochastics

■ comparison to indices, other stocks.

News   *free*

■ Market commentary.

Filters   *free*

■ Fundamental:

1   over 20 variables (stocks and mutual funds).

Comment   *This site is sub-titled "Empowering the Online Investor." It lives up to that claim. What is particularly good about it is not necessarily the free material, which is ample, but the way it is organized. From one page you can have a 360 degree view of a stock or mutual fund, to get you well on the way to analyzing a stock or fund.*

Summary

The sites in this chapter are often recommended for more than one service. By keeping all such sites together the intention has been to make it easier for the reader to avoid having to select lots of different sites as part of trading.

You should have visited quite a few sites depending on the skeleton plans and what your particular interests were in light of what you have read in earlier chapters on analysis, brokers, etc.

18

Getting technical: technical analysis only sites

❝ *Every ship at the bottom of the sea was loaded with charts.* **❞**

Jon Najarian
Chairman and CEO
Mercury Trading

In this chapter

The sites in this section deal exclusively with technical analysis sites. This section is separate from the other sites to reduce clutter. This is not an exhaustive list; the skeleton plans will lead you to all the technical sites relevant to you. The chapter is divided into three parts: educational sites; internet charts sites; software companies sites.

To have got this far

- You will have read the chapter on analysis.
- You will have read the appendix on technical analysis.
- You will have been referred to this chapter by a skeleton plan.

Educational sites

The sites listed in Table 18.1 are useful for the information they provide on technical analysis for those interested in learning more. Those together with the recommended reading should be more than adequate for most technical analysts, and should get you well on the way to becoming an expert (Diagrams 18.1, 18.2).

Table 18.1 Educational sites

Name	Address	Comment
Bridge	news.bridge.com	Specialists in data and news but some useful information
DecisionPoint	www.decisionpoint.com	Specialist in technical analysis
Equis	www.equis.com	Specialist in charting software
Market Technicians Society	www.mta-usa.com	The Technical Analysts Society
Stocks & Commodities Mag	www.traders.com	The specialist technical analysis magazine

For other sites, do not forget to check out Section 5, in particular the directories.

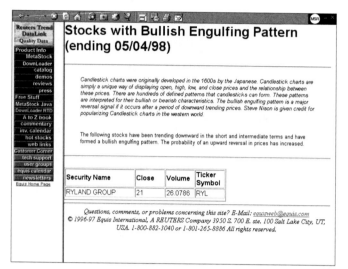

Diagram 18.1

Equis

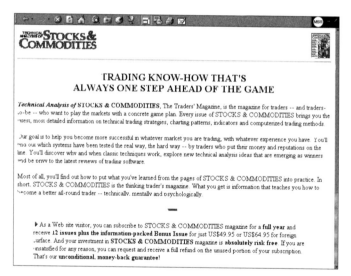

Diagram 18.2

**The Traders'
Magazine**

Internet charts

As mentioned in Section 2, Chapter 10, there are numerous internet sites that provide technical analysis facilities in the form of interactive charts. While the quantity of technical analysis you can perform on these charts is far less than what you
can do with the software mentioned in the next part of this chapter, the sites are
good if your primary interest is fundamental analysis, but you want occasionally
to supplement your fundamental analysis with some technicals.

These sites are included here, together with others mentioned in skeleton plans (see Table 18.2 and Diagrams 18.3, 18.4). For other sites, do not forget to check out Section 5, in particular the directories.

Table 18.2 Typical internet technical analysis chart

Name	Address	Ranking	Charts	Intra-day	Indicators
Alphachart	www.alphachart.com	***	√	√	√
Ask Research	www.askresearch.com	***	√	√	√

*** The site is about as good as technical analysis gets on the web.

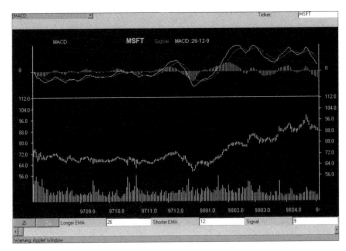

Diagram 18.3
Alphachart

Diagram 18.4
Ask Research

Software

There are numerous companies that provide computer software which can then be used to download quotes from quote vendors and perform technical analysis. Few permit you to download their software from their web sites but you can preview and download demo and find out what they do. Table 18.3 lists some of the best technical analysis software vendors.

Table 18.3 Technical analysis software sites

Product	Company	Address	Ranking	Cost*
Metastock 6.5	Equis	www.equis.com	*** (Recommended)	$349
OmniTrader 3.1	Nirvana	www.nirv.com	***	$395
SuperCharts	Omega	www.omegaresearch.com	**	$199.95
TeleChart 2000	Worden Bros	www.worden.com	**	$29
TradeStation	Omega	www.omegaresearch.com	**	$199.95
Window on Wall St	Window on Wall St	www.wallstreet.net	**	$295

*** Very good software, excellent value for money and recognized as a market leader.
** All round good software, value for money with some features not found elsewhere.
Software lower than ** is not included because the standard of software is so high.
* At time of print.

What to look for

Whatever software you choose look for the following features.

Data included

Are data included in the cost or do you need to go to a supplier – if so which ones (if only a few suppliers supply data then the hidden cost of getting data could be prohibitive).

Data downloader

Do you need extra software to download data from a data provider and get them into your software? If so, what is the cost of that?

Data cleaner

Does the software come with a feature that scans all downloaded data for errors such as dates out of sequence, highs lower than lows, etc.?

Data format

Can you convert different data formats, thereby increasing your choice of data provider and so data costs?

Features

How many indicators and types of charts can be drawn?

Alerts

Can you set price alerts?

Systems development

Is there a programming language permitting you to produce your own system?

Screening

Can you use the software to screen through all data according to a system (Diagrams 18.5, 18.6)?

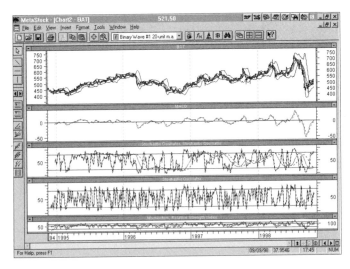

Diagram 18.5

Metastock 6.5 on Equis

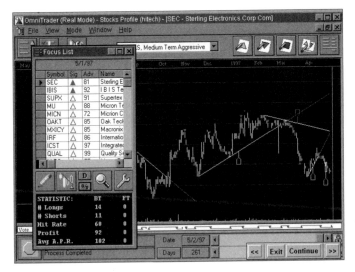

Diagram 18.6

OmniTrader 3.1 on Nirvana

Summary

There are numerous technical analysis resources on the web. The major choice is between using software and a data download or using an online charting service. The latter, with its inherent limitations, is the better choice for the fundamental analysts and/or dabbler in technical analysis. The former is the choice of the serious technical analyst.

Brokers only (a sad and lonely place)

❝ I have probably seen every mistake customers make; what makes them lose money and what makes them successful. ❞

Phil Flynn
Vice President
Alaron Trading

In this chapter

The sites in this section deal exclusively with online brokers. This section is separate from the other sites to reduce clutter and make your navigation easier.

To have got this far

- You will have read the section on online brokers – especially what to look for.
- You will have read the appendix on types of orders that can be placed.
- You will have read the skeleton plans for your chosen product.

Have a look at the tables in the chapter for easy comparison of what the brokers have to offer.

Star ratings in this chapter:

See key at the bottom of Table 19.1.

Recap: what to look for in your broking partner

- Competitive commissions:
  - *1* check for what size trade the advertised "low" commission applies
  - *2* any maintenance or handling charges (i.e. hidden costs?)
  - *3* commissions sometimes vary on the price of the stock, e.g. extra charges for a stock trading less than 50c.
- Account details:
  - *1* minimum initial deposit
  - *2* minimum account balance
  - *3* interest rates for idle funds
  - *4* good brokers ought to automatically sweep excess funds to a high interest account
  - *5* margin and checking accounts:
    - – A margin account will allow you to borrow – what are the rates?
    - – It will be convenient to be able to write checks.
    - – Is there a cost for wiring funds from the account?
  - *6* availability of account data online
  - *7* how often is the account up-dated? Intra-daily may be important for the day trader.
- Established on the net; not new – with potential teething problems.
- Price quotes.

- Methods of confirming orders (an online screen and e-mail at least).
- Emergency back-up.
- Types of orders accepted (see appendix on orders).
- Portfolio monitoring:
  1 How often is your portfolio updated?
  2 Is a tax summary available?
  3 Is an automatic performance measure calculated?
  4 Is a transaction summary available?
- News.
- Research available:
  – what is available, how regular, is it free, is it online or posted?
- Customer support:
  – Phone, fax, e-mail is ideal.

Table 19.1 provides a comparison of the major broking partners.

Table 19.1 Comparison of major broking partners

	Rating	Autosweep	Quotes	Research	Market news	Portfolio tracker	Portfolio alert
E*Trade www.etrade.com	***	√	√	√	√	√	√
Datek www.datek.com	***		√	√		√	
Charles Schwab www.eschwab.com	***	√	√	√	√	√	
Ameritrade www.ameritrade.com	***	√	√			√	
ScoTTrade www.stocktrade.com	***	√	√	√		√	
Charles Schwab Europe www.sharelink.com	***	√				√	
Xest www.xest.com	**	√	√			√	
Stocktrade www.esi.co.uk/trading/	*	√	√			√	
stocktrade Union CAL www.unioncal.com	**	√	√			√	

*** Good value for money, appear on the ball and client oriented.
** Worth investigating, good rates and fair information on the site.
* A little expensive but potentially a good service provider.

E*Trade *** US

www.etrade.com
E*Trade Securities
4 Embarcadero Pl
2400 Geng Road
Palo Alto
CA 94303
Tel: 1 800 786 2575

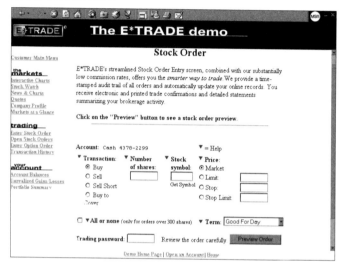

Diagram 19.1

*E*Trade*

Products dealt in

- Stocks
- options
- mutual funds
- bonds.

Minimum commission

- Stocks $14.95 listed market
- stocks $19.95 NASDAQ/limit or stop orders
- options $20 + $1.75 per contract ($29 min.).

Minimum to open an account

- $2,000.

Accounts

- Wide range including margined and retirement
- interest bearing

- autosweep
- checking
- details accessible online.

Quotes

- Real-time ($30 a month).

Research tools

- Mutual funds:
  - prospectus, history, composition, filter/screening facility.
- News:
  - Reuters, Business Wire, PR Newswire, briefing.com (stock analysis, analysts' estimates, market commentary, earnings releases).

Portfolio

- Tracker
- alert.

Orders type

- Wide range including market, limit (good till canceled or day), stop, stop limit, short.

Emergency back-up

- Phone.

Other features

- Options fair value calculations using Black-Scholes.

It is clear from E*Trade's site that it wants your business. The site is easy to navigate and the information is very easy to find. However, it is a broker and I would not recommend it for the news service, etc. In its capacity as a broker it has won a lot of awards and positive reviews making it a must-consider broker.

    Although the commissions are not the cheapest around, you are paying for the security of knowing that it knows what it is doing.

Comment

Datek *** US

www.datek.com
Datek
50 Broad Street, 6th Floor
New York
NY 10004
Tel: 212 514 7531

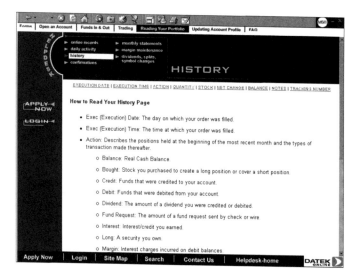

Diagram 19.2

Datek

Products dealt in

- Stocks
- Mutual funds

Minimum commission

- $9.99 listed market or NASDAQ.

Minimum to open an account

- $2,000.

Accounts

- Several types including, margin and IRA available
- interest bearing
- checks
- trading details accessible online.

Quotes

■ Real-time quotes – free to members.

Research tools

■ Mutual funds

■ news

■ research.

Portfolio

■ Tracker.

Orders type

■ Market, limit.

Emergency back-up

■ Phone

■ direct dial-up computer to computer.

You are choosing Datek for its commissions and not much else. But that's fine because there are ample other sites that give you free information anyway. Datek's site also has a reassuring number of positive press reviews. I always find that comforting when considering a site marketing itself on the basis of having a very low cost base.

Comment

Charles Schwab *** US

www.eschwab.com
Charles Schwab
101 Montgomery Street
San Francisco
CA 94104
Tel: 415 627 7000 / 1 800 435 4000

Products dealt in

■ Stocks

■ options

■ mutual funds

■ bonds.

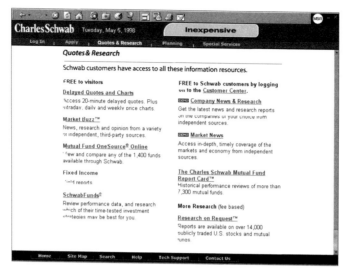

Diagram 19.3

CharlesSchwab

Minimum commission

- Stocks $29.95
- options $35.

Minimum to open an account

- $2,500.

Accounts

- Wide range including margined and retirement
- interest bearing
- autosweep
- checking
- details accessible online.

Quotes

- Delayed (20 minutes).

Research tools

- News (free to public).
- Market Buzz (free to public).
- Stocks:
    - 1   research on request (fee based)
    - 2   S&P company reports.

- Mutual funds:
  - *1* historical performance reviews
  - *2* research on request (fee based).
- Market news:
  - *1* Thomson (market commentary, earning surprises, economic news, company digest)
  - *2* briefing.com
  - *3* market guide (ranks hottest stocks, industry and sector performance).

Portfolio

- Tracker.

Orders type

- Wide range including market and limit.

Emergency back-up

- Phone.

Other features

- Financial planning guides
- asset allocation toolkit.

Charles Schwab is not the cheapest broker around and to a large extent that is because of all the extras in terms of research it offers. Since we will be seeking most of our research elsewhere the commissions will be a big negative factor. However, it is still one of the top e-mail brokers because it is very experienced, and has an enormous number of positive press comments. If you are a little concerned about trading on the net then a broker such as Schwab provides some added security in that you are dealing with an old hand in internet broking. Moreover the off-line broker is, of course, one of the biggest in the world.

Comment

Ameritrade ***   US Int

www.ameritrade.com
Ameritrade
PO Box 2209
Omaha
NE 68103 2209
Tel: 1 800 454 9272

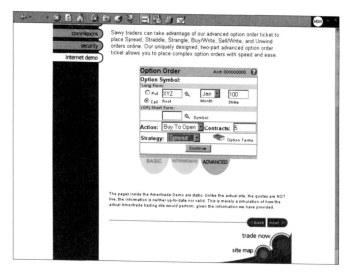

Diagram 19.4

Ameritrade

Products dealt in
- Stocks
- options
- mutual funds
- bonds.

Minimum commission
- Stocks $8
- stocks $13 limit order
- options $29.

Minimum to open an account
- $2,000.

Accounts

- Margin and IRA
- interest bearing
- autosweep
- details accessible online

Quotes

- Delayed 20 minutes (free)
- real-time ($20 a month).

Portfolio

- Tracker.

Orders type

- Market and limit plus others.

Emergency back-up

- Phone (toll-free numbers in 34 countries).

Other features

- The facility to trade in foreign securities, from UK to Singapore.

Comment

Ameritrade is another ultra-deep discount broker offering little else besides cost savings. That's what we like because as I said above, we are not too concerned with getting our research from our broker – it can be a bonus but no great loss if we're making relatively large savings.

You may be unfamiliar with the name of Ameritrade, but it is actually composed in part from the remnant of two of the web's earliest online brokers: K Aughauser and Ceres. So there is security in continuity as well.

ScoTTrade *** US

www.scottrade.com
Nationwide

Diagram 19.5

ScoTTrade

Products dealt in

- Stocks
- options.

Minimum commission

- Stocks $7 listed and NASDAQ
- stocks $12 limit/stop orders
- options $20 + $1.60 per contract.

Minimum to open an account

- $2,000.

Accounts

- Margined, IRA
- interest bearing
- autosweep
- details accessible online.

Quotes

- Dallied (free)
- real-time.

Research tools

- Stocks:
    1 Zacks earnings estimates
    2 market guide quick facts
    3 Vickers insider trading.

- Options:
    – Option analytics screening; chains; quotes.

Orders type

- Market, limit (good till canceled or day), stop, stop limit.

Portfolio

- Tracker.

Emergency back-up

- Phone
- 71 offices nationwide.

ScoTTrade claims its online site has "the lowest online commission of any national discount brokerage firm." Having searched and scoured the net, I have to report that I agree. But there are two things which are astounding. First, these low commissions do appear to be a temporary "loss-leader" of a new market entrant – the off-line broker was established in 1980 and has 71 offices throughout the USA. Second, there is a wealth of research information for free to members – something more expensive discount brokers fail to provide.

I liked this site a lot; it gets straight to the point: commissions. If you've got it – flaunt it.

Charles Schwab Europe * * * UK

www.schwab-worldwide.com/europe
Charles Schwab
Cannon House
24 The Priory, Queensway
Birmingham B4 6BS
UK
Tel: +44 121 200 7788

Products dealt in

- Shares.

Minimum commission

- £10.

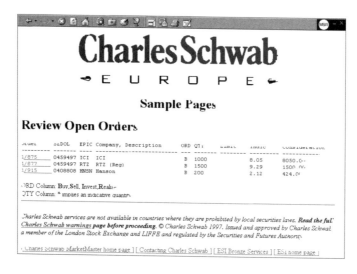

Diagram 19.6

Sharelink sample order page

Minimum to open an account

■ No minimum.

Accounts

■ Interest bearing

■ autosweep

■ details accessible online.

Portfolio

■ Tracker.

Orders type

■ Limit, market.

Emergency back-up

■ Phone.

Comment

It is interesting how much less Charles Schwab Europe offers its European customers compared to the parent Charles Schwab of the USA. This is partly due to UK laws, of course. There is no margining, no checking accounts, the web site is sparse and functional. Since Charles Schwab Europe (formerly Sharelink) offer online trading in collaboration with ESI access to online trading is through that site.

Charles Schwab Europe is essentially an off-line broker who has offered the conservative UK public an online service for those who want it. Commissions are the same for on- or off-line. It's cheap and it's a very well known brokerage – that's all there is to say.

Xest ** 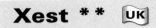 UK

www.xest.com

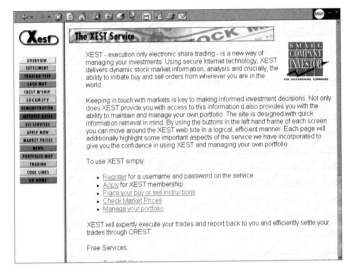

Diagram 19.7

Xest

Product dealt in

■ Stocks.

Minimum commission

■ Stocks £20 (one-off registration fee of £20; annual service charge of £45).

Minimum to open an account

■ No minimum.

Accounts

■ Interest bearing

■ autosweep

■ details accessible online.

Quotes

■ Through ESI (see Electronic Share Information Site).

Portfolio

■ Tracker (through ESI) (see Electronic Share Information Site).

Orders type

▪ Market.

Emergency back-up

▪ Phone.

Comment

A miserable, sparse site with a smattering of color which in place of cheering it up makes it look slightly childish. However, given the few online brokers available servicing the UK this site just squeezes into the listings because it is a subsidiary of Charles Stanley & Co., an established and respected brokerage firm. Most of the online services, such as news and research do not come from Xest at all but from ESI. You're not missing much whether you join or not.

Stocktrade * UK

www.esi.co.uk/trading/stocktrade
Stocktrade
PO Box 1076
10 George Street
Edinburgh EH2 2PZ
Tel: 0131 529 0101

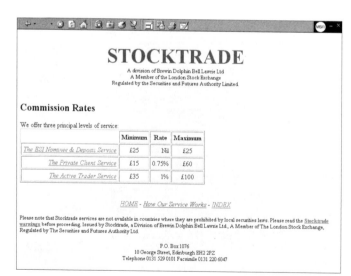

Diagram 19.8

Stocktrade

Products dealt in

- Stocks.

Minimum commission

- Stocks £25.

Minimum to open an account

- No minimum.

Accounts

- Interest bearing
- autosweep.

Quotes

- Through ESI (see Electronic Share Information Site).

Portfolio

- Tracker (through ESI) (see Electronic Share Information Site).

Orders type

- Market.

Emergency back-up

- Phone.

This site offers a reassuring amount of information about the company. Although one gets the impression Stocktrade are still new to online broking, they have a relatively competitive commission, and ample experience in traditional brokerage.

Comment

Union CAL ** Int

www.unioncal.com
Union CAL
39 Cornhill
London EC3V 3ND
Tel: +44 171 522 3333
Fax: + 44 171 522 3317

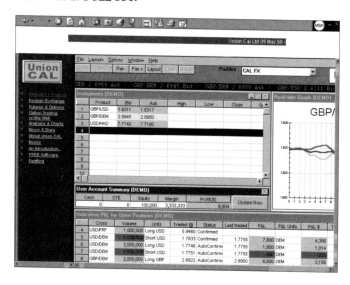

Diagram 19.9

Union CAL currency demo

Products dealt in

- Forex
- futures
- options.

Minimum commission

- Foreign exchange nil
- options £5.

Minimum to open an account

- Foreign exchange $30,000
- options £5,000
- futures $25,000/£15,000.

Accounts

- Interest bearing
- autosweep
- details accessible online.

Quotes

■ Real-time.

Portfolio

■ Tracker.

Orders type

■ Wide variety, including all popular.

Emergency back-up

■ Phone.

Union CAL offers extensive proprietary market comment and technical analysis. With the minimum account sizes it is more geared towards the professional/experienced trader.

Comment

Off and on: off-line brokers with online presence

In this section we examine some brokers that, while they do not offer online trading, do have internet sites which you can inspect to find out more about them before deciding to open an account (Diagram 19.10). These are some of the more prominent brokers. I have not listed US ones because the market is so well catered for by online brokers (see Table 19.2).

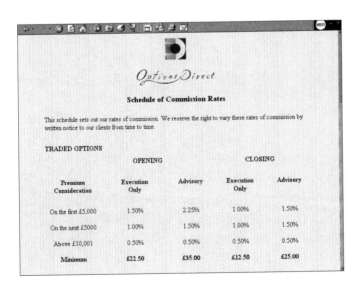

Diagram 19.10

Options Direct

Table 19.2 Comparison of some brokers with online presence UK

Name	Web address	Products traded	Minimum to open account	Minimum commission	Research commentary*	Rating
Berkeley Futures	www.bfl.co.uk	Futures, options	£3000	£20	√	***
Options Direct	www.options-direct.co.uk	Options	–	£22.50	√	***
Charles Stanley	www.charles-stanley.co.uk	Options, stocks	–	£22.50	√	**
Durlacher	www.durlacher.co.uk	Stocks, options	–	£30	√	**
Killick	www.killick.co.uk	Stocks	–	£40	√	*

* Refers to whether the broker offers research online on products dealt in or a commentary on recent price movements.

Of course there will be many brokers local to you that may have a web site. To find out, look in the yellow pages or local phone book under "Brokers" and ask them what their web address is. Alternatively, do an internet search (see later).

Summary

With online brokerage competition heating up commissions are dropping. Online trading is often cheaper and more convenient for trading. However, it is of prime importance to visit sites and check they meet all your criteria and those listed in this chapter. If you do not prefer online trading, the internet remains a useful source of information on off-line brokers.

20

Mutual funds, investment trusts and unit trusts

« The market has intelligence beyond what our minds can comprehend. »

Pat Arbor
Chairman
Chicago Board of Trade

In this chapter

This chapter has a selection of the best mutual fund and investment trust/unit trust (the UK equivalent of a mutual fund sites).

To have got this far

■ **You will have gone through the skeleton plans and been referred to this chapter.**

Please remember that there are some mutual fund relevant sites elsewhere and your skeleton plan is the guide to make sure you are referred to all the relevant sites. The list in Table 20.1 is not exhaustive – your skeleton plan is your guide.

Star ratings in this chapter:

See key at the bottom of Table 20.1.

Table 20.1 Comparison of mutual fund sites

	Ranking	Quotes	News	Filters	Fundamental analysis
Mutual Fund Investor's Center www.mfea.com	**	√	√	√	
Interactive Investor www.iii.co.uk	**	√	√	√	
Morning Star www.morningstar.net	***	√	√		√
Mutual Funds Online www.mfmag.com	***	√	√	√	√
Net Worth networth.galt.com	**	√	√	√	√
Moneyworld www.moneyworld.co.uk	*	√			√
Trustnet www.trustnet.co.uk	*	√			√

*** A very good, model site that is easy to navigate and has a large selection of high-quality information.
** A good site with much information of use provided in a readily accessible manner.
* Some useful bits of information and worth a visit. Could come in useful.
  Any site below * is not listed as it is simply not recommended or the sites already listed cover the same material better.

Mutual Fund's Investor's Center **

www.mfea.com

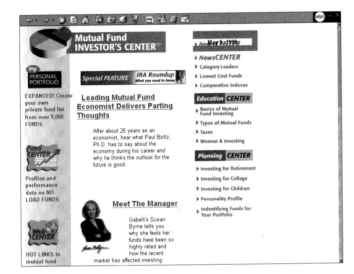

Diagram 20.1

Mutual Fund's Investor's Center

Recommended for

Mutual fund news and search.

Online quotes

■ Fast quotes.

News

■ News items and commentaries on funds.

Filters

■ Based on numerous variables.

This site is produced with the mutual fund investor in mind and is an excellent resource. The Mutual Fund Education Alliance has produced it and the principal aim is to provide high-quality information for the individual mutual fund investor.

Comment

Interactive Investor ** UK free

`www.iii.co.uk`

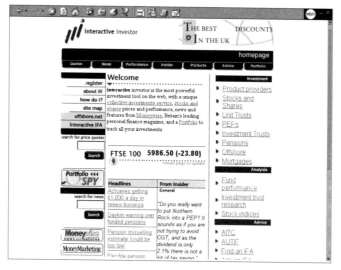

Diagram 20.2

Interactive Investor

Recommended for

Investment trust and unit trust news and search.

News

■ News items and commentaries.

Filters

■ Numerous criteria, provided by Micropal
■ performance rankings.

Comment *Micropal is a definitive source of quality information relating to investment trusts and unit trusts. This site also has links to some leading trust such as GAM, M&G and Fidelity.*

Morningstar *** [US]

www.morningstar.net

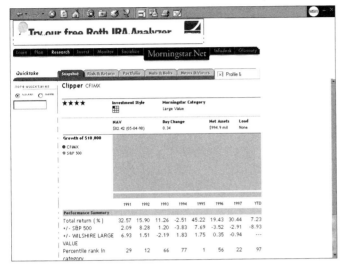

Diagram 20.3

Morningstar

Recommended for

Quotes, fundamental analysis, news and charts of mutual funds.

Online quotes *free*

■ Fast quotes.

Fundamental analysis (some free)

■ Key financial information
■ composition details
■ profiles
■ performance.

Technical analysis

■ Charts.

News *free*

■ News and commentary.

Morningstar is one of the most respected providers of mutual fund data and analysis and its research reports are some of the most thorough available. This site is excellent for the serious mutual funder.

Comment

Mutual Funds Online ∗∗∗ US

www.mfmag.com

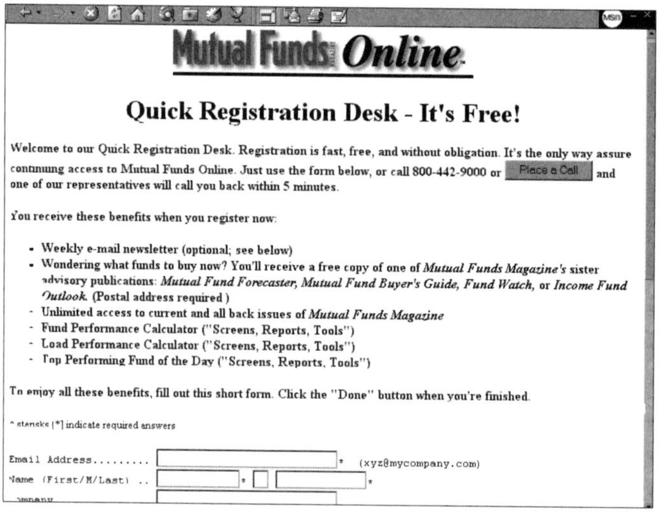

Diagram 20.4

Mutual Funds Online

Recommended for

Fundamental analysis, news, charts and filters.

Online quotes   *free*

■ Fast quotes.

Fundamental analysis (some subscription)

■ Profiles

■ financial information

■ composition

■ performance

■ filters (see later).

Technical analysis

■ Charts.

News

■ News and commentaries.

Filters

■ Numerous search criteria.

I like this clear and easily navigable site. There is ample information and while some of it overlaps with other sites a lot of it complements the information on other mutual fund sites.   **Comment**

Net Worth*** US

networth.galt.com

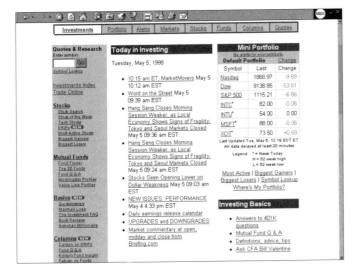

Diagram 20.5

Net Worth

Recommended for

Quotes, fundamental analysis, filters.

Online quotes   *free*

Fundamental analysis (some subscription)

- Profile
- financial information
- composition
- filters (see later).

Technical analysis

- Charts.

News

- News and commentaries.

Filters

■ Ranking of leading funds

■ criteria based on size, fees, performance.

 Comment

One of the earlier and most reputable sites to have an internet presence. It covers all the major categories of information we would look for in a mutual fund site.

Moneyworld * UK

www.moneyworld.co.uk

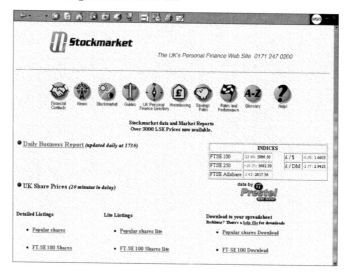

Diagram 20.6

Moneyworld

Recommended for

Fundamental analysis (investment trusts).

Online quotes

■ Quick quotes (stocks, investment trusts) (delayed).

Fundamental analysis

■ Rankings.

Comment

It does its job, without bells or whistles. This is more a personal finance site and has some excellent educational material – well worth an examination.

Trustnet* UK

www.trustnet.co.uk

Diagram 20.7

Trustnet

Recommended for

Fundamental analysis (investment trusts).

Online quotes free

■ Quick quotes (stocks, investment trusts) (delayed).

Fundamental analysis   free

■ Rankings.

Search free

■ By name

Since you are starved of choice in the UK for investment trust information, this is as good as it gets. There is little wrong with the site, but by mutual fund site standards it is impoverished.

Comment

Summary

With so much money invested with fund managers, there is an incredible amount of information on the internet about such funds, much of the information being free. Even if your money is fully invested, the internet can be a good way of keeping an eye on things.

21

The future and its options: futures and options sites

Fewer and fewer traders trade by the seat of their pants and the traders that do tend to be futures traders.

Jon Najarian
Chairman and CEO
Mercury Trading

In this chapter

In this chapter the most helpful sites for futures and options traders are listed and described. As before, they are placed in a separate chapter to help the reader navigate the book a tiny bit easier. Of course, futures and options exist in relation to underlying products and these sites deal not only with the futures and options but the many underlying products, e.g. equities, commodities. However their emphasis tends to be on the nature of futures and options. The skeleton plan leads you through the various sites that you should examine whatever your underlying product interest to ensure you cover all the best and pertinent sites.

To have got this far

- You will have gone through the skeleton plans and been referred to this chapter.

Please remember that there are some futures and options sites elsewhere and your skeleton plan is the guide to make sure you are referred to all the relevant sites. The list in Table 21.1 is not exhaustive – your skeleton plan is your guide.

Star ratings in this chapter:

See key at the bottom of Table 21.1.

The mark of quality: good futures and options sites

Quotes

Given the vast number of futures and options contracts available on just one underlying asset, quotes and "chains" can be very useful. Real-time would be most helpful since we're talking leverage and want to keep a close eye on prices.

Market commentary

Market commentary – the more frequent the better. A good site will be quite detailed and be produced by a competent trader.

Charts

Again, preferably intra-day.

Education

A peculiarity of futures and options sites is the wealth of educational material. This is where the internet comes into its own: free education, 24 hours a day. A good site will have well designed and easy to understand articles and essays.

Discussion groups

Always useful for bouncing ideas.

Table 21.1 Comparison of futures and options sites

Name and web address	Ranking	Quotes	Market commentary	Charts	Education	Discussion forum
1010 Wall Street www.1010wallstreet.com	***		√		√	
Commodity Futures Trading Commission www.cftc.com	*		√		√	
Futures Net www.futures.net	***	√	√	√	√	√
Futures Online www.futuresmag.com	***	√	√	√	√	√
Futures Source www.futuresource.com	***	√	√		√	√
INO Global www.inoglobal.com	***	√	√	√	√	√
MarketPlex www.cbot.com/mplex	***	√	√	√	√	
Options Direct www.options-direct.co.uk	*		√	√	√	

*** A very good, model site that is easy to navigate and has a large selection of high-quality information.

** A good site with much information of use provided in a readily accessible manner.

* Some useful bits of information and worth a visit. Could come in useful.

Any site below * is not listed as it is simply not recommended or the sites already listed cover the same material better.

1010 Wall Street*** US Int

www.1010wallstreet.com

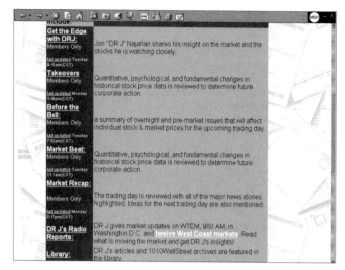

Diagram 21.1

Wall Street

Comment

Jon Najarian, profiled in The Mind of a Trader, *is a director of the Chicago Board Options Exchange and a leading options trader as well as chairman of Mercury Trading and he founded this site. The commentary is excellent because it is provided by him and not only is he phenomenally successful at what he does, he is experienced and actually trades, he doesn't just stand on the sidelines. The downside is that all the commentary is subscription only. But you would not expect it for free when it's that good would you?*

Commodity Futures Trading Commission * US Int

www.cftc.gov

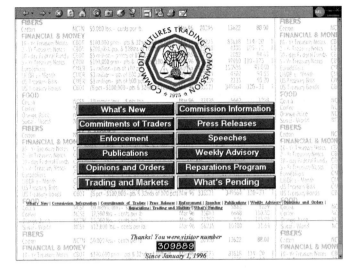

Diagram 21.2

Commodity Futures Trading Commission

This regulatory body is mainly useful for industry news and legal matters concerning futures. Your aim in visiting it is mainly to keep half an eye on the future of futures.

Comment

Futures Net *** US Int

www.futures.net

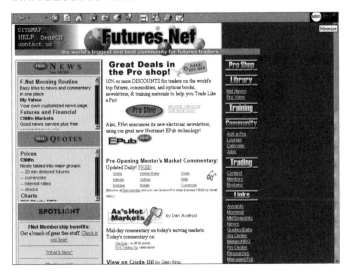

Diagram 21.3

Futures.Net

Comment

The main attraction of this site, which claims to be "the world's biggest and best community for futures traders," is its discussion group. While it will not be useful for all futures traders, it is a dedicated and focused area.

Futures Online*** US Int

www.futuresmag.com

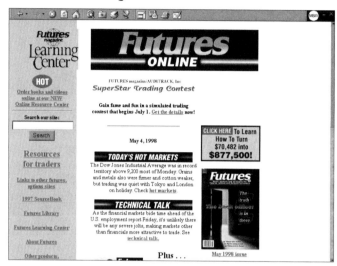

Diagram 21.4

Futures Online

Comment

This online version of the off-line magazine has useful and professionally written market commentary and full articles of the magazine.

FutureSource*** US Int

www.futuresource.com

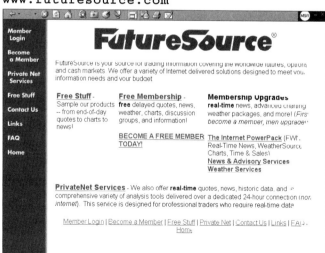

Diagram 21.5

FutureSource

Future's World News provides the news and market commentary for this site which is its key feature. Worth a visit if you are looking for market commentary to see how it ties in with your needs compared to the other sites.

INO Global*** US Int

www.ino.com

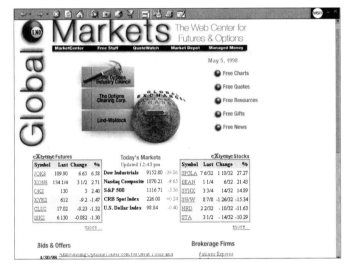

Diagram 21.6

Global

Global is correct. This is an umbrella site with ample links and its own content which taken together provide comprehensive coverage of futures and options-related materials.

Market Plex*** US Int

www.cbot.com/mplex

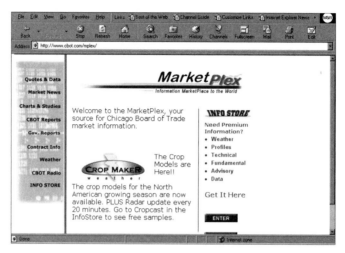

Diagram 21.7

MarketPlex

Comment

This site is part of the Chicago Board of Trade's excellent web site. Market Plex is another umbrella site and an excellent resource of information for the futures and options trader.

Options Direct* UK Int

www.options-direct.co.uk

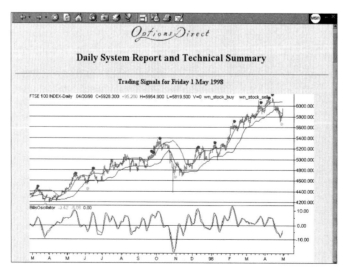

Diagram 21.8

Options Direct trading signals

Options Direct is actually a brokerage firm but provides useful information and analysis for the UK options trader. While anemic compared to US sites, if you're trading LIFFE products this site is actually one of the best!

Summary

Futures and options sites cover a wide range of underlying products because there is a wide range of products on which futures and options are available. The choice and coverage of markets is diverse for the trader and the individual considering derivatives. Because most derivatives traders tend to be more experienced than stock traders, sites tend to be more professional. There is certainly no shortage of quality information.

22

Exchanges

❝ Nobody ever achieved greatness by doing nothing. You have got to step out and do something and take a chance and get your teeth kicked in. ❞

Pat Arbor
Chairman
Chicago Board of Trade

In this chapter

*This chapter contains all the internet sites operated by the exchanges. The best thing about them is that they are **all free**.*

An exchange is basically a marketplace which trades in financial products in place of fruit, vegetables, meat and fish. The financial product may well relate to those more traditional market products, however, for instance the Chicago Mercantile Exchange trades in frozen concentrated orange juice futures.

To have got this far

- You will have read the chapter on keeping abreast/education.
- You will have been referred to this section by the skeleton plans.

Top exchange sites

As you will have noted from the skeleton plans, exchanges can be a good source of free or heavily subsidized educational and background material. A good exchange site should have the following characteristics.

Exchange history/working

A section in the site tells you more about how the exchange came into being and why, and also how it works today, how orders are routed, the main products it deals in, etc.

Publications list

A good site should have a list of recommended reading for both beginners and more advanced traders. It should also provide a wide variety of free educational materials including videos and printed matter which can be ordered from the site. Where possible I have ordered a selection of free publications to gauge their value.

Data download/quotes

Although the skeleton plans will rarely refer to an exchange as a source of data, they are, of course, the source for all commercial data providers and sometimes – if the exchange is on a sufficiently commercial and experienced footing – the exchange itself can be a good and efficient source of historical and daily price quotes.

hot tip *Remember, the product you are interested in may be traded on several different exchanges, so if you want to know more about it, check for free information available from each of the exchanges, that way if there is something you do not understand from one of the exchange's free publications, you may understand it from another.*

Table 21.1 Comparison of major US exchanges

Name and web address	Rating	Products	Exchange history/ workings	Publications	Data download quotes	Market reports	Additional comments
American Stock Exchange www.amex.com	**	Stocks and derivatives	✓	✓	✓	×	
Arizona Stock Exchange www.azx.com	*	Stocks	✓	×	✓	×	
Chicago Board of Trade www.cbot.com	***	Bonds, financial futures and options, commodities	✓	✓	✓	✓	The world's largest futures and options exchange
Chicago Board Options Exchange www.cboe.com	***	Options on stocks and all futures	✓	✓	✓	✓	
Chicago Mercantile Exchange www.cme.com	***	Futures and options on financial products and commodities	✓	✓	✓	✓	The world's third largest futures and options exchange
Chicago Stock Exchange www.chicagostockex.com	**	Stocks, warrants, notes, bonds	✓	×	✓	×	The second largest stock exchange in the USA. A good source of free stock research information
Coffee, Sugar, & Cocoa Exchange www.csce.com	**	Futures and options on milk and coffee, sugar, cocoa	✓	✓	✓	×	
Kansas City Board of Trade www.kcbt.com	**	Futures and options on wheat, gas, value line stock indices	✓	✓	✓	✓	
Mid-America Exchange www.midam.com	**	Liquid futures contracts	✓	✓	✓	×	
Minneapolis Grain Exchange www.mgex.com	*	Grain and fish futures and options	✓	✓	✓	×	
Nasdaq Exchange www.nasdaq.com	**	Mainly technology stocks	✓	✓	✓	✓	Good basics for stock investors
New York Cotton Exchange www.nyce.com	**	Futures and options on cotton, oranges, potatoes, financials	×	×	✓	✓	
New York Mercantile Exchange www.nymex.com	***	Futures and options on energy, Eurotop, metals	✓	✓	✓	✓	
New York Stock Exchange www.nyse.com	**	Over 2,500 stocks	✓	✓	✓	✓	The largest stock exchange in the USA
Pacific Exchange www.pacificex.com	**	Stocks and options	✓	×	✓	×	
Philadelphia Stock Exchange www.liffe.com	***	Stocks and options on sectors, stocks, currencies	✓	✓	✓	✓	A good site for educational materials

***   A very informative site with ample free educational material, easy to navigate and a model exchange site.

**   A very good site with some free material. Should be informative.

*   Worth a visit and most traders should end up learning something about the exchange or the products it trades.

Market reports

Although these tend to be a little bland on exchange sites, often only reporting volume and describing chronological price changes, they can be a good way to get a better feel of what actually happened that day. Exchanges rarely attempt to place a journalistic spin on a day's market activities, leaving you to make your own mind up.

Rules

Some exchanges list their membership rules, for most readers this will be of intrigue value only.

Others

Some exchanges are beginning to realize that there is nothing stopping them developing internet sites similar to those provided by commercial financial sites and so including charts, fundamental research, news, listing of the most active products, etc.

Table 22.1 shows a ranking of major US exchanges (see also Diagrams 22.1, 22.2, 22.3).

Try and visit an exchange near you, and get on the mailing list. It is a great way to learn and keep abreast of developments. Also, many exchanges provide educational courses, check your nearest one – these are usually heavily subsidized by the exchange and so can be great value for money.

Diagram 22.1

Chicago Board of Trade

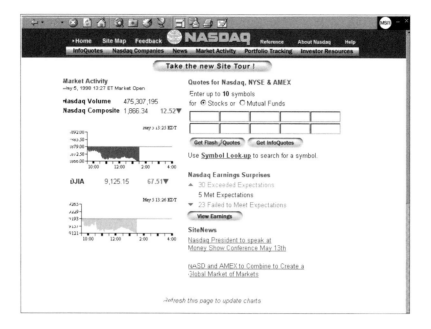

Diagram 22.2

Nasdaq

Diagram 22.3

Nymex

Table 22.2 contains a ranking of the major global exchanges (see also Diagrams 22.4, 22.5, 22.6, 22.7).

Table 22.2 Comparison of major global exchanges

Name and web address	Rating	Products	Exchange history/ workings	Publications	Data download quotes	Market reports	Additional comments
Australian Stock Exchange www.asx.com.au	**	Stocks and bonds	✓	✓	✓	✓	
Bombay Stock Exchange www.bseindia.com	**	Stocks	✗	✗	✓	✓	Portfolio manager
Deutsche Terminboerse www.exchange.de	**	Futures and options	✓	✓	✓	✗	
Hong Kong Futures Exchange www.hkfe.com	**	Futures and options on financial products	✓	✓	✓	✓	
Italian Stock Exchange www.robot1.textnet.it/finanza	*	Stocks	✗	✗	✓	✗	
Kuala Lumpur Options & Financial Futures Exchange www.kloffe.com.my	*	Financial futures and options	✓	✓	✓	✗	One of the world's newest exchanges
Kuala Lumpur Stock Exchange www.klse.com.my	**	Stocks	✓	✓	✓	✓	
Lisbon Stock Exchange www.bvl.pt	*	Stocks	✗	✗	✓	✗	
London International Financial Futures Options and Commodities Exchange www.liffe.com	***	Futures and options on most products	✓	✓	✓	✓	The world's second largest futures exchange
London Stock Exchange www.stockex.co.uk	*	Stocks	✓	✓	✗	✗	
London Metal Exchange www.lme.co.uk	**	Metal futures and options	✓	✗	✓	✗	
Madrid Stock Exchange www.bolsamadrid.es	**	Futures and options	✓	✓	✓	✓	
MATIF www.matif.fr	**	Financial futures and options	✓	✓	✓	✗	Based in Paris
MEFF www.meff.es	**	Fixed income futures and options	✓	✓	✓	✗	Based in Barcelona. Some excellent internships
Montreal Exchange www.me.org	**	Stocks, options and futures	✓	✓	✓	✗	
OM Stockholm www.omgroup.com	**	Futures and options	✓	✓	✓	✗	Some information in Swedish only
Paris Stock Exchange www.bourse-de-paris.fr	**	Stocks	✓	✓	✓	✗	
South African Futures Exchange www.safex.co.za	**	Futures and Options	✓	✓	✓	✗	
Santiago Stock Exchange www.bolsantiago.cl/ingles	**	Stocks, futures and options	✓	✓	✓	✗	
Singapore International Monetary Exchange www.simex.com.sg	***	Futures and options	✓	✓	✓	✓	
Sydney Futures Exchange www.sfe.com.au	*	Futures and options	✓	✓	✓	✗	

continued overleaf

Table 22.2 continued

Name and web address	Rating	Products	Exchange history/ workings	Publications	Data download quotes	Market reports	Additional comments
Tokyo Grain Exchange www.tge.or.jp	**	Commodity futures and options	✓	✓	✓	✓	
TIFFE www.tiffe.or.jp	**	Futures and options	✓	✓	✓	✗	
Tokyo Stock Exchange www.tse.or.jp	**	Stocks, options, futures	✓	✗	✓	✗	
Vancouver Stock Exchange www.vse.com	*	Stocks	✓	✓	✓	✓	
Warsaw Stock Exchange yogi.ippt.gov.pl/gielda/gielda	*	Stocks	✗	✗	✓	✗	

*** A very informative site with ample free educational material, easy to navigate and a model exchange site.
** A very good site with some free material. Should be informative.
* Worth a visit and most traders should end up learning something about the exchange or the products it trades.

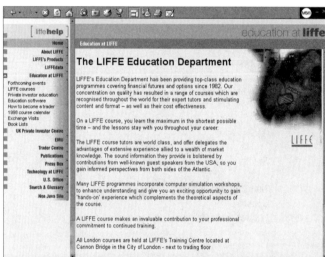

Diagram 22.4

LIFFE

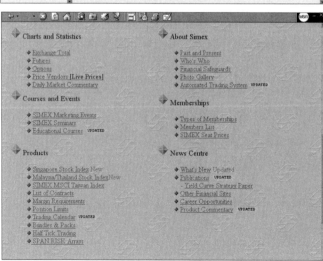

Diagram 22.5

SIMEX

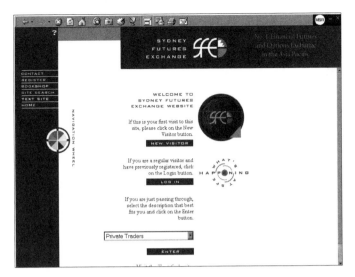

Diagram 22.6

Sydney Futures Exchange

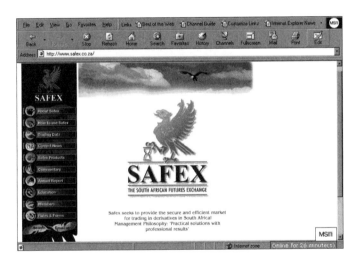

Diagram 22.7

SAFEX

Summary

In many respects the world's exchanges are an often forgotten source of top-notch information. They are improving all the time and beginning to recognize their unique positions and roles on the financial internet. Unlike commercial sites these sites are funded with the non-profit motive of encouraging trading. I feel added comfort when using these sites.

23

Bonds and only bonds

❝ There are others as well who put their balls on the line but aren't good traders and they promptly have them taken off them. ❞

David Kyte
Chairman
Kyte Group

In this chapter

In this chapter you will find a collection of sites dealing only with bonds. The reason they are kept here is for overall ease of using the book. Bond traders will be concerned with many more sites than the ones listed here and the skeleton plan is their guide.

The problem with bonds is that the term covers a multitude of products and timeframes. There are treasuries, long-dated, emerging market, company, mortgage backed, asset-backed, repos, municipal bonds to name the most popular types. If you are interested in bonds, given its specialist nature, you will probably already have an idea of the area you are interested in. If you are a novice wanting to know more about this area then the educational sites in the skeleton plans and the recommended reading will undoubtedly come in handy.

To have got this far

■ **You will have gone through the skeleton plans and been referred to this chapter.**

Please remember that there are some bond-relevant sites elsewhere and your skeleton plan is the guide to make sure you are referred to all the relevant sites. The list that follows is not exhaustive – your skeleton plan is your guide.

Star ratings in this chapter:

See key at the bottom of Table 23.1.

Good bond sites

A good bond site should have the following characteristics.

Quotes

Delayed and historical quotes would, of course, be very useful.

Commentary and charts

Market analysis, from reputed analysts, both in terms of past movement and prospective market changes would add considerable value.

Search engine

The ability to search for bonds based upon numerous variables is an added bonus. This can be considered the same as filtering or screening.

Table 23.1 Summary of good bond sites' provision

Name and web address	Ranking	Quotes	Commentary	Charts	Search engine	Credit rating	Discussion forum
Bonds Online www.bonds-online.com	***	✓	✓	✓	✓	✓	
Brady Net www.bradynet.com	**	✓	✓		✓		✓
PC Trader www.fixedincome.com	**	✓	✓				

*** A very good, model site that is easy to navigate and has a large selection of high-quality information.
** A good site with much information of use provided in a readily accessible manner.
* Some useful bits of information and worth a visit. Could come in useful.
Any site below * is not listed as it is simply not recommended or the sites already listed cover the same material better.

Credit rating

A site providing credit rating from a reputable source is, of course, a good bonus.

Discussion forum

A discussion forum is a definite bonus.

Table 23.1 provides a summary of these points.

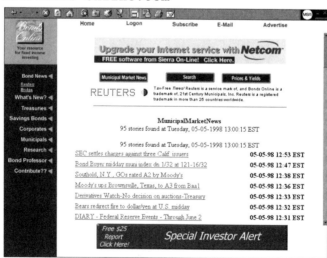

Diagram 23.1

Bonds Online

Comment

The credit rating information available here is exceptional. Overall, the site is very slick and the information diverse and of a high standard. The Bond Professor is an excellent source of information if you have queries regarding bonds.

Brady Net** US Int

www.bradynet.com

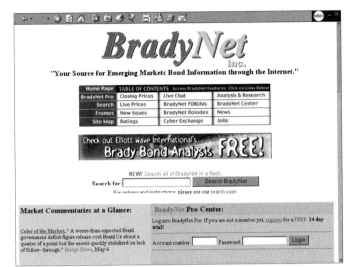

Diagram 23.2

BradyNet

As can be discerned from the name of the site, this site specializes in emerging market bonds. It is a good site with good-quality information and worth a visit if your particular fetish is the emerging market.

PC Trader** US Int

www.fixedincome.com

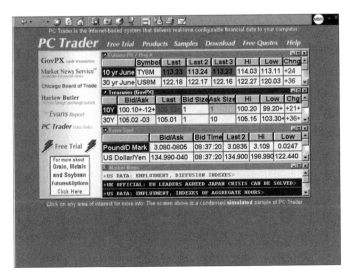

Diagram 23.3

PC Trader

Comment   *The quotes for this site are from GocPX, a popular and reliable source. The market news and commentary are very good and professional (hence some are fee based).*

Summary

I was pleasantly surprised at the quality of bond sites. Although some were very technical, most were very generous in the information they provided.

24

Money, money, money: foreign exchange sites

It's all about dollars.

Bill Lipschutz
former Global Head of Foreign Exchange
Salomon Brothers

In this chapter

In this chapter the leading forex sites for traders that way inclined are listed and critiqued. As before, they are placed in a separate chapter to help the reader navigate the book a tiny bit easier.

To have got this far

■ **You will have gone through the skeleton plans and been referred to this chapter.**

Please remember that there are some currency-relevant sites elsewhere and your skeleton plan is the guide to make sure you are referred to all the relevant sites. The list that follows is not exhaustive – your skeleton plan is your guide.

Star ratings in this chapter:

See key at the bottom of Table 24.1.

Good currency sites

Good currency sites will have the following characteristics.

Quotes

In the fast moving world of forex these have to be real-time.

Market commentary

Market commentary – the more frequent the better.

Technical commentary

Since many forex traders use technical analysis, we need sites with technical commentary.

Charts

Again, preferably intra-day.

Discussion groups

Always useful for bouncing ideas.

Table 24.1 provides a summary of these points.

Table 24.1 Summary of good currency sites provision

Name and web address	Ranking	Quotes	Market commentary	Technical commentary	Charts	Discussion forum
Economeister www.economeister.com	***	✓	✓	✓		
Currency Management Corpn www.forex-cmc.co.uk	***	✓	✓	✓	✓	

*** A very good, model site that is easy to navigate and has a large selection of high-quality information.

** A good site with much information of use provided in a readily accessible manner.

* Some useful bits of information and worth a visit. Could come in useful.

Any site below * is not listed as it is simply not recommended or the sites already listed cover the same material better.

Economeister**

`www.economeister.com`

Diagram 24.1

The Economeister

This site specializes in economic and currency news. It caters well for the forex trader's need for macroeconomic and political analysis.

Comment

Forex Watch** US Int

www.forex.co.uk

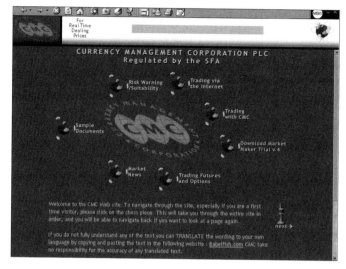

Diagram 24.2

Forex Watch

Comment

This is a specialist site providing both currency-related news and technicals. It is intended for the trader offering pointed advice on buy and sell points.

Summary

Forex trading is particularly complicated, because of the impact of politics and economics, and particularly fast moving. The internet is well suited to providing the type of timely and global information forex traders require and the sites listed here are no disappointment.

Options analysis
software

❝ *You do not need to risk a lot to profit a lot.* **❞**

Bernard Oppetit
Global Head of Equity Derivatives
Banque Paribas

In this chapter

Whether they use fundamental analysis or technical analysis or a combination of both, and whether they trade stocks, futures, indices, or currency options, many options traders also use special options analysis software which helps them in making their trading decisions. Such software relates specifically to the technicalities of options. The details of the sites explain what the software does. This will, of course, make most sense to you if you have an understanding of options, for which see the appendix on understanding options basics and the educational sites in the skeleton plans.

Although it is often possible to trade successfully without such software, the calculations should be undertaken by options traders whether they use the software or not. Consequently such software is most useful if:

- *You plan to undertake more complex strategies, e.g. butterflies, rather than simple calls and puts purchases.*
- *You are not confident (despite reading the options basics appendix and following the options educational sites listed in the book) with the mathematical calculations.*
- *You require to do the calculations speedily.*
- *You would prefer a graphical representation of likely option scenarios.*
- *You are concerned you may be missing out on greater profits by using different strategies.*

In this chapter are listed sites of the most popularly considered best options analysis software vendors.

To have got this far

- You will have read the skeleton plan relating to options.

What to look for

Options analysis software needs to be able to do certain things in order to be more than a mere unnecessary add-on.

Option pricing model

The software will calculate a fair value for the option based on industry standard option pricing models. This can be a useful benchmark guide for comparing prices with the market price.

Auto-position search

Good software should be able to search, based on the user's trading objectives, which options strategies are the most suitable. The search should be based not only on common strategies, such as call and put purchases, but also less common ones such as butterflies and strangles.

Usually the user can enter his assumptions about target price, volatility, expiry. The software will then apply each strategy to the assets available, given the user's assumptions. A list should then be produced ranking each strategy by corresponding likely profit (and sometimes maximum profit, risk). The more ranges the user can input the better. For example, instead of having to input a target price, can the user input a range, or can the user input a date and, based on the underlying asset's historic volatility, will software use the most likely price at that date.

Option breakdown

Any software in this category should be able to totally analyze any given option, providing information such as volatility, Greek risk measurements (delta, gamma, vega, theta, rho, lambda), time and intrinsic value, open interest.

Position charts

This can be a helpful visual aid. It graphically shows how the position's profit/loss profile will look as time passes. Software should display "what if" scenarios based on the user's own assumptions, so a best, worst and most likely case scenario can be built. These charts help understand risk better.

Probability calculator

This calculates the probability of the underlying or option price being at a certain price level by a certain time (inputted by the user).

Major quote vendors supported

We obviously want a software package that supports data downloads from the major quote vendors. That reduces additional costs. It also means that we are not tied to the software provider's own data.

Other features

These can be a useful but non-essential bonus. Two common ones are pager alerts, i.e. you are paged when certain price targets are met, and the portfolio tracker, to track your option positions.

Table 25.1 contains a breakdown of various options analysis vendors and their products (see also Diagram 25.1).

hot tip *Check it out*
Although many of the top options analysis software providers deliver the same services, there are, after all, only so many ways to calculate an option's theoretical fair value. It is the way they display the information and how user-friendly the software screens are that make the major difference. So, make sure you take the time, and have the patience, to try their demos first.

Table 25.1 Summary of options analysis vendors and products

Name and web address	Option pricing model	Auto-position search	Option breakdown	Position chart	Probability calculator	Products*	Major quote vendors	Other features
OptionStation (Omega Research) www.omegaresearch.com	✓	✓	✓	✓	✓	csifb	✓	Alert
OptionVue V (Option Vue) www.optionvue.com	✓	✓	✓	✓	✓	csifb	✓	Portfolio tracker
Optionscope (Equis) www.equis.com	✓	✗	✓	✓	✗	csifb	✓	
Option Pro (Essex Trading Co) www.essextrading.com	✓	✓	✓	✓	✓	sf	✓	Portfolio tracker
Options Lab (Mantic Software) www.manticsoft.com	✓	✗	✓	✓	✗	csifb	n/a	
OptionTrader98 (AustinSoft) www.austin-soft.com	✓	✓	✓	✓	✗	csifb	✗ included	Portfolio tracker

* c = currency options; s = stock options; i = index options; f = futures options; b = bond options

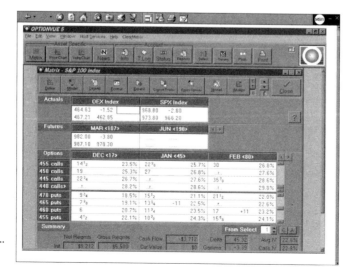

Diagram 25.1

OptionVue 5

Summary

The internet sites of options analysis software provide detailed online brochures and often downloadable demos. The chances of making a bad decision should be negligible. The key thing to remember is to take your time in making your decision because the chances are you will be using the software for a long time.

Recommendation peddlers: gurus and their newsletters

❝ My experience is that the hottest person on the floor is just about the worst teacher. ❞

Jon Najarian
President and CEO
Mercury Trading

In this chapter

The sites in this section deal exclusively with newsletters and gurus. Again, the reason this section is separate from the other sites is to reduce clutter and make your navigation easier.

To have got this far

- ■ You will have read the chapter on keeping abreast – especially on newsletters.
- ■ You will have read the skeleton plans for your chosen product and been referred to this chapter.

Key site features

Do not forget the checklist in Table 26.1 (explained in more detail in Section 2 Chapter 14).

Table 26.1 Checklist

	My choice	Newsletter 1	Newsletter 2	Newsletter 3
Product				
Strategy				
Analysis				
Timeframe				
Method of delivery				
Comprehensible (score)				
Trial period				
Cost				

The sites referred to here are "umbrella" sites. They have in aggregate the following features.

Search criteria

The facility to search for newsletters by publisher, author, product, strategy.

Free samples

The facility to view or order many of the newsletters for free for a trial period.

Track record

A comparison of the newsletters based on their performance.

Investools** US

`www.investools.com`

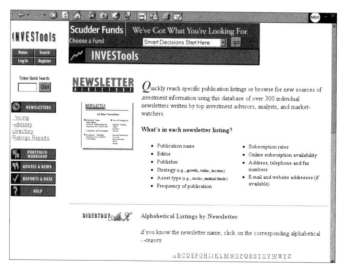

Diagram 26.1

INVESTools

Search according to strategy, product, analysis (eg. charts)
Free issues of some of the listed newsletters

Comment

A wide selection of newsletters here, but no ranking except by a link to Hulbert Financial.

Hulbert Financial*** US

www.hulbertdigest.com

Diagram 26.2

Hulbert Financial

Analysis of investment approaches of newsletters

Profiles of strategy and methods used for recommendations

Addresses of all listed newsletters

Ranking of past performance of all newsletters

Hulbert Financial is well known for its ranking of newsletters. It is a very comprehensive service; however you will have to pay for it.

Newsletter Network** US

www.margin.com

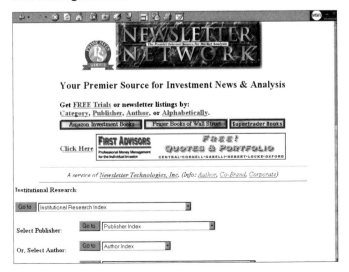

Diagram 26.3

Newsletter Network

hot tip **Diamonds in the dirt**

Many prospectors for newsletters think that if they find some esoteric and little known newsletter they may find something everyone else has missed and so strike oil. Don't kid yourself: the newsletter writer wouldn't be writing the letter if he was sitting on a potential oilfield littered with diamonds!

Search the extensive database according to publisher, letter, author
Free samples

Comment   *Similar to Investools and it may be that the sites do not cover exactly the same newsletters, so it is worth using both sites as search tools.*

Summary

As you will have guessed, I am not a great fan of newsletters. But at least with the resources described in this chapter you have more information than ever before about how good they are. At least your choice will be informed.

27

Can we talk? discussion forums

In this chapter

Here are listed some popular newsgroups and web-based discussion forums (see Table 27.1).

To have got this far

- You will have read Chapter 8 (Section 2) dealing with discussion forums.
- You will have been referred to this chapter by one of the skeleton plans.

Table 27.1 Newsgroups from a general internet search

Name	Content
alt.invest.penny-stocks	Low-priced stocks talk
misc.invest	Investments
misc.invest.commodities	Commodities
misc.invest.emerging	Emerging markets
misc.invest.forex	Foreign exchange
misc.invest.funds	Mutual funds
misc.invest.futures	Futures
misc.invest.stocks	Stocks
misc.invest.technical	Technical analysis
uk.finance	UK personal finance

Some popular web-based discussion forums

Table 27.2 lists major web-based discussion sites and their properties (see also Diagram 27.1).

Table 27.2 Major web-based discussion sites

Name and web address	Stocks	Mutual funds	Futures	Options	Bonds	Technical analysis	Fundamental analysis
Avid Traders Chat avidinfo.com	✓					✓	
The Financial Center On-Line www.tfc.com/chat	✓	✓	✓	✓	✓	✓	✓
Investors Free Forum www.investorsforum.com	✓	✓	✓	✓	✓	✓	✓
The Motley Fool www.fool.com	✓			✓			
Quicken People & Chat quicken.excite.com/forums	✓	✓					
The Stock Club www.stockclub.com	✓						✓
Yahoo! Finance Message Boards messages.yahoo.com/yahoo/ Business_and_Finance/	✓	✓	✓	✓	✓	✓	✓

One of the best collections of web-based discussion is located within Yahoo! at:

`messages.yahoo.com/yahoo/Business_and_Finance/Index.html`.

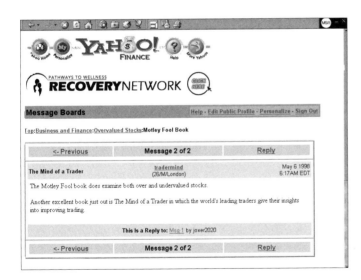

Diagram 27.1
Yahoo!

Newsgroups exist on:

- brokerages
- market trends
- mutual funds
- options
- overvalued stocks
- short-term trading
- stocks (financial, consumer, energy, healthcare, service, technology, transport, utilities)
- company-specific newsgroups, so you can discuss a single stock in splendid isolation.

Summary

Although the quality of content can vary widely in newsgroups and web-based discussion groups they can be a useful source of second opinions. Remember to always query motives of those posting messages. Their opinions carry more weight if independently verifiable (e.g. a news item you may otherwise have missed), rather than hope or spurious argument. Overall, the web-based discussion groups are of a higher quality than the newsgroups and my advice would be to choose 1 or 2 at the most, otherwise you will not be able to keep abreast of them all.

28

E-zines

❝ Most of the new traders read the newspapers ... so they do not have a plan, they just have a general feeling that due to a situation they read in the paper they want to do this or that. What I try to do is to help them make a plan. ❞

Phil Flynn
Vice President
Alaron Trading

In this chapter

The sites in this section deal exclusively with quality online financial magazines. This section is separate from the other sites to reduce clutter and make your navigation easier.

To have got this far

- You will have gone through the skeleton plans and been referred here as part of keeping abreast.

The top e-zines

Table 28.1 lists the top e-zines and their addresses (see also Diagrams 28.1, 28.2).

Table 28.1 The top e-zines

Name	Address
Applied Derivatives Trading	www.adtrading.com
Business Week Online	www.businessweek.com
The Economist	www.economist.com
Forbes	www.forbes.com
Fortune	www.fortune.com
Inc. Magazine	www.inc.com
InvestorGuide Weekly	www.investorguide.com
Stocks & Commodities	www.traders.com
US News Online	www.usnews.com
Worth	www.worth.com

Diagram 28.1

Fortune

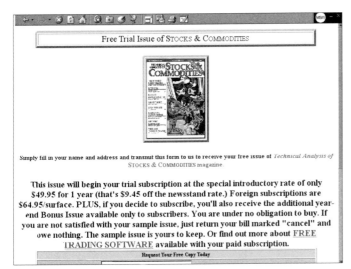

Diagram 28.2

Stocks & Commodities

Summary

Select one or two top magazines to keep in touch with more market background information. Personally, I prefer reading them off-line. However, you could use the online magazines as a cheaper alternative or supplement.

The truth is out there

29

Net trawlers: search engines

" *If you meet a trader who is very, very successful, and he truly, honestly believes it is because he is smarter and faster and more insightful and more aggressive than all of his peers, I don't believe him. I truly don't.* **"**

Bill Lipschutz
former Global Head of Foreign Exchange
Salomon Brothers

In this chapter

We examine one of the most used methods of finding information on the internet: the search engine.

Objectives

- Familiarize ourselves with the workings of search engines
- know when to use searches.

What is a search engine?

A search engine is simply a site that "searches" other sites depending on keywords entered by a user (Diagram 29.1).

Search engine fortunes

Search engines were created in the early days of the popular internet by Silicon Valley students who decided to collect listings of sites. Several years later they had floated their companies (use of the engine being free, but advertising bringing in revenue) and become multimillionaires.

Diagram 29.1

A search engine

Some things to know

- Since pages on the internet change quickly, a search engine is unlikely to be up-to-the-minute, and some results returned may be outdated.
- Just because an engine does not find a site does not mean it does not exist.
- Because of the different way each engine works each will return different results.
- Results are ranked according to closeness of match to your request, and not, of course, according to best available site in terms of content.
- If you are not satisfied with the results try a different engine.

How to search

Very simply: type in the keyword and press enter. If you want to be technical, most search engines will have options which allow you to specify whether the engine is to provide results that contain the keywords as a phrase or any one of the keywords.

Advanced searching

- To search for sites that are country related, go to the search engine's home page and look for the link to the appropriate country, usually at the foot of the page or try typing **domain:country code**, e.g. in the search box for AltaVista **domain:de** lists web sites which display the domain **de** (Germany).
- The asterisk (*) can often be used as a wild card e.g. trad* would look for "trader," "trade," "traditional," etc.
- In the keyword box of the search engine if you enter two words then be careful as to what you are looking for (see Table 29.1).

Beyond this different search engines will all have their own language to assist searches, but in most cases the pure and simple keywords will do.

Table 29.1 Keywords and sample results

Keyword	Result
Dow Jones	All sites containing somewhere in them the words Dow or Jones or both, not necessarily together
Dow AND Jones	All sites containing somewhere in them the words Dow Jones, not necessarily together
Dow OR Jones	All sites containing somewhere in them the words Dow or Jones or both, not necessarily together
"Dow Jones"	All sites containing somewhere in them the words Dow Jones together
+Dow -Jones	All sites containing the word Dow but not those containing the word Jones

Top search engines

Table 29.2 lists the major search engines with addresses and ratings (see also Diagrams 29.2, 29.3, 29.4).

Table 29.2 Major search engines

Name	Address	Rating
AltaVista	altavista.digital	*** (recommended)
Excite	excite	***
Lycos	lycos	***
Yahoo!	yahoo	***
Deja News	dejanews	***
InfoSeek	infoseek	***
WebCrawler	webcrawler	**
MetaCrawler	metacrawler	**

*** Means the search engine lists a very large number of sites, the amount of information displayed can be altered, supports complex searches, includes directories and other category-based searching links.

** As above but fewer results and category links may not be as good.

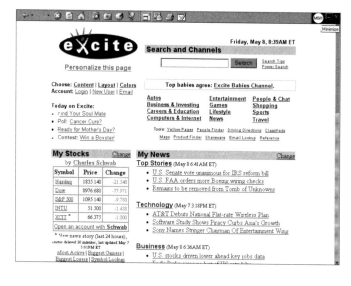

Diagram 29.2

Excite

Diagram 29.3
MetaCrawler

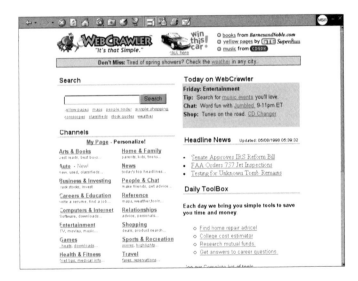

Diagram 29.4
WebCrawler

Summary

We have seen the basic operation of search engines. Today they are sophisticated sites providing a wealth of information beyond merely search facilities. They are worth checking out for that alone. Next, we move onto directories of sites, which may further assist in finding information on the internet.

30

The directory approach: web financial directories

ff *One has to have an interest to understand what is going on in his market. That is a characteristic which very few people have.* **JJ**

Bernard Oppetit
Global Head of Equity Derivatives
Banque Paribas

In this chapter

Continuing our examination of tools that will help us effectively and efficiently find trading information and sites we examine internet financial directories (sometimes referred to as umbrella sites – maybe because the contain everything under the sun).

Objective

■ **Familiarity with directories as means of research.**

Star ratings in this chapter:

See key at the bottom of Table 30.1.

What a directory is

An internet directory simply organizes and lists sites according to category (Diagram 30.1).

The downside is that they rarely rank, review or give much detail about sites. Nevertheless, they can add more focus to a search than a search engine necessarily can.

hot tip — **Save it**
You never know when you will need an umbrella site and so good advice is to bookmark/add the site to favorites (perhaps for a rainy day).

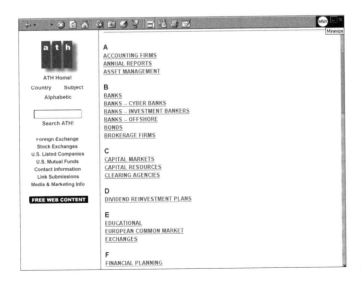

Diagram 30.1

A typical directory

Which directories?

Some of the best directories are listed in Table 30.1. They are all worth a visit and possibly even bookmarking for a rainy day. It can be great fun just surfing these. I consider them the internet equivalent of a candy store – you walk in and there is so much to try, yet no plaque.

Table 30.1 Leading finance directories

Directory	Address	Ranking
AltaVista	altavista.looksmart.com	***
Dow Jones Business Directory	bd.dowjones.com	**
Finance Wise	www.financewise.com	**
Finance Watch	www.finance.wat.ch	*** (recommended)
Investorama	www.investorama.com	***
Yahoo! Finance	quote.yahoo.com	*** (recommended)

*** An excellent selection of categories and links. Comprehensive, diverse and easy to navigate.
** Many good features and a fair selection of sites and categories.
    Anything lower than ** is not included because the standard is so high.

AltaVista ***

altavista.looksmart.com

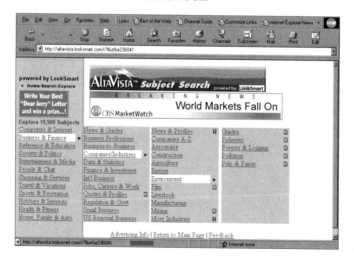

Diagram 30.2

AltaVista

Comment *The tree structure to this directory is very useful: you can see where you have been, what else is available and where you may want to go next. It saves a lot of time avoiding the need to go back and forth in the browser. The directory content itself is also pretty extensive.*

Dow Jones Business Directory**

bd.dowjones.com

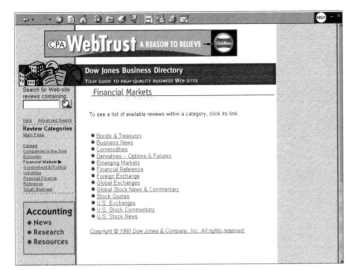

Diagram 30.3

Dow Jones Business Directory

The chief benefit of this directory is that unlike virtually any other finance site it actually ranks each and describes them in some detail. However, it does include relatively few sites.

Comment

FinanceWise**

www.financewise.com

Diagram 30.4

FinanceWise

FinanceWise provides both a search engine and a directory. The directory is not too bad and does have categories others do not. Covers both finance and trading well.

Comment

Finance Watch***

www.finance.wat.ch

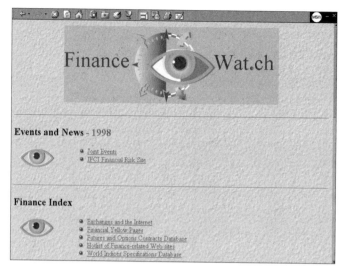

Diagram 30.5
Finance Watch

Comment   *This Swiss-based site (hence the .ch) is massive, nay, it is humungous. I am tempted to say, "If it aint 'ere, it aint nowhere!"*

Investorama***

www.investorama.com

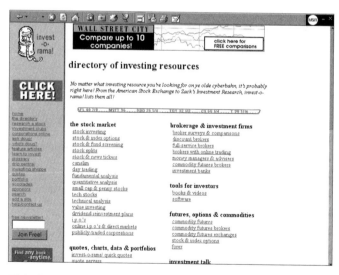

Diagram 30.6
Investorama

Comment   *This directory has a vast number of categories and because the structure is fairly flat (i.e. there are few sub-directories) you can quickly get a very good overview.*

Yahoo! Finance***

`quote.yahoo.com`

Diagram 30.7

Yahoo! Finance

This is how a web site should be designed. The amount of information on the screen without the need for excessive scrolling, eye strain or clutter is remarkable. The financial directory is also comprehensive for a non-finance company. Excellent. I think I'll buy me some shares in Yahoo!

Comment

Summary

In this chapter we have seen some of the powerful and useful service provided by directories as a potential source of trading information and research. While their listings can be extensive we nevertheless need to monitor for quality.

31

Virtual bookworming: internet bookshops

❝Another way [to improve trading] is reading books and reading magazine articles to see which trader has a style that would work for you.❞

Jon Najarian
Chairman and CEO
Mercury Trading

In this chapter

When you want to research a trading topic a little deeper it is worth considering non-internet resources, namely books. But even here the internet has changed things greatly. Online bookstores can very often undercut normal bookstores because of lower operating costs. In this chapter we examine looking for and buying books online.

Objectives

- Awareness of internet bookshops
- how to get value for money
- how to use the bookshops.

What are online bookstores?

An online bookstore is a site which permits you to look for books and buy them. The best sites have several features.

Search

All the sites permit you to search for books. The better sites permit searches based on:

- author
- title
- subject
- publication date
- publisher
- ISBN.

Categories

Many of the online bookstores have books listed according to categories, which can help surfing if you are not quite sure what you want.

Jacket pictures

I always find this helpful.

Reviews

Reviews of the book from either online readers or taken from the jacket is a useful feature.

Table of contents

Sadly, few include this, but many should given that in a bookstore this is really the first thing you will examine.

Synopsis

Vital, unless you know what the book is about.

E-mail notification

Some sites monitor titles similar to ones that you tell them interest you and notify you of new releases. This can be useful, but sometimes tedious.

Other features

Since some internet bookstores are massive businesses they will often have lots of other features: guest speakers, best-seller guides, reviews from magazines, "books in the news," etc. With other sites you can pay in several different currencies. Most deliver anywhere in the world.

Things to bear in mind

When buying books online there are several pieces of advice worth bearing in mind.

hot tip **Mix and match**
Since the prices of books and information about them vary between sites, why not get all you want to know from one site and place the order with another site?

Check out several sites

The price of a book between online stores can vary significantly. Bookmark or add to favorites all the bookstores listed in the table and check them out if you are making a purchase. Another reason to check out different stores is because the amount of information varies from site to site.

Beware P&P

Prices quoted exclude postage and packaging, some sites only tell you those charges after you have placed a provisional order. Remember to factor in the cost. Most sites offer a variety of delivery times and if you are not in a hurry take the slow and cheap option.

Delivery

Find out what the delivery times are. Sometimes online books can take up to 3 months to be delivered.

Worried about giving credit card details online?

All the sites in the table, if viewed through Internet Explorer 4 or Netscape Navigator 4, should encrypt and keep secure your credit card details. You can also visit the sites and view their reassurances on online security if not convinced. Some sites provide a phone number for phoning or faxing orders. Alternatively, if you are still unhappy, look for the book online and ask your local bookstore to order it from its supplier – of course, it won't be as cheap as the online order.

Table 31.1 list major online stores and includes a ranking (see also Diagrams 31.1, 31.2).

Table 31.1 Major online stores

Name and address	Ranking	Price of The Mind of a Trader	Search	E-mail notification	Categories	Jacket picture	Reviews	Table of contents	Synopsis
Amazon www.amazon.com	*** (recommended)	$24.47	✓	✓	✓	✓	✓		✓
Barnes & Noble www.barnesandnoble.com	*** (recommended)	$24.46	✓	✓	✓	✓	✓		✓
The Bookpl@ce www.bookplace.com	**	$37.49 (£24.99)	✓		✓				✓
Booksite www.booksite.com	*	$31.46	✓	✓	✓	✓			✓
Internet Bookshop www.bookshop.co.uk	**	$41.00	✓	✓	✓		✓		✓
Numa Web www.numa.com	**	$37.49 (£24.99)	✓		✓	✓	✓	✓	✓
Traders Library www.traderslibrary.com	*	$34.95	✓	✓	✓				
Wordsworth www.wordsworth.com	**	$29.71	✓		✓	✓	✓		✓

*** A model site, with deep discounts, excellent stock range, search facilities and book details.

** Good prices and fair range and reasonable search facilities.

* Use if all else fails.

Diagram 31.1

Amazon

Diagram 31.2

Barnes & Noble

Summary

The best advice when it comes to buying books online is:

- Amazon and Barnes & Noble are likely to always be the cheapest, and are certainly the largest.
- Check out Numa Web for tables of contents.
- Visit other sites to do category searches and possibly for non-trading-related books and reviews.

SECTION

Appendices

APPENDIX 1

Technical analysis: what and why

In this appendix

For those of a technical persuasion, we shall examine some common technical indicators that can be found in all the major software packages. After briefly describing each one, there will be a description of how it is popularly interpreted. At the end I provide my list of what I consider to be the most popular indicators.

Objective

■ A thorough overview of technical analysis for further study with confidence

Use of this appendix

You will probably find this appendix most useful if you:

■ are considering investigating technical analysis further

■ have bought technical analysis software and want to know more about interpreting some of the indicators on that software

■ are looking to refresh your memory about some indicators

■ are looking to add more technical indicators to your current usage.

 To properly understand technical indicators you should examine them in far more detail than is provided in this appendix, especially if you are considering making trading decisions based on them. See the recommended reading lists for some good books on technical analysis.

Ways of displaying prices

When a price chart is constructed, time is always plotted on the x-axis and price levels on the y-axis. The line chart simply joins each consecutive day's closing price to produce lines.

A bar chart displays the asset's open, high, low, and close. A straight vertical line is drawn joining the low to the high of the day and the open and close is displayed by having a tiny horizontal line to the left (for open) or the right (for close) of the said vertical line.

There are numerous other ways to draw prices, one of the most popular being Japanese candlesticks and Point and Figure (see recommended reading).

Bollinger Bands

Bollinger Bands are plotted at certain standard deviations above and below moving averages (see later). They bind the price charts like tunnels or envelopes.

Interpretation

Generally they are interpreted so that

- price tends to move from one band to the opposite band
- sharp price changes are indicated as imminent once the bands contract.

Correlation

Correlation measures the extent to which one variable, e.g. a securities price, is connected to another variable, for example the price of another security. The aim is to predict movements in one, given movements in the other.

Interpretation

If we know one set of variables is highly correlated to another we can use that to predict movements in the latter after movement in the former.

Ease of movement

This calculates how easily prices are moving, on the basis that the larger the price move, and the lighter the volume then the easier prices are moving (see Diagram A1.1).

Interpretation

A buy signal is indicated when the ease of movement indicator line crosses the zero center line upwards because the security is moving upward easily. A sell signal is indicated when the indicator line crosses the zero center line downwards.

Diagram A1.1

Ease of movement, Bollinger Bands

Envelope

The envelope is two moving averages (see later), one shifted above and one shifted below the price by a certain percent (see Diagram A1.2).

Diagram A1.2

Envelope, Fibonacci, Gann

Interpretation

The idea is that the envelope lines are boundaries of the prices range. So, if the price hits its lower range it is relatively unlikely to go lower. The thinking is that prices revert to more "normal" levels after reaching extremities.

Fibonacci Numbers

Fibonacci Numbers (named after the 12th-century Italian mathematician) are numbers starting with 1 and 1 which are the sum of the two previous numbers. The Fibonacci sequence begins: 1, 1, 2, 3, 5, 8, 13, 21, 34, 55, etc. They exist in nature. On this basis, traders have adopted the relationships for interpreting price charts.

Interpretation

In technical analysis, Fibonacci Fans, Arcs, Lines and Time Zones are but four indicators using this numerical relationship. Fibonacci Lines for instance are drawn by first marking a line between two extreme price points, and then your software will draw in the remaining lines at Fibonacci levels above and below this level. Prices will often retrace to a Fibonacci support level after a significant move.

Gann Studies

These are named after one of the most famous market technicians of all time, WD Gann (1878–1955). Gann believed that the best relationship between prices and time occurred when the angle at which prices rose or fell was that of 45 degrees to the horizontal time axis.

Interpretation

Very simply, if prices are above the 45 degree line then they are bullish, and if they are below the 45 degree line then they are bearish. Gann also gave the values of other angles at which prices ought to find support or resistance, namely 7.5, 15, 18.75, 26.25, 45, 63.75, 71.25, 75, 82.5 degrees.

Gann developed Gann Lines, Gann Fans, Gann Grids, which most technical analysis software which deals with Gann will also include.

Linear regression

A linear regression line can be considered a line of best fit around a set of prices. It is drawn by the computer so that "on average" the distance between the price and the line is the narrowest it can be compared to any other line over the same period for the same price.

Interpretation

If we consider the linear regression line the "equilibrium" price then if prices move too far from the linear regression line they ought to return to it. A buy signal is generated when prices move relatively far from the linear regression line to the bottom and a sell signal when prices move relatively far above the linear regression line.

Moving average convergence divergence (MACD)

This (indicator line) is plotted by subtracting the value of one exponential moving average (see later) from that of another exponential moving average. Another exponential moving average (signal line) is then drawn on top of this.

Interpretation

The simple rule is to buy when the signal line crosses above the indicator line, and sell when it goes below it.

Momentum

The momentum an asset's price exhibits is measured by the ratio of today's price compared to the price a certain number of days ago (see Diagram A1.3).

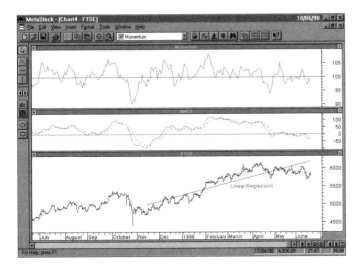

Diagram A1.3

Momentum: MACD linear regression

Interpretation

There are many ways to interpret the momentum indicator. Some of the most popular are:

- Buy when it hits an extreme low value (oversold). Sell when it hits an extreme high value (oversold).

- Buy when the momentum indicator crosses above a moving average of itself. Sell when the momentum indicator crosses below a moving average of itself.

Moving averages

A moving average is calculated by taking the average of an asset's price over the last x days. It is "moving" because as each day progresses you can determine what the last x prices changes are.

As well as this type of moving average – a simple moving average – there is also an exponential moving average. This is calculated so that more weight is given to the latest price and so on until least weight is given to the last price being considered.

Interpretation

There are several popular methods of interpreting moving averages, a buy signal being generated when the price moves above the moving average and a sell signal when it moves below.

Another popular method is to display two moving averages of different time periods and buy when the shorter time period moving average crosses above the longer time period moving average.

The important thing is to experiment with various time periods of moving average and attempt to find one that is consistently good at predicting moves.

On-balance volume (OBV)

This indicator attempts to depict the relationship between volume and price. If the asset's price rises then the day's volume is added to a cumulative total. If the asset's price falls then that day's volume is subtracted from the cumulative total. Therefore, when there is a price rise, the whole day's volume is assumed to have contributed to it by being up-volume. When there is a price fall the whole day's volume is assumed to have contributed to that by being down-volume (see Diagram A1.4).

Interpretation

OBV is designed for short-term trading. The OBV can be considered in a rising trend when each successive low is higher than the previous low and each new high is higher than the previous high. A sell signal is generated when the trend is broken.

Similarly, the OBV can be considered in a falling trend when each successive low is lower than the previous low and each new high is lower than the previous high. A buy signal is generated when the trend is broken.

Diagram A1.4

On-balance volume; moving average

Open interest

This is only applicable to futures. It measures the number of open transactions in a particular contract.

Interpretation

If open interest and prices rise then that tends to indicate new buyers. Similarly, if open interest and prices move in opposite directions or if open interest and prices fall then that tends to show a warning signal.

Parabolic SAR

This indicator is often known as the stop-and-reversal indicator. It is in fact a moving stop that rises with prices.

Interpretation

This indicator is popularly used so that if the price is above the SAR then buy or stay long, if the price is below the SAR then sell or stay short.

Price rate of change

This indicator is calculated by dividing the price change over the last x periods by the closing price of the security x periods ago.

Interpretation

The price ROC tends to be interpreted in the same manner as the momentum indicator. Namely:

- Buy when it hits an extreme low value (oversold). Sell when it hits an extreme high value (oversold).
- Buy when the price ROC indicator crosses above a moving average of itself. Sell when the price ROC indicator crosses below a moving average of itself.

Relative strength index

The RSI measures the current price against the price x periods ago. It is similar in that respect to the other oscillators such as the momentum indicator, price ROC, and Stochastic. It is based on comparing the average of upward price changes with that of downward price changes (see Diagram A1.5).

Interpretation

This indicator tends to be popularly interpreted in the same way as the momentum, price ROC and Stochastic indicators.

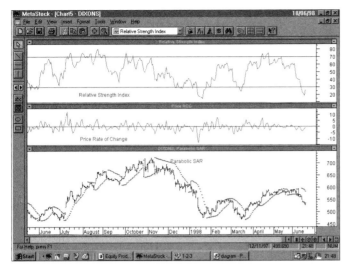

Diagram A1.5

Relative strength index: SAR, ROC

Standard deviation

The standard deviation is a mathematical notation. In oversimple terms it is the average by which the price moves from its own average. It is therefore a measure of volatility.

Interpretation

Relatively low standard deviation values, i.e. low volatility, tends to warn of an imminent price move, on the theory that volatility will increase and revert to its longer term average.

Stochastic oscillator

This oscillator compares today's price with the trading range over the past x days (%K line). A moving average of this line is also taken (%D line).

Interpretation

Like the other oscillators we have discussed buy signals are generally considered to occur when the main line (%K) rises above the %D line. A buy signal can also be indicated when the %K hits a relatively extreme level. If it is a high level then this indicates a sell signal on the basis the asset is overbought; if the %K hits a relatively low level then this indicates a buy signal on the basis the asset is oversold.

Trendlines

A trendline is a line between two points in a chart drawn so that it also touches at least one other. Their purpose is to illustrate areas of price support and resistance. An up trendline is drawn so that it touches three successive rising price troughs. A down trendline is drawn so that it touches three successive price peaks.

Interpretation

The common assumption with trendlines is that prices will bounce off them, unless they don't, in which case they will not! Isn't technical analysis wonderful? Although this appears frustratingly nonsensical, it makes sense when we consider probability. The idea is that there is a probability greater than 1/2 that the price will rebound off the trendline. Therefore the odds are slightly in your favor when trading off a trendline.

Williams %R

The Williams %R is another oscillator and is similar in construction to the Stochastic Oscillator (see Diagram A1.6).

Interpretation

This oscillator is interpreted in much the same manner as the other oscillators. In particular a buy signal is generated by a relatively low extreme reading of the indicator and a sell signal by a relatively high reading of the indicator.

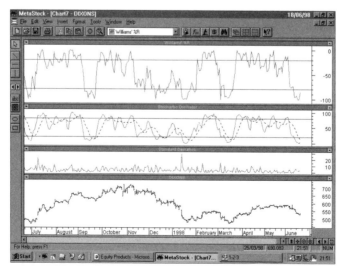

Diagram A1.6

Williams %R, standard deviation, stochastic oscillator

The most popular indicators

Popular among most technical analysts is the use of at least one oscillator indicator, such as the ROC, momentum, Stochastic, William's %R, MACD. Of these the most popular is probably the Stochastic. However, since the way in which the MACD is calculated is different from the other oscillators it is often used in conjunction with the Stochastic.

In terms of displaying charts the old bar chart method remained most popular with Japanese candlesticks a close second.

Trendlines and moving averages are "meat and veg" for the technical analyst and although few rely on them exclusively, they will consider them in their overall analysis of an asset.

Of the volume indicators, the on-balance volume is probably the most popular, although many technical analysts will simply examine a histogram depicting daily volume to get a feel of what volume is doing.

Summary

In this appendix we have seen an outline of some of the most popular technical indicators. However, I cannot repeat often enough: there is a lot more to technical analysis and you are strongly advised to see the recommended reading list and the educational sites for technical analysis in the skeleton plans to find out more.

APPENDIX 2

Fundamental analysis: stocks

In this appendix

We cover some basic good practice advice for those interested in using fundamental analysis for prospecting for stocks.

Objectives

- Detail some rules of good fundamental analysis practice
- Provide a framework for more professional approach to fundamental analysis
- Give you a base for more detailed examination and reading

To have got this far you will have read the chapter on analysis and specifically the section on fundamental analysis.

The rules

There are eight basic rules with which will come in handy when using fundamental analysis. When visiting internet sites it is a good idea to bear these in mind as part of your stock selection. While they do not guarantee success they undoubtedly help increase your success rate.

Do not over-diversify

If you are trying to follow too many companies you will lose focus and simply not have enough time to devote to researching each one.

Diversify sensibly

While you do not want to put all your eggs in one basket, for instance by having too many companies in the same sector, remember that while it is sensible to diversify from 3 holdings to 10, the marginal benefit diminishes as you diversify from 10 to 100.

Go for business you can understand

If you understand a product, then the chances are you will be able to rate the company's prospects a little bit better. If it is a car manufacturer, go visit a few showrooms, does it look like a good product, better than the competition, or stale?

What fundamental analysts look for

Check Table A2.1 to see what fundamental analysts commonly look for.

Table A2.1 What fundamental analysts look for

Item	What signifies positive for the security
52-week high	A new high
Revenue percent change	An increase (acceleration)
Sales growth rate	An increase (acceleration)
Earnings per share growth rate	An increase (acceleration)
Dividend yield	An increase (acceleration)
Dividend rate	An increase (acceleration)
Institutional percent owned	An increase (acceleration)
Institutional net shares purchased	An increase (acceleration)
Long-term debt to total equity	A decrease (deceleration)
Gross margin	An increase (acceleration)
Operating margin	An increase (acceleration)
Net profit margin	An increase (acceleration)
Earnings per share	An increase (acceleration)
Price to earning ratio	A decrease (deceleration)
Cashflow per share	An increase (acceleration)
Insider shares purchased	An increase (acceleration)
Insider ownership %	An increase (acceleration)
Return on assets	An increase (acceleration)
Return on investments	An increase (acceleration)
Return on equity	An increase (acceleration)
Company in the news	Unexpected positive story
Sector in news	Unexpected item not in price of individual stocks
Broker report	Upgrade; positive news
Total operating expenses	A decrease (deceleration)
Free cashflow	An increase (acceleration)
Sales per employee	An increase (acceleration)
Income per employee	An increase (acceleration)

Cashflow

Look for stocks with a relatively large flow of income. This together with low borrowings should feed into a cash-rich company increasing the potential for increased shareholder value.

Accelerating profit margins

Increase in profit margins is something the market looks for when valuing a company, but an accelerating profit margin usually takes the market unexpectedly and can lead to strong share price rises.

Acceleration of net profit and retention of earnings

This can then be used by the company for reinvestment, dividend payment, acquisition or stock buy-back all adding to shareholder value.

Strong sales

Look for a company that is in a market where sales growth is increasing and not under pressure.

Summary

Stock picking is complicated and this appendix together with the chapter on analysis should have given you an idea of what it is you should look for in companies you seek to invest in. This together with the resources available from the sites listed in the skeleton plans and the recommended reading should provide you with the professional tools and information to get you well on the way to increasing the chances of successful investment.

APPENDIX 3

The basics of futures

In this appendix

Many people are intrigued by futures; this is a painless guide to those derivatives. Remember to see the recommended reading and the educational sites under the skeleton plans.

Objective

- A thorough basic understanding of futures for on-going study

What is a futures contract?

A futures contract has several features:

- It is a legally binding contract.
- It is usually traded through a recognized exchange (e.g. Chicago Mercantile Exchange).
- One party agrees to take delivery and the other party agrees to make delivery of the underlying asset.
- The specific quality and quantity of the underlying asset to be delivered is agreed in advance.
- The date of delivery is fixed in advance.
- The price of delivery is fixed in advance.
- The place of delivery is fixed in advance.

In other words, a futures contract is simply an agreement to deliver a specific quantity and quality of an asset at a predetermined price, place and date. If you "long" a futures contract then you have bought a futures contract and so are the party that will take delivery. You may already have entered into very similar contracts; ever bought something and asked for it to be delivered? If you "short" a futures contract then you have sold a futures contract and so are the party that will make delivery.

The product range

Nowadays futures are available on:

- **Metals:** silver, gold, copper, platinum.
- **Energy:** crude oil, heating oil, natural gas, unleaded gasoline.
- **Wood:** lumber.
- **Index futures:** NYSE Index, S&P 500 Stock Index, US Dollar Index, CRB Futures Index, Municipal Bond Index.
- **Currencies:** British pound, US dollar, French franc, Eurodollars, Swiss franc, Deutschmark, Japanese yen, Canadian dollar.
- **Interest rates:** treasury bonds, treasury bills, treasury notes, Eurodollars.
- **Foods and fibers:** coffee, cocoa, sugar, cotton, orange juice.
- **Meats:** live cattle, feeder cattle, hogs, pork bellies.
- **Grains:** wheat, corn, oats, soybean complex.

For every futures contract the most important information is:

- minimum contract size, e.g. 100 troy ounces of gold per contract
- how the price is expressed, e.g. $ per ounce
- effect of minimum tick movement, e.g. a $1 move in the contract price equals $100 difference in profit/loss per contract.

So for example a typical futures contract might look like this:

Cattle (CME): 40,000 pounds; cents per pound, quoted at 72 for December delivery.

What this means is that each cattle futures contract on the Chicago Mercantile Exchange is for 40,000 pounds of live cattle, and prices are expressed in cents per pound. The price of 72 means 72 cents per pound. Therefore a 1 cent price move causes a $400 change in equity (i.e. 1 cent x 40,000).

Note, however, that only about 1% of all futures contracts are held until delivery; they are usually "closed" before then. That is, an equal and opposite futures trade is made which cancels out your delivery obligations. The reasons vary as to why most futures contracts are not held to delivery, but the major one is that the futures contract is used for speculation and the speculator does not care about the underlying asset; another reason is because the future can be used as a hedge (see glossary).

Futures contracts are available in hard and soft commodities, such as various types of grain and metals. There are also futures in financial products such as interest rates, currencies and indices.

Gold futures contracts are traded on the New York Commodity Exchange (COMEX).

Minimum contract size is 100 troy ounces.

Price expressed in $/oz.

Therefore a $1 change in the contract is worth $100.

	$/oz	Contract value	Margin
May 2 Bought 1 contract COMEX gold June delivery	342	$34,200	$2,000
May 23 Sold 1 contract COMEX gold June delivery	352	$35,200	

Profit is $1,000 on an initial margin of $2,000. That is, $10 per oz across 100 ounces that a contract consists of.

Why are there futures contracts?

In the USA, between the Great Lakes and the grain-growing, livestock-rearing Great Plains lies Chicago. A natural port for access to the world's markets for most US farmers, Chicago soon became and remains the home of the largest commodities exchanges in the world.

Picture Chicago in the 1850s. As a farmer growing wheat in rural America each harvest I reap the rewards of my annual toils. I sell most of my wheat to a few farmers who use it to feed their livestock. Each year I pray for wheat prices to rise so that I may make greater profits when it comes to sell my wheat, and each year I worry that the prices might fall. Each year they pray for bumper crops so that the price might fall and their costs drop, and each year they worry that the price might rise. Then, while in our respective fields, it occurs to us to fix our prices several months in advance so that we may plan ahead. While we are at it, we should also fix when, where and what quality our wheat should be. What we have stumbled across is the futures contract.

Essentially, the futures contract was created to meet a business need. That need still exists today; the need for certainty in an uncertain world. The futures contract permitted hedges (i.e. protection) against adverse price movements by fixing the sale price today. Of course, it soon occurred to some non-farmers with stripy shirts, braces, slicked back hair and fast red Italian and German sports cars that futures could also be used to speculate.

How are futures prices fixed?

A future is a derivative. That is, its price is derived from the price of the underlying asset it refers to. A gold future's price is derived from the price of gold. The cash or spot price of the underlying asset is the price at which the underlying asset is currently being bought and sold in the market. The price of the cash asset changes with supply and demand. The futures price responds to changes in the spot price.

Obviously, at delivery, the futures price and the spot price are the same. If they were not then you could buy one and sell the other for instant profit (arbitrage). Before delivery, the futures price equals the cash price plus the cost of holding the cash commodity until delivery. A little thought makes it clear why this must be so. If it were not so, suppose the futures price of wheat is high relative to the cash price of wheat, you could buy the cash wheat, store it and pay interest on the money you borrowed to pay for it, and sell ("go short") the future (i.e. promise to deliver the wheat in the future.) Basically, your costs (of buying and storing the wheat) would be less than your receipts (from selling the wheat) and you would make a profit.

example

Price, above cash wheat price, of wheat future per bushel for delivery in 1 month	20 cents
Costs of holding cash wheat per bushel for 1 month	13 cents

Therefore, sell the future and buy the cash stock. Deliver the cash stock against the future in one month.
Locked in profit = 7 cents per bushel.

What is margin?

Initial margin is a small fraction of the contracts value paid at the time the position is opened. For example, to trade a futures contract worth $20,000 may require initial margin of $2,000, just 10% of contract value. A 5% movement in the contract value, i.e. $1,000, would result in a gain or loss of 50% of the sum invested. This is what is meant by leverage. Margin requirements are set by the exchange.

Variation margin is the further payments that need to be made if the price moves adversely.

Speculation

A futures speculator is like a speculator in any other asset. He seeks to profit from price changes. How he comes to decide what price changes are likely is his business; there as many different methods as traders. A trader may think that the UN is about to relax oil sanctions against Iraq and so the price of oil is likely to fall. As we saw before, all other things being equal, if the price of the cash commodity falls then the price of the future is also likely to fall. Consequently, our trader may short oil futures. However, he will have to be careful that there are not countervailing price-raising forces which may swamp the effects of the UN decision.

The trader will also have to ensure that the expectation of an imminent fall in oil prices is not already discounted in the price, in which case when the event eventually occurs the price will be unaffected.

---

example

			Margin
April 10	Buy 1 December copper contract at	97.25	$1,250
May 31	Sell 1 December copper contract at	102.25	

Here the speculator made a profit of 5 cents per pound or 5 x $250 = $1,250. That is a 100% profit on the original margin from a 5 cent move. But losses can be equally spectacular.

Speculators also use spread positions. A simple spread involves a long and short position so that a gain on the long position is offset partly by a loss on the short position or vice versa. The spreader desires a net gain.

---

example

March	Buy 1 May wheat contract at $2.85 per bushel	Sell 1 July wheat contract at $2.80 per bushel
April	Sell 1 May wheat contract at $3.20 per bushel	Buy 1 July wheat contract at $2.90 per bushel

The net result is a gain of $0.25 per bushel. Gain of $0.35 on the long position and loss of $0.10 on the short position.

Why spread?

The major benefit of spreading is that the downside risk is reduced considerably compared to a net long or short position. Consequently, margin is also reduced.

The hedger

A hedge is a futures position that is roughly opposite and equal to the position the hedger has in the cash market. If you long (own) the cash commodity, your hedge would be to short futures. The hedge is, in effect, an insurance contract.

> *example*
>
> A farmer notes that the price of wheat is $2.85 per bushel in the cash market. He wants to ensure he can get that price in 7 months when it comes to harvest.
>
> | | Cash market | Futures market |
> |---------|-------------|-------------------------|
> | October | $2.85 | Sell wheat future at $2.90 |
> | May | $2.44 | Buy wheat future at $2.49 |
>
> In May the farmer sells his crop in the cash market for $2.44. He also got a gain of $0.41 per bushel from the futures hedge, i.e. he received $2.85 per bushel. If he had not hedged he would have received only $2.44.

Summary

The most basic thing to remember about futures is that you buy them (go long) if you think the price will rise and sell them (go short) if you think it will fall. There is unlimited risk with futures and they should not be traded without a substantial period of paper trading for a full appreciation of the monetary risks.

APPENDIX 4

The basics of options

In this appendix

For those who are interested in options or have just started out, this appendix explains some of the fundamentals. The recommended reading and educational sites in the skeleton plans will augment your knowledge.

Objective

■ A thorough, basic comprehension of options as the basis of further study

What is an option?

An option is a contract between the holder and the grantor (called writer of the option). A holder pays the writer a premium for entering into the contract. There are basically two types: call options and put options.

A call gives the holder the right, but not the obligation, to buy from the writer:

1 within a fixed period of time (the exercise period)

2 a fixed quantity of the underlying security

3 at a fixed price (being the exercise price or strike price).

Key terms

Writer

Strike price or exercise price

Exercise period or expiry date

Premium

In the USA equity options relate to the right to buy or sell 100 shares, and in the UK to 1,000 shares.

 example

In the UK, "1 contract of the Barclays July 1,100 calls priced at 67p" would give the holder the right to buy, any time before a fixed date in July, 1,000 shares in Barclays Bank from the writer at a price of 1,100 pence (or £11) each. To purchase the option in the first place the holder would have to pay the writer £670 (1,000 x 67 pence) as premium.

The premium is the maximum loss the option holder can ever suffer.

example

ABC Corp. July 80 calls entitle the holder to purchase 100 shares of ABC Corp. common stock at $80 per share at any time prior to the options expiration in July.

What's the big idea 'ere?

The general idea is, of course, to make money! The flexibility of options (see later) provides many ways in which this can be done. One of the simplest ideas is (in the case of a call option holder) to buy shares in the future from the option writer at the fixed exercise price and then immediately sell them in the market at a profit, assuming the market price is greater than the exercise price. In the Barclays example, if the underlying price of the stock was 1,200 at expiry in July, the holder would call for his 1,000 shares (at a cost of £11 each) and then sell them immediately in the market at £12 each. Call holders therefore want the underlying share price to rise.

From the point of view of the writer or seller of the option he is obliged if "called" upon to sell the 1,000 shares in Barclays Bank and would receive the £11 per share in return. The writer wants to profit from receiving his premium, and not having to have to sell the holder any shares in the future. The call writer, therefore, does not generally want the market price to rise above the strike price, otherwise he will have to sell to the call holder at a price lower than he could get in the market. In the earlier example a call writer would have to sell at £11 under the option, when in the market he could otherwise have received £12. Call writers, therefore, do not want the underlying share price to rise.

Whether or not the option is exercised the writer keeps the premium.

Similarly, a put option provides the holder the right, but not the obligation, for a fixed period of time, to sell to the writer a fixed quantity of the underlying security at a fixed price.

Most people trade in traded options. That means they can sell the option contract itself to someone else if they so wish, without ever exercising it.

Strike price

Each common stock will have numerous options with differing strike prices. The strike price for an option is initially set at a price which is reasonably close to the current share price. The exchange introduces other strike prices at fixed intervals from that initial strike price.

Read the press

Premiums for exchange traded options are often printed in major financial newspapers. Typically, the listing may look as shown in Table A4.1 (only calls have been shown).

Table A4.1 Typical premiums listing

Option and closing price	Strike price	May	June	July
ABC	105	7 ½	9 ¼	10 ⅛
112 ⅜	110	3	4 ¾	6 ¼
112 ⅜	115	¹³⁄₁₆	2 ⅛	3 ½
112 ⅜	120	¹³⁄₁₆	⅞	1 ¾
112 ⅜	125	¹⁄₁₆	no option	¹³⁄₁₆

In this illustration ABC May 115 calls are trading at 13/16 or $81.25.

How is the option price calculated and how can I profit?

The price at which an option is bought and sold is called the premium. In the Barclays example the option premium was 67p. This is a little like a margin payment.

    An option's premium has two components: the intrinsic value and the time value.

(Share price) < (strike price)
= put option has
  intrinsic value
(Share price) > (strike price)
= call option has
  intrinsic value

Intrinsic value

A call option has intrinsic value if the underlying security price is greater than the option's strike price. A put option has intrinsic value if the underlying security price is less than the strike price.

So, for instance, in our earlier example, if the price of Barclays' shares was 1,110p then the option's intrinsic value would be 10p. That is, if you exercised the call you could buy Barclays' shares from the writer at 1,100p (strike price) and sell them in the market at 1,110p (underlying security price.) That is also why an option can never be worth less than its intrinsic value.

A call option would have no intrinsic value, and so only time value, if the underlying price was lower than the strike price. If an option has intrinsic value it is in-the-money. If an option has no intrinsic value it is out-of-the-money. An option whose strike price is nearest to the underlying price is at-the-money.

Time value

The second component of option premium is time value. It is the difference between the option premium and its intrinsic value, i.e.:

$$\text{Time value} = \text{premium} - \text{intrinsic value}$$

So, in our previous example time value would total 57p. Time value essentially represents the price the holder pays the writer for the uncertainty. It is the cost of risk which the writer faces. Time value erodes as expiry approaches. Therefore, an option is a wasting asset in the hands of the holder.

Time value can be calculated using complex mathematical option pricing models, such as the Cox-Rubenstein Model. The variables are risk-free interest rates, strike price, underlying security volatility and underlying security price, any dividends which would be paid if the underlying security were held.

From Table A4.2 it follows that at expiry (when time value equals zero) an out-of-the money option is worthless and an in-the-money option is worth its intrinsic value. Note than since an option cannot have negative intrinsic or time value the most an option holder can lose (and the most a writer can make) is the premium, no matter how much the underlying price changes.

Table A4.2 Factors affecting time value

Interest rates	Higher interest rates tend to result in higher call premiums and lower put premiums
Dividends	Higher cash dividends imply lower call premiums and higher put premiums
Volatility	Volatility of the underlying stock places a greater risk on the writer that the stock will expire in the money and so volatility raises premium

Relationship between the option price and the price of the underlying security

The most important thing to remember is that the price of a call tends to rise as the underlying security price rises and the price of a call tends to fall as the underlying security price falls. The price of a put tends to rise as the underlying security price falls and the price of a put tends to fall as the underlying security price rises.

So why buy an option and not the security? Because an option is leveraged. That means that for a given percentage change in the underlying price the option price can change by a greater percentage. You get a bigger bang for your buck.

Going back to our previous example: if the price of Barclays moved from 1,110p to 1,150p the option price may move from 67p to 97p. That means there would have been a 3.6% change in the underlying price and a 44.7% change in the option price. You could then decide to sell the option or as before exercise it. There would be more money to be made from selling it.

The price of an option rarely has a 1:1 correlation with the underlying security price. The delta is the rate of change of the option price to the rate of change of the underlying price. So, for example, a delta of 0.5 means that if the underlying price rises by, say, 10 cents then the option price will change by 5 cents. Obviously, the greater the delta then the greater the bang for your buck. However, the delta is greatest for in-the-money options, i.e. those with the most intrinsic value and therefore the most costly options. Consequently, a balance has to be drawn when calculating potential returns between the delta and the price of the option.

example

Barclays' shares are trading at 1,110p
July 1,100 calls are 51p; July 1,200 calls are 16p
If tomorrow the price of Barclays' shares were to be 1,200p then it may be that the July 1,100 calls trade at 123p (average delta of 0.8) and the July 1,200 calls trade at 22.5p (average delta of 0.25).

The return from the July 1,100s is 141% and from the cheaper 1,200s is only 41%. Of course, in this example we have only estimated deltas and have ignored costs and bid ask spreads. Nevertheless, it gives you some idea of the balances that need to be drawn. For modest moves you are likely to profit most from just in-the-money options.

example

Leverage

To own 100 shares of a stock trading at $30 per share would cost $30,000. On the other hand to own a $5 option with a strike price of $30 would give you the right to buy 100 shares for $30 at any time up to expiry. The option would cost only $500 ($5 x 100 shares).

If one month after the option is purchased the stock price has risen to $33 then the gain on the stock investment is $300, or 10%. However, for the same stock increase the option may have increased to $7 for a return of $200, or 40%.

Leverage of course has parallel downside implications. If, as in the last example, the stock fell to $27, the loss on the stock investment would be $300, or 10%. For this $3 fall the option may now be worth $3 itself, i.e. a 40% loss.

Vive la différence

Options are in many respects similar to stocks for the purposes of trading for profit.

Similarities	*Differences*
Orders to buy and sell are handled by brokers	Options have a limited life
Trading is conducted on regulated exchanges	There are fewer options than stocks
Pricing mechanisms are open and transparent	Option owners have no rights over a company; they are not shareholders
Investors have the opportunity to follow price movements second by second if they so wish	Option holders receive no dividends

Strategies

Although there are only two types of options, calls and puts, there are a lot of option strategies. With options you can protect your stock holdings from a price decline, you can prepare to buy a stock at a lower price, you can increase income on your current stock holdings, you can participate in a large market move, even if you are unsure beforehand which way the market is going to move, and, of course, you can participate in a stock rise or fall.

Kids' stuff

The simplest strategy is to go long a call or a put. That means you buy to open a call or put. If you go short (write the option) then you sell to open a call or put. In the latter case you have to post margin since your losses are potentially unlimited. It is a lot safer for the lay investor to be long puts than short calls even though on both you profit from falling prices. A common options strategy already discussed is to purchase calls to participate in an upward price movement.

Locking in a price

Another popular use of calls is to lock in an attractive stock purchase price. Imagine that ABC is trading at $55 and you believe it is about to increase in value, but you do not have the funds to buy 100 shares. You know you will have the funds in 6 months, but you are afraid that if you wait that long the shares will increase in value.

You see that the option expiring in 8 months, hence at the strike price of $55, costs $3, i.e. $300. If you buy one contract and then in 6 months the price of the stock is $70, you could exercise your option and buy the stock for $5,500 + $300. Whereas if you did not have the option and had to buy the option in the open market, it would have cost you $7,000. So you just made a saving of $1,200.

Puts to protect unrealized profit in a stock position

Imagine you bought ABC stock at $50 and it is now trading at $70. You fear there may be a short-term fall in the price but do not want to sell your holding on the hunch. By buying an ABC put option with a strike of $70 for $2 you are assured of being able to sell your stock at $70 no matter what happens to the stock price. If the price does not collapse, then you will have lost the premium, $2 x 100 = $200. Consider it an insurance premium.

But if the stock had fallen to, say, $55, you could have sold it at $70 per share, less $2 per share for the option premium. That means you would have earned an extra $13 per share with the option than if you had not taken out the insurance policy.

Option strategies

Option strategies are beyond the scope of this book, but I will mention a few to give you some idea of what the professionals and experienced non-professional can do with options.

Hedge

A hedge is a position where one profits if the other loses. So a hedge can be thought of as an insurance against being wrong. For example, a hedge against a long call: you could sell short a different call or go long a put.

Straddle

Buy to open an at-the-money call and buy to open an at-the-money put. You profit by increased volatility in the underlying price irrespective of direction. The strategy is a guts if the options are both in-the-money and a strangle if they are both out-of-the-money.

Bull call spread

Long in-the-money call and short out-of-the money call. Profit from upward price movement. This becomes a bull call calendar spread if the short call is nearer a month than the long call.

Key terms

Leverage

In-the-money

Out-of-the-money

Time value

Intrinsic value

Call and put

Exercise period

Writer

Premium

Volatility

Strike price or
exercise price

Bear put spread

Long in-the-money put and short out-of-the money put. Profit from downward price movement. This becomes a bear put calendar spread if the short put is nearer a month than the long put.

Various other strategies exist depending on your views as to volatility and direction and extent of risk you wish to take. These strategies have some unusual names, e.g. butterfly, condor, iron butterfly (buy a straddle and sell a strangle because you expect a limited size move), combo, ladder, box, conversion, and reversal.

See the further reading section if you want to investigate options further.

Summary

The essential things to remember about options are that they are leveraged; they decrease in value the longer they are held. Calls increase in value with the underlying asset and puts do the opposite.

APPENDIX 5

Orders

In this appendix

There are many different ways to place an order to enter or exit a trade. In this appendix we examine some of them.

Objective

- Familiarize ourselves with types of orders and usage

All or none order

A command to either "fill" the entire order, or none of it.

Example
Buy 500 McDonalds at 59½ all or none.

When used
When you want to buy all 500 shares at the specified price, but not less, or want to average out at the price.

Day order or good for day order

If the order cannot be executed before the end of the day, it is canceled.

Example
Buy 500 McDonalds at 59½ good for day. If the current price is 60–60⅛ and the bid price fails to reach 59½ then the order will not be executed.

When used

If you want to enter at a specific price, but only for the day in question, because the next day you may revise the order.

Good till canceled order or open order

This order stands until the customer cancels it or it is executed.

Example

Buy 500 McDonalds at 59½ good till canceled. If the current price is 60-60⅛ and the bid price fails to reach 59½ then the order will not be executed until the price reaches 59½ or the order is canceled by the customer.

When used

As with the good for the day order except the customer wants to keep the order open until he cancels it.

Limit order

An order to buy or sell at a specific price or a better price.

Example

Buy 500 McDonalds at 59½ limit. This means the broker can pay a maximum of 59½.

When used

Where the buyer or seller wants to place a limit on the price he wants to buy or sell.

Market order

The order to buy or sell at the best price available in the market.

Example

Buy 500 McDonalds at market.

When used

When the buyer or seller wants to buy or sell as soon as possible.

Stop order

An order that becomes a market order as soon as the price is reached. Can be buy stop or sell stop orders.

Example

Buy 500 McDonalds at 59 stop.

When used

When the buyer or seller wants the order executed at market price only after a certain price level has been reached.

Summary

Although many types of orders have been examined, most traders only ever find the need for one or two types, usually market and limit orders.

APPENDIX 6

Alphabetical list of sites

1010 Wall Street
www.1010wallstreet.com

Alphachart
www.alphachart.com

AltaVista
www.altavista.digital.com

American Stock Exchange
www.amex.com

Ameritrade
www.ameritrade.com

Applied Derivatives Trading
www.adtrading.com

Arizona Stock Exchange
www.azx.com

Ask Research
www.askresearch.com

AustinSoft
www.austin-soft.com

Australian Stock Exchange
www.asx.com.au

Avid Traders Chat
www.avidinfo.com

Barnes & Noble
www.barnesandnoble.com

Berkeley Futures
www.bfl.co.uk

Bloomberg
www.bloomberg.com

Bombay Stock Exchange
www.bseindia.com

Bonds Online
www.bonds-online.com

Bonneville Market Information
www.bmiquotes.com

Bookpl@ce
www.bookplace.co.uk

Booksite
www.booksite.com

Brady Net
www.bradynet.com

Bridge
www.bridge.com

BridgeFeed
www.bridge.com

Briefing
www.briefing.com

Business Week Online
www.businessweek.com

Charles Schwab
www.eschwab.com
www.schwab-worldwide.com/europe

Charles Stanley
www.charles-stanley.co.uk

Chicago Board of Trade
www.cbot.com

Chicago Board Options Exchange
www.cboe.com

Chicago Mercantile Exchange
www.cme.com

Chicago Stock Exchange
www.chicagostockex.com

Coffee, Sugar, & Cocoa Exchange
www.csce.com

Commodity Futures Trading
Commission
www.cftc.gov

CNN
www.cnnfn.com

Currency Management Corporation
www.forex-cmc.co.uk

Data Broadcasting Corporation
www.dbc.com

Datek
www.datek.com

Decision Point
www.decisionpoint.com

Deja News
www.dejanews.com

Deutsche Terminboerse
www.exchange.de

Dial/Data
www.tdc.com

Dow Jones Business Directory
bd.dowjones.com

Durlacher
www.durlacher.co.uk

Economeister
www.economeister.com

Economist
www.economist.com

Electronic Share Information
www.esi.co.uk

Equis
www.equis.com

Essex Trading Company
www.essextrading.com

E*Trade
www.etrade.com

Excite
www.excite.com

Finance Watch
www.finance.wat.ch

FinanceWise
www.financewise.com

Financial Center On-line
www.tfc.com/chat

Financial Times
www.ft.com

Forbes
www.forbes.com

Fortune
www.fortune.com

Futures Net
www.futures.net

Futures Online
www.futuresmag.com

Futures Source
www.futuresource.com

Hemmington Scott
www.hemscott.co.uk

Hong Kong Futures Exchange
www.hkfe.com

Hulbert Financial
www.hulbertdigest.com

Inc Magazine
www.inc.com

Infoseek
www.infoseek.com

Infotrade
www.infotrade.co.uk

INO Global
www.inoglobal.com

Interactive Investor
www.iii.co.uk

Internet Bookshop
www.bookshop.co.uk

Investorama
www.investorama.com

InvestorGuide Weekly
www.investorguide.com

Investors Free Forum
www.investorsforum.com

Italian Stock Exchange
www.robot1.textnet.it/finanza

Kansas City Board of Trade
www.kcbt.com

Killick
www.killick.co.uk

Kuala Lumpur Options & Financial
Futures Exchange
www.kloffe.com.my

Kuala Lumpur Stock Exchange
www.klse.com.my

Lisbon Stock Exchange
www.bvl.pt

London International Financial
Futures Options and Commodities
Exchange
www.liffe.com

London Metal Exchange
www.lme.co.uk

London Stock Exchange
www.stockex.co.uk

Lycos
www.lycos.com

Madrid Stock Exchange
www.bolsamadrid.es

Mantic Software
www.manticsoft.com

MarketEdge
www.marketedge.com

Market-Eye
www.market-eye.co.uk

MarketGuide
www.marketguide.com

MarketPlex
www.cbot.com/mplex

Market Technicians Society
www.mta-usa.com

MATIF
www.matif.fr

MEFF
www.meff.es

Metacrawler
www.metacrawler.com

Microsoft Investor
investor.msn.com

Mid-America Exchange
www.midam.com

Minneapolis Grain Exchange
www.mgex.com

Moneyworld
www.moneyworld.co.uk

Montreal Exchange
www.me.org

Morningstar
www.morningstar.net

Motley Fool
www.fool.com

Mutual Funds Investor's Center
www.mfea.com

Mutual Funds Online
www.mfmag.com

Nasdaq Exchange
www.nasdaq.com

NetWorth
www.networth.galt.com

Newsletter Network
www.margin.com

New York Cotton Exchange
www.nyce.com

New York Mercantile Exchange
www.nymex.com

New York Stock Exchange
www.nyse.com

Nirvana
www.nirv.com

Numa Web
www.numa.com

Omega
www.omegaresearch.com

OM Stockholm
www.omgroup.com

Options Direct
www.options-direct.co.uk

Pacific Exchange
www.pacificex.com

Paris Stock Exchange
www.bourse-de-paris.fr

PC Trader
www.fixedincome.com

Prestel Online
www.prestel.co.uk

Quicken People & Chat
www.quicken.excite.com/forums

Quote.com
www.quote.com

Reuters MoneyNet
www.moneynet.com

Santiago Stock Exchange
www.bolsantiago.cl/ingles

ScoTTrade
www.scottrade.com

South African Futures Exchange
www.safex.co.za

Standard & Poor
www.stockinfo.standardpoor.com

Stock Club
www.stockclub.com

Stockpoint
www.stockpoint.com

Stocks & Commodities Magazine
www.traders.com

Stocktrade
www.esi.co.uk/trading/stocktrade

Sydney Futures Exchange
www.sfe.com.au

TIFFE
www.tiffe.or.jp

Tokyo Grain Exchange
www.tge.or.jp

Tokyo Stock Exchange
www.tse.or.jp

Traders Library
www.traderslibrary.com

Trustnet
www.trustnet.co.uk

Union CAL
www.unioncal.com

US News Online
www.usnews.com

Vancouver Stock Exchange
www.vse.com

Wall Street Journal Interactive
www.wsj.com

Warsaw Stock Exchange
yogi.ippt.gov.pl/gielda/gielda

Webcrawler
www.webcrawler.com

Window on Wall Street
www.wallstreet.net

Worden Brothers
www.worden.com

Wordsworth
www.wordsworth.com

Worth
www.worth.com

Xest
www.xest.com

Yahoo!
www.yahoo.com

Yahoo! Finance
www.quote.yahoo.com

Yahoo! Finance Message Boards
www.messages.yahoo.com/yahoo/
Business_and_Finance/

Zacks
www.zacks.com

APPENDIX 7

Recommended reading

Key to star ratings

*** Excellent; comprehensible and comprehensive as well as value for money. Should be on your bookshelf.

** A useful read with very much to offer.

* A good read if, having read the others, you want to continue looking into the subject.

Trading psychology

The Bhagavad Gita ***

Various editions

Although written 5,000 years ago, and not directly about trading, I found it to be one of the most useful "trading" books I have ever read. It largely discusses discipline – how and why – and the benefits of discipline. Since a lack of mental discipline is one of the major downfalls of traders this is likely to be a very profitable read.

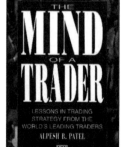

The Mind of a Trader ***

Alpesh B Patel
FT Pitman Publishing 1997

Advice on becoming a better trader from the world's leading traders, including Pat Arbor, Chairman of the Chicago Board of Trade and Bill Lipschutz, former Global Head of Forex at Salomon Brothers who made on average $250,000 each and every trading day he was there, for 8 years!

The Disciplined Trader **

Mark Douglas
Prentice Hall 1990

An extremely good book. Written in a very intelligent fashion and gets away from Mickey Mouse fashion psychology. Deserves a far higher profile than it has to date received.

The Inner Game of Trading ***

Robert Koppel and Howard Abell
Irwin Professional 1997

Includes interviews with some leading traders, but its value comes from the analysis of the psychological difficulties traders are likely to encounter. Definitely recommended.

Classics

Reminiscences of a Stock Operator ***

Edwin Le Fevre
Wiley 1994 (reprint edition)

An undoubted classic. The fictionalized trading biography of Jesse Livermore, one of the greatest speculators ever seen. While dated (it was written in 1923) it nevertheless provides some insight into the difficulties encountered by traders. A very enjoyable read.

Extraordinary Popular Delusions and the Madness of Crowds and Confusion de Confusiones **

Charles Mackay and Joseph de la Vega
Wiley 1995

Explores crowd psychology and how that affects market movement. While its examinations are 300 years old, it is highly relevant today. Short and interesting.

The Art of Speculation **

Philip L Carret
Wiley 1997

Apparently highly regarded by Victor Niederhoffer. Despite that, I would recommend it as a good read.

Manias, Panics and Crashes **

Charles Kindleberger
Wiley 1996

Why do the economists and statisticians and government nerds always get it wrong? This book does not provide any answers but it does provide some insights.

The Battle for Investment Survival **

Gerald Loeb
Wiley 1996

Although written in 1935, and that is partly what makes it a classic, it is fascinating to read how the more things change, the more they stay the same. Good fun to read.

Common Stocks and Uncommon Profits *

Philip Fisher
Wiley 1996

Warren Buffett is a fan – need I say more. The book is dated because, having been written in 1958, everyone has read it and used what it has to teach. But, nonetheless, I would recommend it as an insight into how unconventional but rational thinking can lead to superior analysis and greater profits than the crowd.

Stocks

Getting Started in Stocks **

Alvin D Hall
Wiley 1997 (3rd edition)

A very good primer for stocks. Hall has a clear style and injects humor now and again to alleviate the rigor.

Stocks for the Long Run **

Jeremy Siegal
McGraw-Hill 1998

A very popular title for the buy and hold investor in stocks. Sensible and easy to understand.

Investing with the Grand Masters **

James Morton
FT Pitman Publishing 1996

Morton meets with leading fund managers and discusses investment strategies.

Principally a book for those interested in Britain, but with some thought can be applied to foreign stock pickers as well.

The Global Guide to Investing*

James Morton (ed.)
FT Pitman Publishing 1996

This is a tome of most relevance to those interested in more than one country.

The Motley Fool Investment Guide *

David Gardner and Tom Gardner
Fireside 1997

I can't take the Gardners seriously, but they have followers and they have a brand and a different, more fun style than most stock books. What's more, there is useful information and insight in this book as well as a fresh perspective – then again it may all be fluke. (I jest not.)

Winning on Wall Street *

Martin Zweig
Warner Books 1997 (revised edition)

Zweig is famous for his market reports and for being one of Schwager's market wizards. I found a copy of this book for $11.99 – you can't go wrong.

Beardstown Ladies *

Hyperion 1996

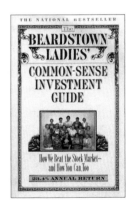

Isn't it annoying when you spend hours, days, nay a lifetime learning something, perfecting it, and then some dear old grandmas come along and turn everything on its head. The idea behind this huge seller is that you don't need to know much to earn in stocks. Damn, blast, confound it! There was I thinking that studying the markets and poring over world and market affairs made a difference. Go figure! A good light-hearted read, and, depending on who you are, uplifting even.

What Works on Wall Street*

James O'Shaughnessy
McGraw-Hill 1998 (revised edition)

O'Shaughnessy goes through a host of investment strategies that seem to "work." The problem is they probably only work for some people, some of the time under complex circumstances that cannot be fully detailed in any book. Nevertheless, it is a useful background read for examining how others are handling the "making money through stocks" problem.

Futures

Getting Started in Futures **

Todd Lofton
Wiley 1997 (3rd edition)

Very clear and easy to understand as well as giving lots of information for delving deeper.

A Complete Guide to the Futures Markets ***

Jack Schwager
Wiley 1984

This book covers fundamental analysis and technical analysis as well as spreads and options. Characteristic of Schwager's books it is very thorough.

Commodities trading

Mastering Commodity Futures and Options **

George Kleinman
FT Pitman Publishing 1997

This book is very well presented indeed. A little like a textbook in style, but covers the ground very well for both the beginner and the intermediate user.

The CRB Commodity Yearbook **

Knight-Ridder
Knight-Ridder annual

A very useful reference guide to commodities. Filled with data, charts, tables, and articles on trends and strategies. If you are serious about commodities, you should have this.

Soybean Trading and Hedging **

Wheat Trading and Hedging **

Investing in Wheat, Soybeans, Corn **

Corn Trading and Hedging **

William Grandmill
Irwin Professional 1988, 1989, 1991, 1990 (respectively)

A series of books by the appropriately named Grandmill for commodity traders.

Grandmill provides details of the commodities, and his own systems for picking entry and exit points. If you think it is best to become an expert in one area of commodity trading then books such as these should be a good starting point to develop your skills and understanding.

Options

Traded Options **

Peter Temple
Rushmere Wynne 1995

For those trading options on LIFFE. Thorough and explains all the basics, from what options are to buying software.

Getting Started in Options ***

Michael Thomsett
Wiley 1993

Again, very clear and easy to understand. An excellent start for beginners.

McMillan on Options ***

Lawrence McMillan
Wiley 1996

Brands itself as the "Bible" of the option's markets. Why do publishers refer to their books as the "Bible" of something? I wonder if they mean only a minority of people will ever read the book but more are supposed to and it competes with equivalent books for the rest. Anyway, that aside, McMillan goes beyond explaining the basics about options and actually applies a degree of critique. Should consider if you are a beginner.

Option Volatility and Pricing Strategies *

Sheldon Natenberg
Probus (1994 edition)

Natenberg is a leader in this field. This book is definitely for the more advanced trader wanting to dig into option mechanics.

The Options Markets *

John Cox and Mark Rubinstein
Prentice Hall 1985

This is a classic text on options. The book is about valuing options – these authors, of course, created the famous Cox-Rubinstein option pricing model.

All About Options **

Russell Wasendorf and Thomas McCafferty
Probus 1993

The good thing about this book is that it covers both strategies and some of the background mechanics behind options, such as what happens on the trading floor.

Advanced Options Trading **

Robert Daigler
Probus 1993

This book moves beyond basics and discusses some strategies generally used only by the professionals. That does not mean a private investor using them will have hit upon some sector – so beware. But if you are interested in knowing more than just the basics, this book is better than most.

Trading Options on Futures *

John Labuszewski
Wiley 1998

This covers treasuries, currencies and commodities. I think if you are trading options on futures there is more to it than simply understanding options and understanding futures. The whole is greater than the sum of the parts and therefore a book such as this is added value in being exclusively written for one trading sector.

How to Make Money with Corn Options *

Make Money with Soybean Options *

Make Money with S&P Options *

William Grandmill
Irwin 1990, 1990, 1989 (respectively)

If you are concentrating in one of these areas and feeling like you need something specifically addressing your trading needs, then these books were written with you in mind. Grandmill is a prolific writer and knows what he is talking about.

Trading and Investing in Bond Options *

M Anthony Wong
Wiley 1991

This title covers strategies, pricing models and details the peculiarities of trading this market using options.

Options on Foreign Exchanges *

David DeRosa
Probus 1992

Not to leave out the currency option boys and girls this market specialist covers valuation of options, pricing of currencies as well as how the various markets work. Probably useful for the beginner and intermediate level trader in forex options.

Commodity Options **

Larry Spears
Marketplace Books 1985

This one is for beginners who may not have settled on a particular commodity and who want an overview.

Technical analysis

Technical Analysis Explained **

Martin Pring
McGraw-Hill 1991

The first half of this book is more relevant than the second half. While a little disappointing, nevertheless provides insights not available elsewhere.

The Investors Guide to Technical Analysis **

Elli Gifford
FT Pitman Publishing 1995

While the book uses UK companies to illustrate points it nevertheless is useful to traders in any country. Thorough, comprehensive and easy to read and understand. Good as a starter and for more advanced study, however it is not mathematical.

Technical Analysis from A to Z **

Steven B Achelis
Probus 1995

A good introductory guide which is comprehensive. Lot of pics of indicators.

The Visual Investor **

John Murphy
Wiley 1996

Former CNBC presenter provides a good primer on technical analysis. He draws on one of the key aspects of technical analysis – it is visual.

Encyclopedia of Technical Market Indicators **

R Colby and T Meyers
Business One Irwin 1988

As you would expect of a book claiming to be an encyclopedia, this is an exhaustive study. It will be most useful if you want a good overview before settling down on a few chosen indicators.

Martin Pring on Market Momentum *

Martin Pring
McGraw-Hill 1993

Aimed at the user who has chosen momentum as one in his arsenal of technical indicators and wants to learn more, this book is typical Pring: clear and useful. Unfortunately, Pring maintains his habit of stylized artificial charts instead of giving more real market illustrations to make his points.

Momentum Direction and Divergence *

William Blau
Wiley 1995

Definitely for the advanced user. If after learning about oscillators you want to take things further and uncover some mathematics to better understand their weaknesses then this is a good book.

Stock Market Trading Systems **

Gerald Appel and Fred Hitschler
Dow Jones Irwin 1980

This is a classic and discusses the price ROC and moving average trading systems among others. It is always best to go to the original source to gain insights which later secondary texts are likely to miss.

The Moving Average Convergence–Divergence Method ***

Gerald Appel
Signalert 1979

Appel is the creator of this highly popular trading method and this book explains it straight from the source's mouth. Useful if you plan to place large weight on this indicator in your own trading.

Volume Cycles in the Stock Market **

Richard Arms
Equis 1994

Arms is a well known technical analyst and this book delves in depth into volume. If volume analysis is something you intend using then this a very good source of information.

How to use the Three-Point Reversal Method of Point and Figure Stock Market Trading **

AW Cohen
Chartcraft 1984

Despite the cumbersome title this is a useful book on a popular method of drawing charts.

Understanding Fibonacci Numbers **

Edward Dobson
Traders Press 1984

Not too difficult to understand if Fibonacci fascinates.

New Strategy of Daily Stock Market Timing for Maximum Profit **

Joseph Granville
Prentice Hall 1976

Another one of the technical analysis gods. This book discusses on-balance volume in particular. Granville created that indicator, so who better to learn more about it from?

Japanese Candlestick Charting Techniques ***

Steven Nison
New York Institute of Finance 1991

Steve Nison is regarded as the expert on Japanese candlesticks. This book is very clear and easy to understand. Nison uses actual charts and not stylized fictional ones. He also focusses on how and when the chart indications fail. The book helps you to understand the rationale behind technical analysis, why it works, and why it does not. Excellent.

New Concepts in Technical Trading Systems **

Welles J Wilder
Trend Research 1978

Wilder is very highly regarded in the technical analysis world. Here he explains and interprets numerous indicators including RSI.

Fibonacci Applications and Strategies for Traders *

Robert Fischer
Wiley 1993

Taking Fibonacci study further with this book. While you do not necessarily need such detailed knowledge, if you are going to use it, you may as well know all there is.

Volume and Open Interest **

Kenneth Shaleen
Irwin 1996

A good starter to investigating these two popular statistics in technical analysis. Probably unavoidable if you are trading futures.

Point and Figure Charting **

Carroll Aby
Traders Press 1996

Both a beginners' guide and a reference book for this method of plotting prices.

Fundamental analysis

Schwager on Futures: Fundamental Analysis ***

Jack Schwager
Wiley 1995

While expensive, it is certainly comprehensive, although confined to futures.

One Up on Wall Street **

Peter Lynch
Penguin 1990

The stock picking guru provides some useful "what to look for" rules. Written in an easy-to-digest style and fun to read.

Valuation, Measuring and Managing the Value of Companies **

Tom Copeland, Tim Koller and Jack Murrin
Wiley 1995

This goes into some of the serious stuff. It is quantitative and fundamental analysis should be. Runs to over 500 pages, but has useful diagrams and charts.

Security Analysis **

Benjamin Graham and David Dodd
McGraw-Hill 1996

Another quantitative and densely analytical book. If you are serious about fundamental analysis this book should be read.

Guide to Global Economic Indicators **

The Economist
Economist 1993

The increased globalization of markets makes an understanding of economic indicators essential. If the Asian flu can give Americans a chill then what is going on everywhere and anywhere matters. The *Economist* is one of the most authoritative sources of such information.

Financial Times Guide to Using the Financial Pages ***

Romesh Vaitilingam
FT Pitman Publishing 1996 (3rd edition)

If you can't understand the financial pages then you can hardly be applying fundamental analysis effectively. This book is comprehensive and up to date.

Fundamental Analysis Worldwide *

Haksu Kim
Wiley 1996

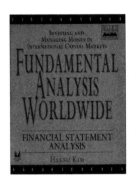

This is a title for the global investor who may be investing in more than one country. It details how to get local information and at the same time maintain the necessary global perspective.

Bonds

Mastering Government Securities **

Stephen Mahony
FT Pitman Publishing 1997

One of FT Pitman's Mastering Market editions, and as such very clear and easy to understand. Great for the beginner to take him or her well into the intermediate stage.

How the Bond Market Works *

Robert Zipf and John Allen
Prentice Hall 1997

This is written almost as a text book, but despite that is useful for beginner, intermediate and reference.

The Bond Book **

Annette Thau
Probus 1994

Covers virtually every type of bond from treasuries to zeros. If you are planning to specialize in bonds then this has got to be one of the books you read.

Currency markets

Mastering Foreign Exchange and Currency Options **

Francesca Taylor
FT Pitman Publishing 1997

One of the clearest books on the subject. It gets you up to speed with speed!

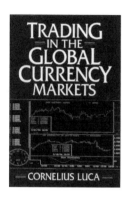

Trading in Global Currency Markets **

Cornelius Luca
Prentice Hall 1995

A useful behind-the-scenes look at the mechanics of forex trading. Who does what and why? It is helpful in the area of understanding risk.

Foreign Currency Trading **

Russell Wasendorf Sr. and Russell Wasendorf Jr.
McGraw-Hill 1997

The father and son duo go from basics to reference material. Pretty detailed.

Traders' profiles

The Mind of a Trader ***

Alpesh B Patel
FT Pitman Publishing 1997

As noted earlier, the world's leading traders share their insights, not merely in a question and answer format but in an easy-to-understand category-based layout. You can see at any point what exactly is being discussed and with a summary at the end plus author comment, the conclusions are made clear.

Market Wizards and New Market Wizards ***

Jack Schwager
Harper Business 1993, Wiley 1995 (respectively)

Absolute musts. Fascinating, although since they are in a question and answer format you are left to draw many of your own conclusions.

100 Minds that Made the Market *

Kenneth Fisher
Business Classics 1991

Biographical in nature and the profiles are somewhat short, but nevertheless a good bedtime or holiday read.

The Super Traders *

Alan Rubenfeld
Irwin 1992

Nine profiles of traders from a diverse background. While a little bit too biographical, nevertheless makes for a good read.

Warren Buffett Speaks *

Janet Lowe
Wiley 1997

If you're into stock picking then it would undoubtedly help to try to get in the mind of one of the all-time greats.

Floor trading insights

Tricks of the Floor Trader ***

Neal Weintraub
Irwin 1996

One of the few books of its kind. Gives the outsider a view of what the insider does. Provides knowledge which is useful to know.

The Trader's Edge **

Grant Noble
Probus 1995

Some very useful insights into what they do on the floor. A good insider's view and useful pointers on some of the advantages.

Trading Rules **

William Eng
FT Pitman Publishing 1995

While some of the rules will be familiar, others provide valuable enough information to justify buying this easy-to-understand book.

The Compleat Day Trader *

J Bernstein
McGraw-Hill 1996

A very good seller, with an unusual title. Not only covers day trading but also risk management.

High Impact Day Trading **

Robert Barnes

Irwin 1996

This book highlights the author's Mountain Valley system, going for longer moves and ignoring shorter ones. It has proved a very popular title.

Glossary

Abandoned option Where an option is neither sold nor exercised but allowed to lapse at expiry.

Acid test ratio A measure of financial strength. Also known as the quick ratio. Cash plus short-term investments plus accounts receivable divided by current liabilities for the same period. All other things being equal, a relatively high figure may indicate a healthy company.

Active channels A feature of Internet Explorer 4. Internet sites that are selected as channels provide special IE4 content. Gates wants to lead internet tv – hence the term channels.

American option An option that is exerciseable at any time within its life. Can be and are traded outside Europe.

Arbitrage The purchase in one market of an instrument and the sale in another market of it or a closely linked instrument in order to profit from the small price differentials between the products in the two markets. Arbitrage profits usually exist for a short time only because someone usually scoops on them since they are "locked in."

Arbitrageur A trader engaged in arbitrage. They seek to make a lot of small, quick profits.

Assign To oblige a call option writer to sell shares to the option holder, or to oblige a put option writer to buy shares from a put option holder.

At the market An order to buy or sell at the best price obtainable in the market.

Averaging Where a price moves against a trader and he trades more of the stock to enlarge his position but to lower his overall entry price. It will mean he will have a lower exit price at which he can make a profit.

Backbone A high-speed connection within a network that connects all the other circuits. Another name for a "hub." A central connection from which "spokes" or connections radiate.

Bandwidth The capacity of a network to carry data. If your pipes are clogged (low bandwidth) then things take forever to load. It's not an issue of length but width.

Basis point Used to calculate differences in interest rate yields, e.g. the difference between 5.25% and 6.00% is 25 basis points.

BBS A bulletin board system. A little like an electronic notice board. You "post" messages to the board and everyone who subscribes to the board can view them.

Bear(ish) An individual who thinks prices will fall.

Bear market A market in which prices are falling.

Bear spread An option position where it is intended to profit from a falling market. Usually, the position involves the purchase of a put at one strike price and the sale of a put at a lower strike price.

Beta This measures the stock's volatility to the market as a whole.

Bid An offer to purchase at a specific price.

Black-Scholes pricing model A mathematical model used to calculate the price in theory of an option. The main input variables are: the risk-free interest rate, volatility, dividends, time to expiry, the strike price, underlying price.

Bounce What happens to mail which for some reason (e.g. wrong e-mail address) cannot be delivered.

Break A sudden fall in price.

Breakout When the price moves out of its recent range. Sometimes signals further moves in the direction of the breakout.

Broker An individual who executes customers' orders.

Bull(ish) An individual who believes prices will rise.

Bull market A market in which prices are rising.

Bull spread An option position where it is intended to profit from a rising market. Usually the position involves the purchase of a call at one strike price and the sale of a call at a higher strike price.

Call option (calls) The right, but not the obligation, existing for a fixed period of time only, to purchase a fixed quantity of stock at a fixed price.

Cashflow per share The trailing twelve month cashflow divided by the twelve month average shares outstanding. All other things being equal, a relatively high figure, growing steadily, is a sign of a growing and healthy company and may indicate a rising share price.

Clerk An employee of an exchange's member firm, who is registered to work on the exchange floor.

Closed When referring to a position this means you have made an equal and opposite trade to one already held and so have no more exposure to the market on that trade.

Contrarian An individual who generally believes it is usually better not to do what the majority is doing, because the majority does not make money.

Cookie According to conspiracy theorists a cookie is a small piece of software that is downloaded from a web site to your computer's hard drive that tells the webmaster all your hidden and deepest secrets. According to everyone other than conspiracy theorists a cookie is a small piece of software that is downloaded from a web site to your computer's hard drive that tells the webmaster your username, password, viewing preference and one or two other things. It means you do not have to enter the same information over and over again.

Current ratio The ratio of total current assets divided by the total current liabilities for the same period. A measure of financial strength. All other things being equal, a relatively high figure would indicate a healthy company.

Cyberspace William Gibson's name in his fantasy novel *Neuromancer* to describe what is now known as the internet.

Day trade(r) A position that is closed the same day it was opened.

Delta The change of the options price for a change in the underlying price. A delta of 0.5 means a 10 point move in the underlying price causes a 5 point move in the option.

Depreciation Not a measure of spousal dissatisfaction but an accounting measure used to reduce the value of capital expenditure for the purposes of reclaiming tax.

Diversification Reducing risk by spreading investments among different instruments, i.e. not putting all your eggs into too few baskets.

Dividend ex-date This is the date from which a purchaser of the stock will not be entitled to receive the last announced dividend. Appropriately, when a stock goes ex-dividend its price falls by approximately the value of the dividend.

Dividend growth rate A measure of corporate growth. The annual positive change in dividend paid to stockholders. All other things being equal, an increase should indicate a growing company and should be reflected in rising share price.

Dividend rate This is the total expected dividend for the forthcoming twelve months. It is usually the value of the most recent dividend figure multiplied by the number of times dividends are paid in a year plus any extra dividend payments.

Dividend yield This is calculated by dividing the annual dividend by the current price and expressing the figure as a percentage.

Domain Part of a web or e-mail address. Separated from the rest of the address by dots.

Dotted quad A string comprising four sets of numbers separated by dots that constitute an internet address, e.g. 123.32.433.234.

Drawdown The reduction in trading capital as a result of losses.

Dynamic HTML This makes web designers very excited. It means that bits of web pages can be made to do things like change color when you point to them. These bits are therefore dynamic and not static (unlike their designers who are definitely not dynamic).

Encryption These scramble data and so keep them private from those who want to sneak a peek or drop an eave (eavesdroppers).

EPS Earnings per share. A measure of corporate growth. The value of corporate earning divided by the number of shares outstanding. All other things being equal, a growing figure reflects a healthy growing company and should be reflected in the share price.

European option An option that is exercisable only at expiry.

Exercise Where the holder of an option uses his right to buy or sell the underlying security. Also means to workout.

Expiry The date up to which a trader can exercise his option.

Flame An e-mail that is abusive or argumentative. Usually includes the words "you are a ..." somewhere in the message.

Flamefest The same as a flame orgy.

Floor broker A member who executes orders for clearing members.

Floor trader An individual who trades on the floor of an exchange either for himself or a company.

Free Speech An issue relating to the internet about which the US Congress spends inordinate quantities of time. Essentially, the concern is to give rights to those that would deny them to others, including those who granted them.

FTP (file transfer protocol) The protocol for sending files through the internet.

Fundamental analysis Forecasting prices by using economic or accounting data. For example, one might base a decision to buy a stock on its yield.

Futures A standardized contract for the future delivery of goods, at a pre-arranged date, location, price.

Gap Where a price opens and trades higher than its previous close.

Geek Also known as a net nerd. They were the kids everyone hated at school, who wore thick blackrimmed spectacles and were extremely uncool. They would also get sand kicked in their faces and were so unpopular no one would be seen dead with them – sometimes not even their parents. Now the sand has settled, and it has become clear that because they were unpopular they spent all their time studying, and can now be considered some of the wealthiest people on the planet, with the fastest, flashest cars. They definitely had the last laugh.

Gross margin A measure of company profitability. The previous twelve month total revenue less cost of goods sold divided by the total revenue. All other things being equal, a decrease in gross margins could indicate troubled times ahead.

Hedge Protection against current or anticipated risk exposure, usually through the purchase of a derivative. For example, if you hold DM and fear that the price will decline in relation to dollars you may go long dollars. You would then make some profit on your long position to offset your losses in holding DM.

Implied volatility Future price volatility as calculated from actual, not theoretical, options prices. The volatility is implied in the prices.

Income per employee The income after taxes divided by the number of employees. A measure of corporate efficiency. All other things being equal, a greater figure, or a growing figure, indicates a more efficient company and should be reflected in a rising share price.

Insider share purchases The number of shares in the company purchased by its insiders – officers and directors – over a stated period of time. All other things being equal, a relatively large move may indicate a forthcoming upward move in the stock price.

Institutional net shares purchased This is the difference between institutional share purchases less institutional share sales in the company over a stated period of time. All other things being equal, a relatively large move may indicate a forthcoming upward move in the stock price.

Institutional percent owned This is the percentage of shares owned by all the institutions taken together. It is a percentage of the total shares outstanding. All other things being equal, a relatively large move may indicate a forthcoming upward move in the stock price.

Intranet This is a collection of computers connected to one another and usually located in a company or other organization. Unlike the internet the network is private and not principally intended for the public.

Java An island or a coffee bean or a programming language developed by Sun Microsystems. It allows users to do lots of clever things with web pages.

LAN (local area network) A network of computers operating up to a few thousand meters from one another.

Limit The maximum permitted price move up or down for any given day, under exchange rules.

Liquid market A market which permits relatively easy entry and exit of large orders because there are so many buyers and sellers. Usually characteristic of a popular market.

Long A position, opened but not yet closed, with a buy order.

Long-term debt to total equity A measure of financial strength. The long-term debt of the company divided by the total shareholder equity for the same period. All other things being equal, a relatively high figure may indicate an unhealthy company.

Margin A sum placed with a broker by a trader to cover against possible losses.

Margin call A demand for cash to maintain margin requirements.

Market capitalization This is the product of the number of shares outstanding and the current price.

Market order *See* At the market

Mark to market Daily calculation of paper gains and losses using closing market prices. Also used to calculate any necessary margin that may be payable.

MIME Multipurpose internet mail extension. This enables you to attach files to e-mail.

Momentum An indicator used by traders to buy or sell. It is based on the theory that the faster and further prices move in one particular direction, the more likely they are to slow and turn.

Moving average A system used by traders to determine when to buy and sell. An average (simple, exponential or other) is taken of the closing (or opening or other) prices over a specific number of previous days. A plot is made based on the average. As each day progresses the moving average has to be re-calculated to take account of the latest data and remove the oldest data.

Net After expenses; or short for the internet.

Netiquette Proper net behavior. For instance, swearing is neither appropriate etiquette nor netiquette.

Net profit margin A measure of profitability. Income after taxes divided by the total revenue for the same period. All other things being equal, downward pressure on the net profit margin could provide advance warning of impending share price decline.

Network A group of computers connected to one another so that their users can access each other's machines.

Offer A price at which a seller is willing to sell.

Off-line browser A browser that permits viewing of sites previously downloaded without being connected to the net.

Open position A position that has not yet been closed; therefore the trader is exposed to market movements.

Overbought/oversold A term used to mean broadly that a stock is likely not to advance further and may decline (overbought) or advance (oversold).

Position Trades which result in exposure to market movements.

Price, 52-week high This is the highest price the stock traded in in the last 52 weeks. It may not necessarily be a closing high, it could be an intra-day high.

Price, 52-week low This the lowest price the stock traded in in the past 52 weeks. Could be an intra-day low price.

Price to book ratio The current price divided by the latest quarterly book value per share. All other things being equal, a relatively low figure may indicate the stock is undervalued.

Price to cashflow ratio The current price divided by the cashflow per share for the trailing twelve months. All other things being equal, a relatively low figure may indicate the stock is undervalued.

Price to earnings ratio The current share price divided by earnings per share before extraordinary items, usually taken over the previous 12 months. All other things being equal, a relatively low figure may indicate the stock is undervalued.

Protocols A set of rules with which two computers must comply in order to communicate.

Push technology The internet can be quite a passive experience, needing the user to log on to a site to determine if changes have occurred or to download information. With push technology the browser can be set to automatically download data from a set site.

Put option A right, but not the obligation, existing for a specified period of time, to sell a specific quantity of stock or other instrument at a specified price.

Pyramiding The increase in size of an existing position by opening further positions, usually in decreasing increments.

Quick ratio A measure of financial strength. Also known as the acid test ratio. Cash plus short-term investments plus accounts receivable divided by current liabilities for the same period. All other things being equal, a relatively high figure may indicate a healthy company.

Return on assets A measure of management effectiveness. Income after taxes divided by the total assets. All other things being equal, a relatively high or growing figure may indicate a company doing well.

Return on equity A measure of management effectiveness. Income available to shareholders divided by the total common equity. All other things being equal, a relatively high or growing figure may indicate a company doing well.

Return on investments A measure of management effectiveness. Income after taxes divided by the average total assets and long-term debt. All other things being equal, a relatively high or growing figure may indicate a company doing well.

Revenue percent change year on year A measure of growth. The revenue of the most recent period less the revenue of the previous period divided by the revenue of the previous period. All other things being equal, a growing figure indicates a growing company and should be reflected in a rising share price.

Sales percent change A measure of corporate growth. The value of sales for the current period less the value of sales for the preceding period divided by the value of sales for the preceding period, expressed as a percentage. All other things being equal, a growing figure indicates a growing company and should be reflected in a rising share price.

Sales per employee A measure of company efficiency. The total sales divided by the total number of full-time employees. All other things being equal, the greater this figure the more efficient the company.

Scalper A trader that seeks to enter and exit the market very quickly and thereby make a lot of small profits.

Seat Exchange membership that permits floor trading.

Server A computer that shares its resources with others. The resources may be disk space or files or something else.

Shares outstanding The number of shares issued less those held in treasury.

Short An open position created by a sell order, in the expectation of a price decline and so the opportunity to profit by purchasing the instrument (so closing out) at a lower price.

Short-term debt The value of debt due in the next 12 months.

SMTP (simple mail transfer protocol) The standard set of rules for transferring e-mail messages from one computer to another.

Speculator An individual who purchases financial instruments in order to profit. Often used to refer to a non-professional. Sometimes used derogatorily.

Spread The simultaneous purchase of one contract and the sale of a similar, but not identical contract. Depending on the exact combination, a profit can be made from a rising or falling market.

Stop order (stop loss orders) An order left with a broker instructing him to close out an existing position if the market price reaches a certain level. Can be used to take profits or stop losses.

TCP/IP (transmission control protocol/internet protocol) A set of rules used to connect to other computers.

Technical analysis Methods used to forecast future prices using the price data alone (for example, by plotting it as a chart and noting direction) or using the price as an input in mathematical formulae and plotting the results. *See also* Fundamental analysis.

Technical rally or decline A price movement resulting from factors unrelated to fundamentals or supply and demand.

Tick The smallest possible price move.

Total debt to equity ratio A measure of financial strength. The total debt divided by total shareholder equity for the same period. All other things being equal, a relatively low figure is a sign of a healthy company.

Total operating expenses A measure of the cost of running the company. All other things being equal, a lower figure is preferable to a higher one.

Trendline A line on a price chart indicating market price direction. The line connects at least three price points which touch the line, with no prices breaking the line.

Volatility A statistical indication of probable future price movement size (but not direction) within a period of time. For example, 66% probability of a 15 pence move in 3 months.

Webcasting This is the internet trying to be older – like tv or radio. Instead of viewing pages, you view a stream of data in the form of radio or video. Unfortunately, the infrastructure is lacking to make this a popular alternative to tv and radio.

Whipsaw A price move first in one direction and shortly thereafter in another direction, thereby catching traders wrong-footed. Such markets may be termed "choppy." Such effects often give rise to false buy and sell signals, leading to losses.

Index